HAWTHORNE
AND HIS PUBLISHER

Æt 50

William D. Ticknor

HAWTHORNE AND HIS PUBLISHER

BY

CAROLINE TICKNOR

BOSTON AND NEW YORK
HOUGHTON MIFFLIN COMPANY
MDCCCCXIII

PREFACE

THE annals of literature contain the record of various memorable friendships which have existed between authors and publishers. The names of Scott and Constable, "Tom" Moore and Longman, Browning and George Murray Smith, are permanently linked together. Yet it is doubtful if among all such notable friendships, any can rival that of Hawthorne and Ticknor.

The value of the fragmentary story of this association, as set forth in the following pages, must of necessity lie in those passages in which the subjects speak for themselves. Especially does Hawthorne in his frank and spontaneous communications, penned from the consulate at Liverpool, reveal himself with a freedom from all restraint, not to be found elsewhere in his letters and journals.

C. T.

CONTENTS

ILLUSTRATIONS

HAWTHORNE AND HIS PUBLISHER

I

IT is said that a hundred years must pass ere a
man, or his work, can be properly estimated. Yet,
when a century has flown, it is apt to be the work,
rather than the man, which challenges the attention of posterity. The "good" achieved is not
"interred," but very often the achiever is; only too
frequently the architect of some fine edifice sinks
wearily to rest before his task is finished, leaving his
fair creation to be completed by other hands. And
in the end, while men admire the finished structure,
they have but little curiosity concerning the architect. Yet no true lover of a work of art, or graceful
structure, is quite content until he has learned something of him who brought forth the fair creation.

Even so, those who to-day reverence the best in
the field of American letters cannot fail to be interested in the creator of that notable publishing-house
which put before the public our great New England
writers and also brought to us from the Old World
so many of its choicest literary offerings.

A century has passed since the birth of William
Davis Ticknor, whose early ambition differed ma-
terially from that of many other enterprising youths

who came to Boston far back in the twenties, to seek
their fortunes; some longed for wealth, others sought
fame, but this young man, whose heritage was a
great love of books, desired that his "imprint upon a
title-page should be the guarantee of a good book."
This was the corner-stone of the notable literary edifice which he was destined to rear; a structure unique
in the history of book-publishing.

Fortunate is the man who is permitted to have his
dreams come true, and who sees a worthy ambition
successfully realized. The publishing-house, which
Mr. Ticknor built up, first alone, and then with the
able assistance of his associate, Mr. James T. Fields,
became a vital factor in the literary life of the whole
nation. It was recognized as a distinction for an
author to have its imprint upon his work, and the
writers of that day, those who belonged to the golden
days of American literature, next to their own tal-
ents, owed their fame to the good offices of their publishers. Together they made Boston the headquarters of the best in literary America.

The "Old Corner Bookstore" became truly the
"Hub" about which literary New England revolved.
Through its portals passed a galaxy of literary stars
such as this nation had never before produced:
Hawthorne, Longfellow, Holmes, Lowell, Whittier,
Emerson, Thoreau, and many others were its hab-
itués, and where else in this broad land have the
American immortals gathered with such frequency,
enthusiasm, and profit?

There in the curtained private office of the firm,
where the fate of so many budding aspirants was

decided, one could habitually encounter a literary coterie unsurpassed anywhere in genius, wit, and wisdom. And authors from across the seas found their way promptly to the famous "Corner," whose hospitality was extended to Dickens, Thackeray, and many others of the Old World celebrities. Well might the foreign authors seek here the welcome of the New World, for Mr. Ticknor had from the first been their warm friend, discerning their literary worth and tendering just payment for its enjoyment. He early won their heartfelt gratitude, for it was to his initiation, undoubtedly, that the first unsolicited payments from American publishers for copyright to foreign authors, and the first regular purchases of "advance sheets" were due. This practice, always maintained by his house, he began in 1842, with a check to Alfred Tennyson, who never forgot to voice his appreciation of this act of literary justice, and it is interesting to recall the fact that he recorded the same when he was eighty years of age. In response to a birthday communication received upon his eightieth anniversary he wrote to the son of the publisher whose first check had reached him almost half a century before: —

DEAR SIR, — I thank you most sincerely for your kind words upon my eightieth birthday. It is an especial pleasure to me to receive them from the son of one who gave so honorable an example to his countrymen of justice in the highest sense.

Truly and gratefully yours,

TENNYSON.

The literary "justice" performed in this instance
was from this time consistently continued towards
other English writers in the face of numerous protests from various American competitors, who maintained that what the law permitted was "fair game"
in any business enterprise, and also that our writers were not receiving any compensation from foreign publishers. But "fair play," and not "fair
game," was the motto embodied in the transactions
of the founder of the "Old Corner Bookstore," for
old and young, for black and white, for foreigners no
less than his own countrymen, and no injustice prac-
ticed by those across the seas towards us was looked
upon by him as justification for our own mainten-
ance of an unfair code. And he strove hard for the
establishment of that long-needed international
copyright, the attainment of which required so many
years of painful effort. It seems almost incredible
that such a measure, first agitated as far back as
1837, should not have materialized for over sixty
years.

Never was man endowed with a warmer affection
for his own, or with the capability of a more truly
unselfish devotion to his friends, than that possessed
by Mr. Ticknor, but when a matter of financial fairness or business integrity was at stake, all men stood
on a plane of absolute equality.

Many were the tributes of sincere appreciation
that were wafted back across the seas from grateful
hearts upon the other side, — and many were the
voiceless prayers of gratitude that never found expression save in some fragmentary reminiscence of

To B. H. Ticknor Esqre   Septr 4th 1889
Aldworth.
Haslemere.

Dear Sir,
        I thank you most
sincerely for your kind
words on my eightieth birthday
        It is an especial pleasure
to me to receive them from
the Son of one who gave
so honourable an example
to his Countrymen of
justice in the highest sense.
Truly & gratefully yours
                    Tennyson

after years; among these unchronicled services may be mentioned the timely aid lent to a tottering London house, which later ranked among the greatest of English publishing establishments, but which would have gone under without the prompt financial help given by Mr. Ticknor.

As one glances over the literary memoirs of that most fruitful mid-Victorian period, the eye falls frequently upon some reference to the generous treatment accorded many English writers by this American publishing-house, where also warm personal interest went hand in hand with ample financial compensation. Now, it is Browning, delighted by an unexpected check from this direction; again it is De Quincey, who voices his debt to his American publishers; or it may be Charles Reade, who found his earliest appreciation here, or yet George Eliot, Trollope, or Anne Thackeray Ritchie.

That this attitude of confidence and respect was heartily reëchoed by the writers in this country, hardly needs verification, for it is constantly reiterated in the biographies and autobiographies of those that formed a part of the charmed circle identified with the "Old Corner." And also, by a responsive public outside the inner shrine, which watched with loyal interest and enthusiasm for the good things to come from off the presses of this publishing-house, whose imprint they regarded as a security in which they placed absolute trust.

And so it was that, ere he reached his fortieth year, William D. Ticknor saw his cherished ideal realized; and the most distinguished writers of the Old World

joined with those of his own land in testifying that
"his imprint on a title-page had become the guarantee of a good book."

Mr. Ticknor possessed great personal charm; he
was a singularly handsome man, with graceful manners and a cordial and sympathetic personality; he
instantly inspired confidence and won in a brief
space of time warm and true friendships which he
never failed to retain. Many young authors, who
later won places of great distinction, came to him for
counsel and guidance, while their elders relied upon
his judgment and advice in regard to the writing as
well as to the printing of their works. Among the
enduring friendships formed with the authors of his
day the most notable was that existing between him
and Nathaniel Hawthorne, which was of closest and
most continuous intimacy, from the beginning of
their acquaintance, when the shy and retiring author
began to depend on his alert and executive publisher
for all manner of services, up to the very end, when
this devoted friend departed with the dying novelist
on that last journey during which the well man was
stricken down at the age of fifty-three, in the full
glory of his powers and activities, leaving the stunned
and shattered Hawthorne to survive him but a few
short weeks.

So closely interwoven were the affections and interests of these two friends that no account of either
one is half complete without the other. Unlike as
these two men were in their physical and intellectual
constitution, they yet coincided in many spiritual
correspondences. Ticknor supplied just that which

Hawthorne felt he lacked and understood precisely
what was needed before the other asked it. Much
the same was true with regard to Hawthorne's other
great friendship, that for Franklin Pierce, who, while
differing equally from the novelist and dreamer, also
gave him the same strong, sturdy companionship to
lean on.

If Hawthorne proposed to take a trip to Washington, he dreaded it until Ticknor had consented to
accompany him, and when President Pierce appointed him to the Liverpool consulship, he would
not embark unless his publisher would go with him
and start him upon the new enterprise. After his
return from Europe his various little journeys were
always made in company with Mr. Ticknor, and he
insisted that his identity should be concealed in all
hotel registers under the incognito of a "friend."

In writing of this long-standing friendship Mr.
Ticknor's eldest son declared: —

"Hawthorne was not a visionary, a student of the
occult forces and processes of man's secret soul, and
a romance writer, only, he was strongly practical
also. He could work hard at common tasks, measure
his earnings, economize, and forecast domestic possibilities; he was a good custom-house officer, and at
daily drudgery, while scrutinizing and recording
character, he could gather historical facts, draw right
inferences, and plan for little readers, résumés of
classic mythology."

"What he needed, sought, and kept was a friend
stronger and more expert in practicality even than
himself, to whom also he could confide upon occasion

his personal thoughts, his professional hopes, and his fancies and criticisms in regard to literature and æsthetics. Nowhere else, not even in his journals, was Hawthorne so frank as in the many intimate letters which he sent to this confidant from abroad. Sometimes it would not be wise to take him absolutely. Everybody who has ventured to jest in writing, knows how risky it is, but in passing sharp, offhand judgments upon some common acquaintances, he evidently relied upon his friend to put a right and fair value upon them.

"That he (Hawthorne) could reach, pounce upon, and draw wisdom from beneath commonplace exteriors and everyday doings, was the explanation of many things which the casual thought strange or unbecoming. His reluctance to participate in the elegant hospitality pressed upon him was derived from no taste for ignoble company, but because at the Old Province House Tavern of Master Waite, he could see and feel, beyond the common men who came to whet their clay in its bar-room, its true ghosts that still qualified the atmosphere of its chambers and stairways, while in the long dining-room of the Bromfield House, where sturdy Crockett stood and carved for his old-fashioned table-d'hote, were to be met stout and shrewd Boston men, through whom were to be traced back, for record and use, traits of person, demeanor, and character, which no fine social gathering could have supplied him, however much it might have delighted and cheered him as a craftsman in composition.

"So, too, in the vacation jaunts of those ante-

European years, he wanted the same companionship. He wanted to conceal the man whose name he bore, and whose features had been portrayed by brush and burin, to be just the personality within that figure, free to think, to watch, to speak, or keep silent, sure that his mood and bent would be respected and sustained.

"He liked best to be taken to such plain, miscellaneous hotels as the Astor, or Bixby's, to be entered anonymously as 'a friend' of his companion, to carry no money, to know nothing of the details of the journey, to make only chance acquaintances whom he could anatomize, but who could have no clue to him, and to be brought back home as mutely as he had been taken away. Often has the writer [Mr. Howard Ticknor] noticed, when the two were starting for some outing, a look on Hawthorne's face of affectionate trustfulness, content, and of such rest as if the profitable trip had been already enjoyed. It was strange to him, a youth, that one grown man should seem so dependent upon another; but life has long ago explained the perplexities."

As one reviews Hawthorne's career, a score of vivid pictures arise before the mental vision; he appears in the Custom-House at Salem, at the "Old Manse," and later at "The Wayside"; then he may be seen briskly engaged in his consular duties; and again, he sits dreamily beside his cheerful fireside in the midst of his family circle, or quietly muses upon the creations of his brain in his own study ; now he is happy in the enchanted realm of Italy, and again glad to set foot once more upon his native heath; these and many more views present themselves in picturesque succession; each one is Hawthorne, yet there is still another picture which more than all the rest seems to impress itself upon the onlooker as truly characteristic of the subject. Hawthorne, not actively engaged in any occupation, but passively gazing out on the world surrounding him, from a half-shadowy hiding-place; Hawthorne alone, withdrawn from outside interruption and uncongenial company, yet close beside his faithful friend at the "Old Corner." Here he sat oftentimes in the small counting-room, over which his companion presided busily, while he dreamed in the shadow. Across the office in the opposite corner was the little green-curtained sanctum of Mr. Fields, where the sociable spirits invariably gathered.

Upon the other hand, the counting-room was elevated two or three steps above the level of the store, where, seated at his desk, the senior partner could command the whole field, and nothing that was taking place escaped his penetrating glance. In some respects the little curtained corner was the literary "throne-room," but here was the power behind the throne, and here the final literary judgment seat.

And "Hawthorne's chair" was here in a secluded niche where he could see and yet be out of sight; here he could observe all without being subjected to outside observation; for he was quite invisible unless one stepped up through the little gate into the counting-room. In this one chair, it was for many years Nathaniel Hawthorne's custom to ensconce himself whenever he visited the "Corner"; he often spent whole hours here, resting his head upon his hand apparently in happy and satisfying sympathy with his environment.

And those that looked upon this picture love to recall this portrait of Hawthorne and his friend, one in the light, brimful of stirring activity, the other watching in the shadow, motionless physically, yet mentally alert, and following with an inward intentness the fantastic trains of thought evoked sometimes by what was passing in the outward world, and again by that which was merely passing within his active brain.

And to the lad in his father's office, who watched him furtively from time to time, Hawthorne gave the impression that while he was conscious of what was passing, and took note even of the shop-frequenters, and back of them of the outside street traffic, yet all the while he was pursuing an orderly and complete train of thought peculiar to himself, and quite apart from that which was taking place about him. If any acquaintance, knowing him to be there, came to claim his attention, his face seemed to cast off an intangible but perceptible veil, and he roused himself to a genial and conversational mood, though still with a suggestion of having come rather unwillingly from a haunt of his predilection, to which he would fain return as soon as he might do so without impoliteness.

He could but rarely be induced to leave his place for a stroll, a bit of luncheon at Mrs. Haven's author-frequented coffee-shop, or to join the animated and

mirthful chatter of the sanctum a few dozen feet
away. As he sat there, perhaps, all through the
morning, he would occasionally address a remark or
a question to the busy man beside him. Mr. Ticknor
was nervously quick in every action; his smile was
brilliant, and his blue eyes, although kindly and
humorous, were direct and piercing. When after a
moment's pause he replied to Hawthorne with a
sudden toss of his head and a swift, keen flash of his
eye, the latter would flush to his thick hair and turn
his dark eyes almost as if asking why the other had
spoken; but an instant later he remembered his own
remark, grasped and adjusted the connection, smiled
warmly and affectionately, and resumed his quiet
reflection; his face always assuming an expression of
rest and content.

Thus it was that Hawthorne and his publisher
spent many hours together in the counting-room of
the Old Corner Bookstore.

II

THE OLD CORNER BOOKSTORE

APART from the interest attaching to the famous literary personages who frequented the Old Corner Bookstore, the antique edifice is in itself worthy of much respectful consideration. It stands a curious and lone representative of the architecture and craftsmanship of two hundred years ago, being the oldest brick building in the city.

It is also a significant milestone on a road whereon moved together the advance of literature, and the progress of commercial dignity and equity in this country. For here the founder of a publishing-house established by his voluntary act the principle that an author, even though a foreigner, had a right to participate in the earnings and profits of his mind, and thus made his business house, not indeed the richest in America, but the most just and highly esteemed, — the exemplar which others soon came to follow and emulate until its policy had become virtually incorporated in international law.

In 1712, the present building was erected on the Old Corner estate, to replace one that had been burned the year previous, and in the course of two centuries it has known many ownerships and occupancies, though it remained a bookstore during the whole of its second century.

Those who desire to follow its early history more

minutely will find the story of its modifications and transfers carefully recorded by the late Dr. Nathaniel B. Shurtleff, once mayor of Boston, who has furnished the material necessary to satisfy the antiquarian and the searcher after titles. The whole tract of land, then extending along School Street nearly as far as the present City Hall site, to where the Niles stable was, and the Niles Block now is, and for quite a distance on Washington Street, then known as Cornhill, was granted about 1630 to William Hutchinson, who took possession of it in September, 1634, when he arrived from England with his family.

Hutchinson was prominent in many ways and may be pointed out as the most distinguished possessor of the property in question. The bold and radical theological attitude of his wife, the famous Anne Hutchinson, caused their banishment from the colony, and the estate passed in part to one Henry Shrimpton, who improved it somewhat. From his descendants it passed in 1707 to the apothecary Thomas Crease, who erected the present building.

After other sales and gifts, the property again came into the possession of descendants of the Hutchinsons, whose reëntry was made about the middle of the eighteenth century. Toward the close of that century Edward Sohier and his wife Susanna [born Brimmer] became the owners, succeeded by the widow of Henderson Inches and by Herman Brimmer.

The neighborhood, although so near to the residences of "the quality" and to various public edifices, was always dedicated to trade, many favorite shops and offices being mentioned as occupying adjacent lots. The savor of Mr. Crease's drug store long hung about these particular premises, the last apothecary there having been Dr. Samuel Clarke [father of the late Rev. Dr. James Freeman Clarke], who retained his shop and residence here until 1828, when the character of the place was finally changed and it began its century dedicated to the world of books.

The building consisted in Dr. Clarke's time, of the Old Corner one, containing the shop, and a western extension of the family quarters, projecting into the garden at the back and offering the real front of the establishment.

The first link in the chain of the bookish associations which made the Old Corner famous, was forged by the late Timothy Harrington Carter, who came from his home in Lancaster, Massachusetts, in 1815, to seek his fortune in Boston; he found employment at the bookstore of Cummings and Hilliard, at the corner of Washington Street and Spring Lane, where such business was continued until the time of James Munroe and Company, some years later. When Mr. Carter came of age he entered the firm as a partner and took the entire management of the business, enlarging its scope and multiplying its profits. In 1827, Mr. Carter, having given a year to study at home and abroad, set about organizing a new book house, in which he intended to be only a silent partner; it was his plan to institute a sort of publication trust for the manufacture and sale of books too costly or extensive for single firms to undertake.

But jealousy and fear were aroused, and there was enough trade influence with the legislature to obtain the insertion in the charter of an innocent-looking clause which was effectually prohibitive.

Mr. Carter then arranged a partnership with a younger brother, and a clerk, under the name of Carter, Hendee and Company, and, being the capitalist, set about securing a business site. He chose the Old Corner, which Buckingham says had already been used by Mr. Benjamin Perkins for a year or so as a bookstore, but could obtain no longer term of lease than six and a half years, although he secured a verbal agreement to restore to him or pay him for any permanent improvement.

Mr. Carter at once lowered the first floor to the street level, and built upon the garden the block which ran along School Street as far as Number 11. In the rear of this extension, concealed by it and known to comparatively few people, he also set up a great wooden building, which he used for the seven presses of the printery, in which he was concerned, for he engaged part of his means in type-founding, printing, and other kindred enterprises. Those presses, although eventually worked by steam, were at first run by a team of Canadian horses.

But Mr. Carter's firm was not alone in creating thus early a literary atmosphere about the place. Mr. Samuel G. Goodrich, afterwards known to the world as "Peter Parley," and to whose initiative was due the first collection made of Nathaniel Hawthorne's fugitive writings, occupied, as author and publisher, the second story of the new School Street building.

Meanwhile the upper story had an associated occupancy, being used as a printing-office by Mr. Isaac R. Butts, who eventually took on authorship, as the shrewd and trusty compiler of various legal and commercial works. At about this period the front upper story was possessed by a skillful, but irascible, and not always punctual bookbinder, Mr. Peter Low.

When Mr. Carter took the estate it was paying about fourteen hundred dollars a year; but when later the owners refused to extend his lease or to carry out the agreements made on their behalf on account of his improvements, it was rendering about four thousand dollars, and was in such a condition that it always afterwards leased at a high rent, the tenant bearing also the taxes and other charges, thus increasing handsomely the temporary and permanent value of the estate for the benefit of the owners who had done nothing to earn it. Perhaps in the whole city one can hardly find a more striking illustration of "the unearned increment" than this, — a mere homestead value having grown to a property of its present magnitude by the character and effort of its occupants, its owners having expended neither money, care, nor labor.

The private fortunes of Mr. Carter suffered somewhat at the time when the collapse of the United States Bank brought about much disaster, but still his firm remained so prosperous that the retail and miscellaneous publishing business could be sold in 1832 at a good price to Messrs. John Allen and William Davis Ticknor, young men with whom Mr. Carter associated himself for a while as a silent partner and adviser. After about a year, Mr. Allen, who seemed not to be thoroughly adapted for the business, withdrew, and Mr. Ticknor conducted it alone until late into the forties, having established himself as a publisher from the very start.

And now, as the character and trend of the house's affairs were established by him, and its publications (in spite of any modifications of the firm upon the title-pages) were known in the trade generally as "Ticknor's books," something more should be said of the modest but strong and positive man who changed the attitude of America towards the world of literature.

William Davis Ticknor was born on August 6, 1810, in Lebanon, New Hampshire; he was the eldest son of William Ticknor, a prosperous farmer, and his wife, Betsey Ellis, who brought her husband a large family of children.

The Ticknor family, originating in England, first appeared on this side of the Atlantic in the person of William Ticknor, of Kent, who settled in Boston in 1646, and in Scituate, Massachusetts, in 1656, and became quite a personage in that town. His "warehouse" is mentioned in the town record in 1660. He held office as selectman, assessor, and surveyor, and was a sergeant of General Cudworth's guard during King Philip's War, in 1676.

His son William removed in 1710 to Lebanon, Connecticut, which was thereafter the headquarters of the race until 1774, when Elisha Ticknor, grandfather of our subject and of his eminent cousin George Ticknor, the historian of Spanish literature,

removed to Lebanon, New Hampshire. One branch
of the stock still remained in Connecticut, however,
and became somewhat noted for the skill in medicine attained by several individuals, especially Caleb,
who was long a distinguished practitioner in Baltimore, and whose son Frank contributed to the cause
of the South, during the War of the Rebellion, some
of the best lyrics which it inspired. Elisha was a
figure of some importance in his time, for he held a
colonel's commission in the New Hampshire contin-
gent to the expedition against Crown Point and in
other campaigns of the Revolution.

In 1827, William D. Ticknor, prompted by the
country boy's perennial desire to try his fortune in
the city, set out for Boston, his material capital consisting in a little sum of profits from the raising of a
few sheep which his father had encouraged him to
keep upon the homestead farm. He was a stranger,
but not without relatives, friends, and probable
supporters, for two uncles were living in the city, —
Elisha, father of the cousin, who was in time to be a
Harvard professor and a famous literarian, and Benjamin, who was a well-to-do broker. In the office of
the latter he at once found employment; and when
his uncle died, a few years later, he conducted the
business so well to its settlement that he was offered
a position in the Columbian Bank, which he accepted
and held for a year or two.

His financial ability being recognized, a better
place was offered him in the bank; but the Ticknors,
to whatever occupation they were bound in order
to make a living, had always bookish tastes and

sympathies, and the young man availed himself of
the opportunity to go into the book business with
Mr. John Allen, who was already established in it.
In 1832, the partnership was formed under the style
of Allen & Ticknor.

Mr. Ticknor was married on December 25, 1832,
to Miss Emeline Staniford Holt, daughter of Master
Benjamin Holt, of the old Mayhew School, and
granddaughter of the Rev. Thomas Baldwin, D.D.
Seven children were born to them, of whom two died
in infancy; the others, all of whom survived their
father, were two daughters, Emeline and Alice, and
three sons, Howard Malcom, Benjamin Holt, and
Thomas Baldwin; the boys all graduated at Harvard
and in turn entered their father's establishment.

Mrs. Ticknor was a woman of great charm of person and nobility of character; she possessed exquisite
literary taste, and was devoted to the realm of books,
always preferring a quiet nook in her library to the
most brilliant social function; in the memory of those
who knew her only in her later years, she remains a
gentle and serene presence with a smile that was
ever a benediction.

Until 1845 the name of William D. Ticknor stood
alone at the foot of the house's title-pages, and it
was his taste which selected the books which those
title-pages introduced. It was during this epoch that
Longfellow, Lowell, and Tennyson among the poets,
and many eminent men among scientists and scholars, were presented to the American public by
Mr. Ticknor. One of his first books was Mrs. Norton's poems, and his early catalogues include many

Aet 30

William D. Ticknor

important volumes such as "Rejected Addresses," "The Confessions of an Opium Eater," the initial volume of Whittier, and the poems of Barry Cornwall and Robert Browning, which last he continued to publish long after it was clear that they would yield his house no pecuniary profit.

During his first decade of publishing, Mr. Ticknor extended his own reading and his acquaintance, increased his influence, and established relations which were strong bases for the future development of his house. He was esteemed not alone as a sound merchant and financier, a warm friend and a strong man in the Baptist denomination, but also as clear, equitable, and authoritative in his literary judgment. He was a director of the Boston Lyceum, treasurer of the American Institute of Instruction, a trustee of the Perkins Institute, and a leading member of the School Committee. It was his own judgment which made known to America De Quincey, Tennyson, Charles Reade, and other great English names on the catalogue of his house, and it was his decision which transferred from the disintegrating establishment of Messrs. Phillips, Sampson and Company the "Atlantic Monthly," although his partner, Mr. Fields, who was abroad at the time, opposed the purchase urgently, prognosticating for it such an unhappy end as came to Putnam's, and other propitiously started periodicals. His warmest indorsement of the purchase was when he wrote resignedly that the "best must be made of it," yet it is only fair to say that subsequently he strove enthusiastically to make it of the "best."

A nephew of Mr. Ticknor, who as a boy served a brief apprenticeship at the Old Corner, recalls with interest his boyish experiences with the frequenters of this popular resort. It was his duty to reach the store at 7 A.M., before which time the negro porter had done the necessary sweeping; he, with the other boys, then did the dusting, so that by 7.30, when Mr. Ticknor appeared, all was in readiness.

Among the literary habitués were some "early birds" who would appear at this favorite rendezvous even before the arrival of the head of the house. In this category was the delightful and eccentric poet, John G. Saxe, who often put in an appearance by 7 A.M., much to the satisfaction of the office boys, to whom he spouted the drollest verses. At the back of the office was a huge packing-table, upon which it was Mr. Saxe's custom to stretch himself at full length; placing a pile of books under his head, he would make himself comfortable according to his taste, after which he proceeded to recite poems to the enchanted boys, who grouped about him, with open mouths and idle dusters. Saxe would lie there composing and reciting one amusing verse after another, and meanwhile the boys would cast stealthy glances out of the window to see if the head of the house was coming. As soon as they caught sight of his erect form briskly approaching, the cry went up, "Here comes the boss," and the poetical séance came to an abrupt end; the poet bestirred himself from his recumbent pose, and the neglected dusting was hastily completed.

Mr. Carter notes in his autobiography that it was

customary during the early part of the last century
for merchants to receive into their families some of
their employees in part payment for their services,
and that he himself began with forty dollars a year
and his board. Among several whom Mr. Ticknor
had at this time, in his home in Pinckney Street, were
two young men, who afterwards achieved noteworthy reputations, — James T. Fields, of Portsmouth, who eventually became Mr. Ticknor's partner, and a prominent and popular man in literary
life, and Thomas Niles, Jr., of Boston, who was in
time the chief director of the house of Roberts Brothers. Both had good business heads, but Fields had
so alert and eager a mind and power of assimilation
and cultivation that, as he grew to manhood and
profited by the advantages at his disposal, he established himself in another home and formed a coterie
of his own friends; foremost among these was E. P.
Whipple, afterwards known as the forcible, influen-
tial, and much-sought essayist, critic, and lecturer.

Young Fields was capable, versatile and ambitious, and possessed many attractive qualities; he
availed himself promptly of every social and commercial opportunity, and in 1845, Mr. Ticknor took
him into partnership together with Mr. John Reed,
Jr., who contributed something to the house's capital, but withdrew after a few years. At this time the
imprint on the house's title-page became Ticknor,
Reed and Fields, being subsequently compressed to
Ticknor and Fields, and continuing so until after
Mr. Ticknor's death.

"Now ensued a period glorious for American

letters," writes a contemporaneous critic, "during which, the Old Corner attracted to itself the greatest of native and English writers, comparatively few Americans of distinction being associated with any other house. The sterling worth, the mercantile dignity and sound judgment of Ticknor, and the swift perception, the brilliancy and the social charm of Fields, gave in their union, power, reliability, and geniality to the establishment, and the Old Corner became the constant resort of wits, poets, scientists, philosophers and the distinguished of all professions.

"Here came Rufus Choate to explain the hieroglyphic memoranda in which he set down the names of the books he wanted to come by the next 'boat' as he always called a steamship. Here came Holmes, to say how he loved to practice medicine and teach anatomy, and how his one difficulty was not to pour out from his stores of knowledge faster than his pupils could absorb. Here Thackeray towered above his admirers and told gaily of his American experiences and impressions, none the less amused because the point of his story made against his own simplicity or ignorance. Like Hawthorne, he was not fond of bookish topics, did not like to 'talk shop,' and was more interested in mere men and women than in authors, caring more for their humanity than their compositions.

"Here Henry Giles scintillated with such brilliant epigram, and outlined his thoughts so incisively that his misshaped form was forgotten, and Whittier's 'thee' and 'thou' greeted his friends shyly and tenderly. Here were seen the burly figure of bluff Henry Ward Beecher, and the slender form of his gentle-mannered sister, Mrs. Stowe, the sweet, kindly face of Lucy Larcom, the spiritual countenance of Ralph Waldo Emerson, and the round, rosy, beardless, boyish face of Thomas Starr King; and here were often to be met jovial John G. Saxe, the herculean, whose talent and touch assimilated him more nearly than any other American to Thomas Hood, in fun and fancy, and bright-eyed little 'Tom Folio,' with a bundle of books and papers clasped in his arms under his short cloak, and ever on the point of some fine literary discovery, of which too often some one with whom he had been over generously confidential gained ultimately the credit.

"Here the great men of the bar, pulpit, platform and university chair exchanged their notions of science, ethics, history, poetry, politics and people, and Gliddon discoursed of Egypt and the latest find in mummies; here Biscaccianti, Kellogg, Cary, and other *prime donne* dropped bits of song; Mrs. Kemble, Murdoch, Mr. and Mrs. Barrow, Warren, Vanderhoff, Forrest, Davenport, and Brougham scattered the bright gossip of the stage, and Ole Bull talked of his northern home and his 'leetle yellow phiolin.'

"John Leitch, one of the great Cunard captains, passed most of his Boston stays reading away for dear life on a square, green-topped stool in a front corner, and here came the village clergyman and the country doctor yearly to replenish their libraries, depending for the profitable expenditure of their

hard savings upon the advice of the clerks, who had
in their turn been instructed, ever kindly and help-
fully, by the theologians, surgeons and doctors who
were daily visitors. Here came the 'solid men of
Boston' to enrich their libraries with fine sets of
standard authors, or to subscribe for new editions of
Scott or Dickens; here, too, came their wives to secure the latest keepsakes and albums of fashion, and
sometimes to request the sending to their houses for
inspection of some illustrated volumes, which occasionally came back with traces of cake and coffee on
their pages, and here came the seekers for big Bibles
for presentation to pulpit, or at weddings, for the
Old Corner kept the only stock of Oxford Bibles in
the town."

Lectures, readings, and many concerts depended
upon the interest of the Old Corner for the sale of
their tickets, and it should be added that in those
primitive days, when a lottery for a good cause was
thought not wrong, many a charity, church, or
library looked hither for an agency to dispense its
tickets even to distant places. These were the
palmy times of the old New England lecture system,
when the cleverest, strongest, and most attractive
speakers were to be had almost for the asking. The
average fee for a lecturer was rarely more than ten
dollars, but a poet or a first-class reader got five, or
possibly ten dollars more. Mr. Ticknor's long connection with the Boston Lyceum and the Institute
of Instruction made the store a headquarters for
speakers and for committees, and many a winter
course was arranged there.

As years passed, the Old Corner became in the right sense great, and the expansion of its affairs necessitated more division of labor. Mr. Ticknor gave especial attention to the manufacturing and financial departments and Mr. Fields devoted himself more to the literary relations. But the two partners always lived and worked in harmonious union, and every enterprise represented a real concert of thought and action. Mr. Ticknor was glad to let his younger associate assume most of the social and hospitable representation, which the joint purse of the house provided; this, however, was because of his retiring disposition and not from any lack of social tact or charm.

When the house began its ultimately long list of entertainments, with the dinner to Charles Mackay, and the following one to Agassiz, Mr. Ticknor was reluctant to take the head of the table, but occupied it with grace and felicity; and a note of Hawthorne's penned while they were together in England, thanks him for responding to a toast on his behalf at a large public banquet.

While the exterior of the Old Corner underwent various changes, the interior remained virtually the same. Beside the Washington Street door stood a tall, slender mirror framed in darkened gilt, which had come down from Dr. Clarke's time, and had in its day reflected beauty, grace, charm, and coquetry, as well as gravity, stability, and philosophic dignity. The upper left-hand corner, looking back from the front entrance, was inclosed with green curtains, behind which Mr. Fields had a cozy nook, whose

broad window-seat was always full of manuscripts,
new books, letters, and elegant trifles. Here there
was always plenteous company of the best and
brightest minds of the time. Had there been any
modern Boswell present to take notes of the conversation there, or could the old walls themselves have
repeated what they had seen and heard, an unriv-
aled "table-book," of wit, wisdom, personal description, and anecdote might easily have been compiled.
But alas, nothing now survives of all that brilliant
and evanescent chat which oftentimes possessed a
charm far greater than that preserved upon the
printed page.

The long School Street building contained a series
of ground-floor shops, and at the end of the sequence
was situated Mrs. Abner Haven's coffee-room, which
was a famous place of resort and refreshment. Originally patrons had the use of only one large back
room, lined with high hard black slippery hair-cloth
sofas before which stood a few great round mahog-
any-framed and marble-topped tables. As custom
increased, a staircase was built to the second story
of the wooden house behind, and the refection rooms
were continued forward to the room over the shop.
The kitchen, where presided the old Italian cook,
David, whom everybody knew, was also in that
house and sent its viands down a narrow archway to
the side door of the shop.

Beside the usual cakes, candies, and ice-creams of
the period, Mrs. Haven's was famous for a few things
which can no longer be easily procured, such as perfect toast, a peculiarly rich thick lemon pie, "jum-

bles," shining Brighton biscuit, Washington pies, "gibraltars," plump cream-cakes, and an exhilarating boiled coffee, which was suspected of owing something of its flavor to a slight infusion of brandy added just as it came to the boil. In time a few cold meats were added to the bill of fare, and such simple provision sufficed for the literarians, artists, merchants, and bankers of that day, who could always be found lunching and hobnobbing there in groups about noontime, or possibly about the middle of the afternoon, having perhaps adjourned from Mr. Fields's sanctum for greater privacy and freedom from social interruption.

There were few radical changes in the occupancy of the various shops contained in the building until the ever-augmenting business of Ticknor and Fields, which required additional space for storage and distribution, caused the dismissal of nearly all of the adjacent tenants. And eventually outgrowing even their extended premises, Messrs. Ticknor and Fields removed to 124 Tremont Street, where a building had been commodiously and finely arranged for their especial use and convenience, and where as many as possible of the old associations and characteristics were perpetuated.

III

WITH the publication of "The Scarlet Letter" in 1850, Hawthorne said good-bye forever to literary obscurity. A broad wave of popular applause greeted his ears from all parts of this country and was wafted back to him from across the seas. Following this success, Hawthorne busied himself with writing "The House of the Seven Gables," upon which he expended about five months. This book was completed in January, 1851, and when it appeared a couple of months later the demand for it was very great.

After finishing this work, Hawthorne allowed himself a vacation of some four months, beginning the "Wonder Book" in June of this year. The latter work was written very rapidly and with keen enjoyment on the author's part; it was the only book produced by him that contained not a single gloomy page. It was finished in the first week of July, 1851, and only a few months intervened between this and "The Blithedale Romance," which was written between the first of December and the last of April, 1852.

With the completion of the latter book, Hawthorne had at first intended penning another romance, upon some theme more cheerful than those heretofore put forth. Instead, however, he produced, in response to many entreaties from young people, a second volume of "Wonder" stories, under the title of "Tanglewood Tales." And it is at this particular period in his career that his correspondence with Mr. Ticknor opens; of these letters about one hundred and fifty have been preserved, and they extend over some thirteen years, the first being dated 1851, and the last 1864, the year of the writer's death, and the first of them touch upon the publication of the last two volumes referred to.

The greater part of these letters were written while Hawthorne was American consul at Liverpool, and they contain so much that is of interest and value that the publication of a portion of them seems very desirable. While many of them are trivial in character and contain no special contribution to the world of letters, yet they cannot fail to appeal to those who desire to become more intimately acquainted with the personality of Hawthorne, which these communications reflect so strongly, and also to those who are students of the social, economic, and political conditions of both England and America fifty years ago.

Hawthorne's personality, which at times impresses the reader as so vague and illusive, is one on which it is of interest to throw all the light possible to be obtained. Mr. Howells has perhaps best expressed these intangible qualities when he writes: —

"I am painfully aware that I have not summoned before the reader the image of the man as it has always stood in my memory, and I feel a sort of shame for my failure. He was altogether so simple that it

seems as if it would be easy to do so; but perhaps a
spirit from the other world would be simple too, and
yet would no more stand at parle, or consent to be
sketched, than Hawthorne. In fact he was always
more or less merging into the shadow, which was in a
few years wholly to close over him; there was nothing uncanny in his presence, there was nothing
even unwilling, but he had that apparitional quality
of some great minds which kept Shakespeare largely
unknown to those who thought themselves his inti-
mates, and has at last left him a sort of doubt. There
was nothing teasing or wilfully elusive in Hawthorne's impalpability, such as I afterwards felt in
Thoreau; if he was not there to your touch it was no
fault of his: it was because your touch was dull, and
wanted the use of contact with such natures. The
hand passes through the veridical phantom without
a sense of its presence, but the phantom is none the
less veridical for all that."

Hawthorne's capacity for "merging into the
shadow" when people sought a closer intimacy with
him, or strove to draw him out in order better to understand him, made him perchance seem more a man
of mystery to casual acquaintances than the facts
warranted. Hawthorne was no doubt often prone to
slip away from the prosaic world of substance for the
delightful realm of shadows; but there were times
when he was merely shy, and others when he was
only determined not to be bored.

To those most intimately acquainted with this
writer he showed another phase of Hawthorne, one
which laughed at the shadowy apparition, poked fun

at his own foibles, and at long-cherished institutions, and posed (if such a word can be used in connection with one who was childishly natural) as a hard-headed and calculating individual.

For a glimpse of the practical side of a man who was the most impractical of beings, one must turn to the letters which he penned to those closely linked to him both by ties of affection and also of business. In such communications Hawthorne found relaxation from the tension entailed by literary labors, or from wearisome consular duties. He spoke his mind freely and with a kind of boyish irresponsibility. He indulged in cutting and satirical remarks about men, and things, as well as institutions that he truly respected. He set himself forth as a mercenary being, and pretended to a devotion to convivial indulgence that would have shocked the sensibilities of those who did not know the man behind the pen.

During his sojourn in England as consul to Liverpool his letters to his friend Ticknor were most characteristic of this spontaneous, non-reflective Hawthorne. He "ran on" with a careless disregard of anything beyond his present mood. He talked with the freedom of a man who knows that he is so well understood that it does not matter what he says. He made daring comments for the fun of making them, in one paragraph, and took them back or softened them, for truth's sake, in the next.

The correspondence opens a year before the Liverpool appointment, when the writer is in Lenox, and touches upon the removal of the Hawthorne family to Concord. Soon after their establishment in the latter town, the negotiations began in regard to the biography of Franklin Pierce, which caused Hawthorne to lay aside his other work for the time being.

In the following letter, penned from Concord, July 13, 1852, Hawthorne refers to the appearance of "The Blithedale Romance": —

DEAR TICKNOR, — I see you announce the book as to be published to-morrow. Please to send a copy to Mrs. Horatio Bridge, care of F. I. Bridge, Esq., Appraiser's Office, Custom-House, Boston.

I am reduced to a penniless condition; and Mrs. Hawthorne, I believe, has thirteen cents in ready money. Please to send a small supply — say twenty-five dollars — as speedily as possible.

I make no progress with the biography, on account of the sluggishness of the people who ought to furnish the materials.

Truly yours,
NATH'L HAWTHORNE.

A fortnight later he writes that he is about to begin the biography of Pierce. This work was reluctantly undertaken, although the writer was deeply attached to the President-to-be, as Hawthorne was conscious of the fact that Pierce would probably offer him some foreign appointment, and shrank from the suggestion that his biographical work must seem like a shrewd political move. But at the other's urgent request he finally discharged the task, which he was both glad and sorry to undertake. Pierce and he had been faithful friends since their college days, and

Hawthorne loved and respected the future President, and never to the end of his life did he find any cause to alter his sentiments towards him.

In the letter which follows Hawthorne refers jocosely to his preparations for a trip into Maine: —

Concord, July 24th, 1852.

Dear Ticknor, — I am glad you have got rid of so many of the new books. Sweep them off as fast as you can. Don't let your shelves be disgraced with such trash.

As for the biography, I have just been supplied with the materials for commencing it. I shall set to work to-morrow in good earnest, and shall not show my face till it is finished.

Your claret was most excellent and acceptable, and has already given me a great deal of comfort. Some other friends have sent me some sauterne, some champagne, and some sherry; and I have laid in a supply of first-rate brandy on my own hook; so that I hope to keep myself pretty jolly in spite of the Maine Law.

Truly yours,

Nath'l Hawthorne.

Hawthorne wrote later, in regard to his "Life" of Pierce: "I was terribly reluctant to undertake this work, and tried to persuade Pierce, both by letter and viva-voce, — that I could not perform it so well as many others; but he thought differently, and of course, after a friendship of thirty years, it was impossible to refuse my best efforts in his behalf, at

this great pinch of his life. . . . Before undertaking
it, I made an inward resolution that I would accept
no office from him; but, to say the truth, I doubt
whether it would not be rather folly than heroism to
adhere to this purpose in case he should offer me
anything particularly good. We shall see. A foreign
mission I could not afford to take. The consulship at
Liverpool I might. I have several invitations from
English celebrities to come over there, and this office
would make all straight." And this dream of the
Liverpool consulship was realized immediately after
General Pierce's election to the Presidency.

One needs only to glance over the collection of
Hawthorne's letters to his publisher to realize the
constant thoughtfulness of the latter, who was
untiring in his rendering of small as well as large
services. Hawthorne, who was from the first singularly dependent upon the offices of this devoted
friend, called upon him for a thousand and one small
errands and commissions which would fill the modern publisher with wonder. And Ticknor took pleasure in performing a great variety of thoughtful services which his friend would not have dreamed of
suggesting. The following note voices the author's
thanks for one of those frequent tokens of regard
which gave such pleasure to the sender: —

CONCORD, January 1st, 1853.

DEAR TICKNOR, — I thank you heartily for those
cigars. They will keep your memory fragrant for
many a day to come.

The account arrived to-day. I am glad to see so

good a balance to my credit. It will diminish fast enough.

Could you ask Healy on what day it would be convenient to have me sit? I don't think Mrs. Hawthorne will be able to come again — she being quite ill with influenza.

Yours truly,
NATHANIEL HAWTHORNE.

The month following, Hawthorne writes in regard to the Liverpool consulship, which seems likely to be offered him if the desire of the author is made sufficiently obvious to his friend Franklin Pierce, then in the presidential chair. It devolves upon Ticknor to ascertain how the land lies, and to bring the matter to the President's attention, and so the following suggestion is forwarded: —

CONCORD, February 16th, 1853.

DEAR TICKNOR, — Are you diplomatist enough to find out from the General whether he means to remove young Cass from the Roman chargé-ship? If you could do this before he leaves Boston, it would be doing me a very great favor — not that I have anything personally to do with it. I should not like to have him know that I asked the question; but perhaps you might get the truth out of him by inquiring what he would give me, in case I did not go to Liverpool.

The fact is, I have a friend, who wishes to apply for it, in case Cass is to be removed.

Very truly yours,
N. H.

Ten days later Hawthorne forwards a letter for his publisher to deliver in person to Franklin Pierce.

CONCORD, February 26, 1853.

DEAR TICKNOR, — I enclose you a letter for the Emperor Frank, which I hope you will deliver in person, and follow up its arguments with any better ones that may occur to yourself. For this purpose, I have sent it unsealed.

I rather think you had better not show it to Colonel Miller — not that I care much about it either way; but it was not written for his eye.

I trust you will go to Washington. You ought to be seeing about the red tape and wrapping-paper. You might help Colonel Miller, and very probably, do me a good turn into the bargain. The General means well; but it would be a pity if he should be led into doing a wrong thing as regards that consulship.

Truly yours,

N. H.

Three weeks later the copy for the "Tanglewood Tales" goes forward to its publisher with the following comment: —

CONCORD, March 15, 1853.

DEAR TICKNOR, — I send the "Tanglewood Tales." According to my calculation, they will make rather less than three hundred pages, containing the same number of lines as the pages of the "Wonder Book." I wish you would send it to press immediately, and have the illustrations done after it is printed; otherwise, I may not be able to correct the proofs.

Yours truly,

N. H.

One week before, on March 9th, the writer had penned in his note-book the words: —

"Finished, this day, the 'Tanglewood Tales.' They were written in the following order: —

"The Pomegranate Seeds.

"The Minotaur.

"The Golden Fleece.

"The Dragon's Teeth.

"Circe's Palace.

"The Pygmies.

"The introduction is yet to be written. — Wrote it 13th March."

This book, Hawthorne's only literary production of this epoch, had been relinquished in order that its author might write the "Life" of Franklin Pierce.

The Liverpool appointment which Hawthorne had hoped for, and which Ticknor had been untiring in his efforts to help his friend obtain, was an assured thing before the end of March; and on the 28th of that month, two days after its confirmation, Hawthorne wrote with satisfaction that all uncertainty concerning it was at an end. There were, however, various important matters which could only be attended to in person, and Hawthorne's presence in Washington at this time was an invaluable asset for him; but, as usual, he dreaded making any move alone, and at once appealed to his friend to aid him in this special instance, by taking a trip to the capital with him. Among other things he mentions casually that he would like to have his publisher order a new dress-coat for him.

CONCORD, March 28, 1853.

DEAR TICKNOR, — The President has made the appointment; but it is not to take effect until the first of August — my predecessor having resigned, but wishing to retain his position till that date.

I feel rather inclined to follow our idea of going to Washington in two or three weeks. My best dress-coat is rather shabby (befitting an author much more than a man of consular rank); so, when you next smoke a cigar with our friend Driscoll, I wish you would tell him to put another suit on the stocks for me — a black dress-coat and pantaloons; and he may select the cloth. I shall want them before we go to Washington.

Perhaps I may be in Boston in the course of the week, — perhaps not.

Truly yours,
NATH'L HAWTHORNE.

On the 14th of April the friends set out for Washington; it was Hawthorne's first visit to the capital and proved a new and enjoyable experience for him. During this stay he was greatly lionized, and he and his companion were flooded with invitations and were royally entertained. Hawthorne was fairly tired out with the social festivities, but he was loath to leave Washington, which seemed to give him such an admirable view of this country from a central point, and also offered such ample opportunities for the acquiring of just such information as the new consul desired.

When at last the friends were once more headed for Boston, they journeyed straight homewards without stopping over in New York as they had first intended doing. The letters written at this time by Mr. Ticknor to his wife touch upon their social experiences and also upon the success of the business side of the expedition, which had resulted, as the visitors hoped it would, in augmenting Hawthorne's consular income.

BIXBY'S HOTEL, SUNDAY, NEW YORK, April 17, 1853.

MY DEAR WIFE, — We are thus far on our journey. The ride to-day was rather tedious, though we came without accident and arrived at 12 P.M. It was our intention to have gone to Philadelphia yesterday, but finally concluded to hold over till Monday. I have been occupied every moment . . .

Yesterday we went to see the splendid steamer "Atlantic" off. She took 155 passengers, — quite enough for comfort. She's a magnificent ship.

In the P.M. Mr. Bixby very kindly invited us to visit the Croton Water Works, — some ten miles out of town. The bridge over which the pipes are laid, is a grand affair, 114 feet high and 1450 feet long, and cost one million of dollars. It is built in the most substantial manner and is really one of the best specimens of mason work that I ever saw. We dined at "High Bridge" and got into town about half past five. The ride was very pleasant with the exception of a cold east wind, which furnished us all with slight colds.

We told the Landlord at the "Bridge" that we wanted a plain beef-steak and fried potatoes for dinner. He replied (a colored gemmin): "Don't you want a real nice dinner?" We said, "No, nothing but a plain steak."

In about half an hour we were summoned to dinner. We first found a plentiful supply of soup. Then came broiled shad, — veal cutlets — beefsteak, — roast chicken, and the "fixins" — pudding, pies, etc., a regular laid out dinner. And of course we had to pay, accordingly. And this is the way the New Yorkers shave one.

Last evening we went to a "Literary Club" and spent a very pleasant evening.

It began to rain about eight o'clock and continues a regular cold Northeaster. The bells are now ringing for church, but as I am minus an umbrella I shall hardly venture out, . . . I am engaged to dine with Mr. W. Appleton at half-past one o'clock in company with Bixby. Hawthorne was previously engaged to dine with Professor Hackley. . . .

Three days later Ticknor writes from Washington: —

"We have at length arrived at the end of our journey. We left Philadelphia at half past eight this morning, spent five hours in Baltimore and reached here at nine this evening. Although 't is twelve o'clock I will just apprise you of my safe arrival, as I

shall probably have little time to write during my
stay here.

"Washington is comparatively quiet though there
are still a plenty of office-seekers lingering about the
Hotels. I dare say I may be looked upon as one of
the "needy," especially as I come with Hawthorne.
But I have not yet made up my mind to ask favors of
this sort. Better peddle newspapers.

"We have just taken a walk around the White
House. It far exceeds Hawthorne's expectations.
To-morrow at nine he goes to see the President. I
shall defer my call till a later hour. . . .

"I have been absent seven days. I can hardly
realize where the time has been spent. But so it is.
Oh! how swift the days and weeks pass. Soon will
those allotted us be numbered. May they be filled
with well-performed duties. . . ."

On April 22, two days later, he continues his comments upon the Washington visit: —

"The weather is delightful here, — very warm.
A summer suit would not be uncomfortable. Fruit
trees in blossom. I have just returned from a visit
to the Capitol. The objects of interest are so far
apart that it requires much time to see them, not to
speak of the labor.

"I called upon the President this morning. He
is looking well and in my judgment is doing well.
He was very cordial, and I think he bears his honors with becoming modesty, and yet with proper
dignity.

"I also called on Mr. Young, who is most engaged
in his department. I called with Hawthorne on

Judge Cushing yesterday, where we met the Secretary of the Treasury.

"I told the President that I had been unable to decide what to ask for, — but upon the whole would leave it for him to suggest some liberal 'gift.' He replied that he thought he had better exchange places with me. Believing my position to be the most agreeable. I, of course, declined. Hawthorne is quite a lion here. Much attention is shown, and yet it annoys him very much. He is to take tea with the President to-night. We shall hardly leave here before Monday. . . .

"I left my *business* in Boston and have hardly thought of it, so far as care is concerned. I made up my mind when I left, to leave anxiety behind so far as business is concerned. We intend if possible to go to Mount Vernon. It is about 16 miles from Washington. The Public Conveyance is only three times a week. I shall go over to Alexandria — and enter for once 'Old Virginia.'"

Hawthorne's enjoyment of the visit caused it to be extended beyond the limit at first planned, and Ticknor writes on the 27th: —

"When I last wrote you, I expected ere this to have been at home, — but have been delayed from day to day till I have about concluded to leave Hawthorne behind. I am only waiting for him, and this 'loafing' is more wearisome than work. I have, however, had a very pleasant time thus far in Washington. I expected fully to have left this morning, but the President wished Hawthorne to remain till

Saturday, and although he would not urge me to wait for him, I felt that he would be disappointed if I left him. I therefore telegraphed to Boston to know if I was specially wanted. Mr. Fields says, 'No, stay and enjoy' . . . Had I known that Hawthorne would remain so long I should have left last Saturday.

"Sunday and Monday it rained all the time. Yesterday was a most delightful day. To-day is as warm as June. Hawthorne has gone, with some friends to 'Mount Vernon,' and had I been informed in regard to the 'Boat' (it goes only three times a week) I should have gone also.

"I have had several interviews with the President. He appears very well, and yet I fear he is very far from giving full satisfaction to the 'Progressive' portion of his party. I am perfectly surprised to see to what extent this spirit is carried here.

"I dined yesterday, with several gentlemen (among them Senator Douglas) who represent 'Young America.' I am convinced that old party lines in every section of the country are breaking up and that there is a spirit abroad which is to revolutionize the politics of the country. Whether it will be for the best good of the Nation, I think is a question of very great importance—but the tide is rolling on, —and good men of all parties must control and guide, or we shall 'suffer loss.' I have learnt more of political intrigue and management, since I have been here, than I ever dreamed of, —and I assure you, my dearest E., that I believe that of all men these politicians are the most miserable here, — and they most certainly have poor prospects for the future.

"Dr. Baily of the 'Era' has been very polite to us. We have dined with him. He has taken us to ride twice.

"I shall know to-morrow whether Hawthorne will leave on Saturday, if not I shall leave him, as I feel that I ought to be at home. . . .

"We 'breakfasted' with some friends on Monday at eleven; got through at three."

Ticknor wrote from Washington on April 28, 1853: —

WILLIAMS HOTEL.

DEAR WIFE, — Your letters of 20th and 24th instant I received this morning, and am truly glad to receive them. They have been at Bixby's. I telegraphed yesterday to have my letters forwarded. I think we shall get off on Saturday. I am enjoying my visit very much. I have made the acquaintance of a good many Southern and Western men. Every day adds to the number. If I had a month to spare, I should like to extend my journey, but that must be postponed to a future trip. I am quite ready to go home, and hope Hawthorne will be ready soon. I do not see how we can reach Boston before Monday or Tuesday. If you write me again the letter will reach me at Bixby's. . . .

Hawthorne has accomplished a good deal for himself. In addition to the Liverpool Consulship he has secured the Manchester also, — which adds to his income some $3000 annually. This he would have lost, if he had not come on. I am very glad for his sake.

Much love to all. I have time for no more at present.

Your affectionate husband,
W. D. Ticknor.

Two months later the steamship Niagara steamed out of Boston Harbor, bearing towards the Old World, and the untried diplomatic life, Nathaniel Hawthorne; he was accompanied by his family and also by his friend William D. Ticknor, without whom he had refused to embark upon his new enterprise.

IV

AUTHOR AND PUBLISHER EMBARK

THE nautical architecture of 1853 differed considerably from that with which we are to-day familiar. The Cunard Company had then been in existence less than a score of years, but it had even at that date established its reputation for safety and comfort. The steamship Niagara, upon which the Hawthornes embarked in company with Mr. Ticknor, was a ship only two hundred and fifty feet long, propelled by paddle-wheels, and very simple in its appointments. Its little company of passengers was so small that its milk supply could be amply provided by the one cow which was cozily housed on the deck, as were a coop full of fowls, whose number daily diminished as the good ship neared her journey's end.

And the ship's company surely made up in quality whatever it may have lacked in quantity; in those days the stream of foreign travel was but a tiny rivulet, yet it bore on its surface a much larger proportion of prominent and representative Americans, as well as distinguished tourists from the Old World, than may be found to-day in the great deluge of ocean travel.

One can picture the little group of Hawthornes, with their sturdy guardian beside them, waving farewell to the smiling and genial visage of James T. Fields, who had come down to see them off, and watching "Boston visible" fading from sight. They left behind them dear old New England "as a place," but, standing side by side, as it receded from their view, these two men carried with them most emphatically New England as a "state of mind." Hawthorne stood for poetical and temperamental New England, that which should make its lasting imprint upon this country's literature and flavor all its future artistic output; and his companion and publisher was the personification of the best practical and executive development of a new nation.

Just, clear-sighted and energetic, the latter was prepared to test the Old World standards by the highest New World ideals, but never in the spirit of thoughtless conceit or of censoriousness; he was at all times most keen to discern the best that was in the possession of that older civilization, and he desired to bring back to his own land those treasures both in the field of literature and social welfare that he was privileged to find there.

Among the other passengers in that ship's company was Mr. Crampton, the British minister, bound for Halifax, and the accomplished Field Talfourd, of distinguished family, an artist, and a man of wide culture. Mr. George Sillsbee, of Cambridge and Boston, a most extensive traveler, was another agreeable acquisition to the little coterie which clustered about the Hawthorne party and helped to make this smooth midsummer crossing a most delightful one.

Hawthorne was accorded the honors of the captain's table, and Captain Leitch was one of the most popular of the Cunard commanders, always a favorite with all his passengers. It was a curious coincidence that when, seven years later, Hawthorne sailed away homeward, this same commander was found standing upon the bridge of the vessel in which he then embarked.

Mr. Ticknor pens the following letter describing the ocean voyage: —

11 O'CLOCK, ST. NIAGARA, July 7, 1853.

MY DEAR WIFE, — As we shall have an opportunity to mail letters at Halifax you will not be sorry to receive even a short note. I never left home with so little satisfaction of readiness. I do not really feel prepared to make the most of this journey and yet I shall try to do so. I intended to have taken some of the minutes of my previous tour but this I entirely forgot. It is not important except as a guide. Had not poor H. been sick I should have had all matters nicely arranged. . . .

We were on board at 11.30 o'clock and precisely at 12 were moving. The ship is full, I believe about 150 passengers. Yesterday it was excessively hot. The Captain says he never experienced a hotter day at sea. To-day it is quite cool, but very pleasant. The sea is smooth and the steamer moving on with very little tossing. I believe there are a good many sick. I have not come to that point yet, though very likely I shall get my share for I'm not in very good condition to enter upon a sea voyage.

I can but feel sad to leave my beloved ones for so long a time. Do take good care of yourself. . . .

We are getting on finely to-day and shall probably be at Halifax about six o'clock. A large part of our company, I should think, were English. Very few that I know. Mr. Train the great shipowner, wife and son, Mr. Reynolds, Mr. Gilman the architect, N. Hawthorne and family are about the extent of my present acquaintance. Mr. Crampton, the English resident minister at Washington, is with us on his way to Halifax. He is a very pleasant and agreeable man.

I have not found out my "chum" yet. He did not "turn in" till the lights were out last night and I left him in his "berth" at seven this morning, so that I have n't seen his face.

I heard his voice, from which I judge him to be an "Henglishman."

The prospect is that we shall have a pleasant passage though not as quick as some, as this is not a fast ship. . . .

Kiss the children, dear ones, I would gladly do it myself. Kind regards to the Ellens.

Your affectionate husband,
                                W. D. TICKNOR.

A fortnight later Ticknor writes from London describing the safe arrival of the party: —

                    LONDON COFFEE-HOUSE,
                    LONDON, 22d July, 1853.

MY BELOVED WIFE, — I am once more in this great city: a world in itself. We had a very pleasant voyage over the water. For eight days it was like sailing upon a Lake. We could hardly perceive the motion of the boat. No guards were required on the tables. Very few persons were sick. The number of passengers was large — coming from almost every quarter of the Globe, — but nothing occurred personally to mar the comfort of any one. On Friday morning the wind changed and we had a gale for thirty-six hours. As we had enjoyed the luxury of the table in profusion, this coming upon us so suddenly, nearly all were in more or less trouble! I had a slight touch, but not enough to avoid my dinner.

I had my seat at the Captain's table with Mr. and Mrs. Hawthorne, Mr. E. Train and wife and daughter, Mr. McDonald, Speaker of Canada Parliament, Mr. Hodgkinson and daughter, of England; all very intelligent and social people. The time passed rapidly and pleasantly, and I could hardly realize when we reached the Liverpool dock, at six o'clock Sunday morning, that we had crossed the Atlantic and travelled nearly three thousand miles. Captain Leitch is a man of intelligence and a gentleman, disposed to do all in his power to make the passage agreeable to his passengers (Mr. McKinnens, of "Harper's Magazine" for July, to the contrary notwithstanding). Our luggage was passed with very little ceremony, and we were soon at "Waterloo Hotel." Mr. Hawthorne was disappointed in not finding his lodgings ready and was obliged to go with his family to the Hotel, which is both inconvenient and expensive. In consequence of this, and not wishing to leave Mrs. Hawthorne alone at the Hotel, he did not as he had intended come with me

to London. I remained with him till Wednesday
arranging his business as well as I could until he
enters upon his duties August 1st.

The present Consul is very civil to him and will
give all needed instructions as to the practical duties
of his office.

I remained on deck most of Saturday night to get
a good view of "The Isle of Man," and of the "Irish
coast" as we came through the north channel, and
in so doing took a severe cold, which kept me in the
house most of Sunday and I have not quite got my
head cleared yet.

In Liverpool there is not much to be seen except
the Docks and their Commercial buildings. I would
not have remained twelve hours, but for Hawthorne.
He wished me to stay by him as long as possible.

Mrs. Hawthorne is a very sensible woman. A
better wife he could not have.

I left Liverpool on Wednesday morning at 9.30
o'clock, avoiding the night line, — arriving in London about 5 P.M. This gave me a fine opportunity to
see the country, which I much desired and it is truly
magnificent, — almost enchanting to look on the
splendid farms in the highest state of cultivation.
The grass and trees for richness of color cannot be
described. Fields of grain nearly ready for harvest,
thousands of sheep and cattle grazing in the pastures
or cooling themselves beneath the shady trees, which
are abundantly scattered in every direction; it was
the most picturesque and beautiful sight that I ever
beheld. O my dear wife, that you could have enjoyed this with me, how would it have increased my

pleasure. I hope, should our lives be spared, that your eyes may yet rest on the beauties of Old England. . . .

Mr. Bennoch, Mr. Fields's particular friend, called upon me early yesterday, putting himself at my service and proposing plans, which were I to entertain, and I am sure I should like to do so, would occupy me for a month. I dined with him at six o'clock at Greenwich, after which I went to his residence at Blackheath Park, about seven miles from London.

On our way we called on Mrs. Crosland, who with her husband accompanied us to Mr. B.'s. The conditions before I went, were, that I should spend the night with him. I passed a most delightful evening.

Mr. B. is quite a distinguished man in London. His wife I was much pleased with. They are both whole-hearted Scotch people. No ceremony, but you feel at once at home. Mrs. Crosland is a charming woman, not handsome, but intelligent and very agreeable.

But to add to the pleasure of the visit, I met Grace Greenwood. She is spending a short time with Mrs. B. previous to her departure for home. Of course she was quite in raptures to see me. She desires to send special love to you and the children. She will doubtless call to see you on her return. I have an engagement with Grace and Mrs. Crosland for this evening, to go to some place of amusement. I am sure I don't know where or what.

I have just received very kind notes from Miss Mitford and Miss De Quincey, insisting upon my calling upon them. Miss De Quincey says her "papa" will be greatly disappointed if I do not come and see him. I hardly think I shall go to Edinburgh. It will take time, and I have little at best. It takes a good deal of time to do little business in London on account of distances. Still I should much like to see the old man. . . .

I should like to send home some of the strawberries and cherries which are abundant here just now. Strawberries that you could not put into a common-sized wine glass, although I am not sure that they have so fine a flavor as the smaller kind. As I was out of town last evening and till ten this morning, I am behindhand in my letters and cannot write half I intended. I should like to tell Tommy about the Liverpool Donkeys, and Benj. about the magnificent dray horses as large as small elephants, but I cannot now. . . . Do take good care of yourself and may a kind Providence in mercy watch over and keep you all in safety till the return of your loving husband,

W. D. Ticknor.

A touch of indisposition makes the writer a bit homesick for his family and he asserts: —

"I am really and truly homesick. I would gladly go by the next steamer and if I had not books to buy I would not long remain. I dare say I shall get over this feeling of loneliness in a few days. I have bought nothing as yet, but I shall make a beginning to-morrow.

"On Friday evening I went with Grace to a lecture from Albert Smith on 'Mont Blanc.' A most amus-

ing and entertaining fellow. Just the man to take
with the public in America. I advise him by all
means to 'go over.'

"On Saturday P.M. I went with Mrs. Bennoch and
Grace to the new Crystal Palace. It is some seven or
eight miles from London, and is yet unfinished. It
has been greatly enlarged and is really a very magnificent affair. It is designed to be a grand deposi-
tory of works of art of every description. When completed it will be a great curiosity. They have already
a large amount of statuary in the building, and many
casts from Westminster Abbey and from Paris. I
went to St. Paul's Sunday morning and the remainder of the day spent in my room."

Absorbed as he was in the world of men and of
books, Mr. Ticknor was ever keen in his enthusiasm
for nature and for all growing things. True to his
early training upon the New Hampshire farm, he
noted the ripening of the crops with a watchful eye
and delighted more in the vision of the rolling hay-
fields and picturesque herds of cattle than in the
somber grandeur of the Old World cathedrals. Men
he loved, books he loved, nature he delighted in, but
art and architecture were to him matters of less vital
interest, though he had a great fondness for all objects of beauty, and derived the greatest satisfaction from buying such objects when they came
within his means and presenting them to his friends.

He writes a few days later: —

"It rains about one half of the time. The season in
England has been unusually wet, so that the hay and

grain have suffered a good deal. In fact there has been but little weather for haying. I should think it genuine John Bull weather, but give me Yankee land. . . .

"I have rooms at 35 Norfolk Street, Strand. A large front parlor, quite as large as both of our parlors. A sleeping-room adjoining of good size, for which I pay one guinea per week, including attendance. My parlor is hung with paintings and engravings of a fair order. I should say some twenty in all.

"The *young* lady who waits upon me is not far from sixty! and weighs, I should judge, about seventy-five pounds. She is, however, very pleasant and attentive.

"The Madam of the house appears very pleasant, but her hair is so very red, I am careful not to offend. I think if I had seen this at first, I should have hesitated.

"There is great excitement in London, at present in regard to the 'cabs' and 'hansoms.' The former is a vehicle something like our carriage and drawn by one horse. The 'hansom' is like our chaise somewhat, only quite low with a box behind in which the driver sits. There has recently been a new law passed touching the fare and somewhat reducing it especially for short rides. The cabmen were much dissatisfied and after a few days' experiment they 'struck,' and for two days, the thousands of these most convenient articles, that lined the streets in every direction have entirely disappeared. Not one can be hired at any price. I don't know what will be the result, but I know that at present it is a matter of much personal inconvenience to me. The fare is now

6*d*. or 12½ cents per mile for one or two persons, for the third an extra 6*d*. may be charged. I enclose the 'Cabman's Lament,' just out.

"I took a plain dinner yesterday with Mr. Bohn at his store. I go to Richmond, to dine with him on Sunday. Mr. John Murray invited me to dine with him to-morrow, but I declined the honor. Subsequently I received an invitation to a school examination in the city and to dine with 'The Right Honorable The Lord Mayor' and a number of distinguished persons. I think I shall go, as this will be quite new to me. I am told that it will be a grand affair. I received the invitation through Mr. Bennoch, Mr. Fields's particular friend. He is an officer in the city and a princely merchant. He has been very civil to me and would find occupation for me to fill my whole time, if I had no business on hand. I have therefore to decline many invitations. He goes with me next week to see Miss Mitford. . . .

"A large number of American booksellers have been here this summer and are still 'on this side,' mostly in Paris just now. I have not yet seen Mr. Brown. He is expected in London this week.

"The fashion for boys in London is regular hats. They look very funny. Little fellows not as large as Benny with their narrow brims and high tops, look like miniature men. I can't say that I like it. . . .

"I am engaged to attend a large party at Mr. Bennoch's next Wednesday where I expect to meet a goodly number of the literary people of England as Mr. B. has an extensive acquaintance with that class of individuals.

"I think, by the way, it would suit Mr. Fields quite as well as myself. I find Mr. F. in high reputation wherever I go, and what is a little surprising, they all understood that he was to have been in England this season. They must have received this impression from some source.

"I am satisfied, unless he intends to take up a residence here, that it is as well that he remains at home, for he is evidently so fond of English life that by repeating his visit so soon, he would hardly have been satisfied with Yankee land.

"One very interesting sight about London is some three hundred boys in various parts of the city taken from the prisons, and about ten or twelve years of age, dressed in regular uniform of red flannel shirt and furnished with a bottle of blacking and a brush, and they earn some four or five dollars per week, by blacking the boots and shoes of the passers-by, at a penny each. Each has his appointed station with a little stand for the foot. I am told there is not an instance in which a boy has been known to make improper use of the money. I take frequent opportunity to encourage the little fellows."

It is of interest to compare the features which were familiar to the city of London sixty years ago, with those that we have with us to-day. The boot-black is certainly not such a curiosity as would be the small boy with the top-hat upon the streets of Boston, and the tendency to "strike" in 1853 has certainly developed a lusty progeny.

In view of the fact that the friendship of Francis

Bennoch and that of Henry A. Bright played so important a part in Hawthorne's life abroad, it may be of interest to describe them briefly.

Bennoch was greatly beloved by both Ticknor and Fields, as well as by Hawthorne, in whose journals his name reappears again and again ; while Bright, having at the start taken the new consul under his wing, continued to the end his fond and devoted friend, and when, in 1864, Longfellow penned the details of Hawthorne's death to Bright, he wrote: "I am glad to know how deeply you feel this loss; for I know, having heard it from his own lips, that he liked you more than any man in England."

Henry A. Bright was a university man, son of a wealthy local merchant who sent ships to Australia, and was related to various members of the aristocracy. When he first met Hawthorne, Bright was about thirty years old; he was slender, vivacious and intensely English, though in some ways he suggested the American rather than the British type. He not only knew England, but [he knew how to exploit England in the most delightful manner. He spared no pains to exhibit his friendship to both Hawthorne and Ticknor at all times, yet he quarreled with everything pertaining to the American point of view, and he and Hawthorne frequently displayed their prowess at political and social argument, neither convincing the other in the slightest degree. In eloquent language that was an education to the chance listener, they fought again the American Revolution and thrashed out the subject of monarchism versus republicanism; indeed, Bright and the American

consul would have had less admiration each for the
other had either one been a whit less loyal to his own
land and institutions.

Francis Bennoch was a superb specimen of the
human race and a true lover of his fellow-men. A
warm friendship immediately sprang up between him
and Hawthorne, who soon came to regard him and
Bright as his two closest friends in England. Bennoch was a Scotchman, with a mixture of English
and Irish ancestry, which combination had apparently brought him the best traits characteristic of all
three types. He had a mellow, sympathetic voice,
sparkling black eyes full of sunshine and kindness,
black, wavy hair and a broad, high forehead. He
was a poet of considerable merit and had composed
many songs, lyrics and narrative poems, and had
published a volume of his verse composed in the
spirit of Scott and Burns. He was at this time considered one of the handsomest men in England, and
he had a heart large enough to embrace not only all
of his hosts of friends, but the whole continent of
North America into the bargain. He was a man to
whom all superlative terms seemed fittingly applied,
and if other men were esteemed kind, hospitable and
generous, he was without doubt the kindest, most
hospitable, and above all the most chivalrous of
men.

When Hawthorne's publisher sailed away, after
having done all in his power for his friend, he left
Bright and Bennoch, as it were, standing guard over
the fortunes of Hawthorne in the Old World, and
one only needs to peruse the journals of the latter

to realize how well these two splendid specimens of English manhood stood by him.

Bennoch figures as one of the subordinate characters in the posthumous romance "Doctor Grimshawe's Secret." It is but a brief sketch of him and is very much modified from the vivid and magnetic reality. In one of his communications Hawthorne has penned a description of the home of the Bennochs:—

"Reaching Mr. Bennoch's house, we found it a pretty and comfortable one, and adorned with many works of art; for he seems to be a patron of art and literature, and a warm-hearted man, of active benevolence and vivid sympathies in many directions. His face shows this. I have never seen eyes of a warmer glow than his. On the walls of one room there were a good many sketches by Haydon, and several artists' proofs of fine engravings, presented by persons to whom he had been kind. In the drawingroom there was a marble bust of Mrs. ——, and one of the Queen which Mr. Bennoch said was very good, and it is unlike any other I have seen. It is intended as a gift, from a number of subscribers, to Miss Nightingale. Likewise a crayon sketch of —— looking rather morbid and unwholesome, as the poor lady really is. Also, a small picture of Mr. Bennoch in a military dress, as an officer, probably of cityhorse. By and by came in a young gentleman, son of Haydon, the painter of high art, and one of two ladies staying in the house, and anon Mrs. ——. And so we went in to dinner.

"Bennoch is an admirable host, and warms his guests like a household fire by the influence of his

kindly face and glowing eyes, and by such hospitable
demeanor as suits this aspect. After the cloth was
removed, came in Mr. Newton Crosland, a young
man who once called on me in Liverpool, — the husband of a literary lady, formerly Camilla Toulmin.
The lady herself was coming to spend the evening.
The husband (and I presume the wife) is a decided
believer in spiritual manifestations. We talked of
politics and spiritualism and literature; and before
we rose from table, Mr. Bennoch drank the health of
the ladies, and especially Mrs. Hawthorne, in terms
very kind towards her and me. I responded in her
behalf as well as I could, and left it to Mr. Bowman,
as a bachelor, to respond for the ladies generally, —
which he did briefly, toasting Mrs. Bennoch.

"We had heard the sound of the piano in the
drawingroom for some time, and now adjourning
thither, I had the pleasure to be introduced to Mrs.
Newton Crosland, — a rather tall, thin, pale and
ladylike person, looking I thought of a sensitive
character. She expressed in a low tone and quiet
way great delight at seeing my distinguished self!
for she is a vast admirer of The Scarlet Letter, and
especially of the character of Hester; indeed, I
remember seeing a most favorable criticism of the
book from her pen, in one of the London magazines."

In view of the fact that in many of his letters
Hawthorne makes humorous reference to his fondness for the bottle, it is worth while to quote an
episode which sets forth the truth in this respect as
demonstrated by his friend Bennoch.

At a dinner (occurring some time after Hawthorne's death) at which Mr. Bennoch was present, aspersions were cast by some English critic upon Hawthorne's character; this speaker accused him of being a hard drinker, of having disgraced himself at some English dinner, and of having died while on a spree with his friend Franklin Pierce. When the exponent of this slanderous statement had resumed his seat, Mr. Bennoch rose and spoke as follows: —

"I was the friend of Nathaniel Hawthorne during many years; I knew him intimately: no man knew him better. I was his constant companion on his English excursions and during his visits to London. I have seen him in all kinds of circumstances, in all sorts of moods, in all sorts of company; and I wish to say, to the gentleman who has just sat down, and to you all, that, often as I have seen Nathaniel Hawthorne drink wine, and although he had a head of iron, I have never known him to take more than the two or three glasses which every Englishman drinks with his dinner; I have never known him to be, and I know I am saying the truth when I say that he never was, under the influence of liquor. I myself was present on the occasion to which the gentleman has alluded, and I sat beside Nathaniel Hawthorne, and I am happy to tell you that then, as at all other times, when all were sober, he was the soberest of all. And in conclusion, I will say that the statement which the gentleman has just made to you, and which I am willing to believe he merely repeated upon hearsay, is a lie from beginning to end. Whoever repeats it tells a lie; and whoever repeats it after hearing what I have said, tells a lie knowing it to be such."

Among Mr. Bennoch's contributions in the field of literary benefactions may be cited his services to Mary Russell Mitford. Through his efforts she was enabled to issue "Atherton," and other tales, also a collected edition of her dramatic works.

In glancing through the quaint collection of Scottish verse penned by this truly charming and lovable gentleman, one comes across a poem entitled "Our Ship," which proves to be a tribute to the good ship Niagara, written during Mr. Bennoch's crossing to America in 1849. This, if not a notable poetic production, yet undoubtedly gave much pleasure to the ship's company at the time of its composition.

Bennoch's association with Haydon was one of exceeding interest, and the biography of the latter affords a glimpse of the generosity and friendship of Bennoch for this temperamental genius, who finally took his own life.

At the time of the publication of the "Old Home," Hawthorne had much difficulty in deciding whether to dedicate this volume to Bennoch or to his friend Pierce; he finally decided in favor of the latter, but his desire to express his appreciation of Bennoch's many kindnesses was later voiced by Mrs. Hawthorne, who, after her husband's death, dedicated the "Passages from the English Notes" to "Francis Bennoch, Esq., the dear and valued friend, who by his generous and genial hospitality and unfailing sympathy, contributed so largely (as is attested by the book itself) to render Mr. Hawthorne's residence in England agreeable and homelike."

V

HAVING seen the Hawthornes comfortably settled
in their temporary abode, Ticknor remained for some
time in London, where he hoped that Hawthorne
might presently join him. The latter, however, could
not get away at that time and wrote him to this
effect on July 22, 1853: —

"We have had very dull times here since you left
us; and to tell you the truth, I believe we are all very
homesick. Mrs. Blodgett cannot receive us till next
Wednesday. The children find the hotel a veritable
prison. As for myself, I have had but little enjoyment in a solitary cigar, . . . I wish I could come to
London, but consider it unadvisable at present, for
several reasons.

"My wife, just now, has gone out to walk with the
children or she would certainly send you her warmest remembrances; — so would Una, Julian, and
Rosebud, who all miss you more than they would
their father. Ellen and Mary (especially the former)
have also conceived a great regard for you."

A week later Hawthorne replies to a query regarding "The Tanglewood Tales": —

"If I remember right, there were but 336 pages in
your edition of 'Tanglewood,' and I am sure the last
story ends with a sentence about the departure of
the Argonauts after obtaining the Golden Fleece, —

Orpheus playing on his harp, and the vessel skimming over the water. I left the conclusion to the reader's imagination. I have not the book at hand to refer to.

"My engagements are such that I cannot possibly come to London on the day named by Mr. Bennoch. I wish I could; but it will be just at the beginning of my administration, and it will never do for me to run away at once.

"We did not get to Mrs. Blodgett's till Thursday; and I assure you we were all heartily sick of the Hotel — nor shall we feel at our ease until settled in a house which we can, temporarily, call our own. I have found very little enjoyment, thus far, in my visit to England.

"I long to see you."

Ticknor was in the mean time very busy with his work in London. He writes from there on August 4, to Mrs. Ticknor: —

"I have been hard at work the past week and have bought some books, but find very few that are new and valuable. The London book-trade is very slack, and but for the aid they get from 'Uncle Sam's' boys they would hardly survive. . . .

"On Sunday last I went to Twickenham to dine with Mr. H. G. Bohn. He has a very elegant place, about seven acres of land, and all a most perfect garden. The house is an old-fashioned English house and very comfortable. He lives like a prince. Mrs. Bohn is a very agreeable lady. They have five children, three sons and two daughters. The two eldest

sons are in their father's store. A Dr. Ludlow, of
New York, a fine specimen of a green Yankee, also
dined with Mr. B. Before dinner we took a walk to
Twickenham Church and saw the place where Alexander Pope was buried and the place where he lived.
The villa has been taken down and a new one erected.
It is a private residence, and of course none are admitted on the grounds. It is directly on the bank of
the little Thames, and as we rowed up the river in a
boat we had a fine view. A little farther up is Strawberry Hill, where Sir Horace Walpole wrote his celebrated letters to Horace Mann.

"I was disappointed in not having time to go into
Richmond Park, which is within a mile of Mr. Bohn's
residence. Hampton Court is also within two miles,
and had I gone in the morning, as my friend wished,
I should have seen all of these places. I was very
glad to get out of the smoke and noise of London
even for a few hours.

"Mr. B. is a fine specimen of an English gentleman: warm-hearted and generous. He has a great
passion for old china. . . .

"Mr. Brown, of the firm of Longmans & Co.,
runs on old coins. He has some $40,000 or $50,000
in rare coins . . . but it seems as if the money
could be invested more satisfactorily. It was
really a great curiosity. He spent nearly two
hours in showing them, and we passed over them
very hastily.

"But to return, I had a very pleasant time and
got home about half-past ten o'clock. Monday and
Tuesday I was busy in business, and yesterday till

noon. In the P.M. I went to a garden Collation, at Blackheath at Mr. Bennoch's.

"It was really a very fine affair. A large tent was spread in the garden with tables to seat some sixty or more, and loaded with nice things of which, not feeling quite well, I partook very sparingly. It was a very pleasant arrangement; if any one did not wish to remain long at table, he could retire to the house or walk in the garden. Mr. Bennoch, although a merchant, is also a politician, a poet, and a great patron of the fine arts. His house is filled with elegant paintings and statuary. His company was almost entirely composed of literary people and artists. Soon as I could decently get out, I left the table, as it was crowded, and turned to the garden. A lady soon followed and as we met among the flowers we entered into conversation, and very soon introduced ourselves to each other, when I found my friend to be no other than the famous authoress Miss Pardoe. I found her very social and agreeable. She urged me to call upon her, which if I had time I should like to do.

"Among other names known to you by reputation I will mention Mr. and Mrs. S. C. Hall, Mary Howitt, Mrs. Crosland, Tupper, Bishop, the great musical composer, also the Lord Mayoress, — His Lordship not present, — and our particular friend Grace Greenwood, who has promised to go and see you on her return. She will tell you more of this than I can write.

"I was delighted with Mary Howitt. I would like to have seen more of her but she was obliged to leave early. She, as also did Mr. and Mrs. Hall, insisted that I must call upon them before leaving England. I should be very glad to do so, but I have not time to visit much. Mrs. Hall lives in the country. She said I could come and spend the night with them on the Sabbath.

"There is much less ceremony and formality and far more real cordiality with the English people, when you once know them, than we find among the same class of persons in America. You feel at home with them directly. I spent a most delightful afternoon and evening. I did not get to bed till one o'clock. I intend for the future to be in bed earlier than I have thus far, for I do not get the rest I need. It may do for those who can lie in bed till ten in the morning.

"I have been running from place to place all day without accomplishing much, and I rather hastily promised Mr. Bennoch to spend to-morrow and next day with him, and after this I shall decline all interference with my business arrangements. We go to-morrow to dine with Mr. Tupper, and Saturday to see Miss Mitford. I regret that I made the engagement but must work the harder next week. On Wednesday next, at six o'clock, I am to dine with Mrs. Crosland. This won't interfere with my business. . . .

"I was not surprised to hear of the death of Mr. Appleton. He was very old. As a merchant no one stood higher in Boston. His benevolence was great. Many a poor family will miss his constant and timely aid. I trust he has gone to a better state.

"I shall hardly get home before the middle of September, and I must be industrious if I go to Paris. I have spun out a long story and I hardly think it amounts to much after all. . . .

"Good-night, my dearly beloved. May good angels ever watch over you and our precious jewels."

The promised visit to Miss Mitford was the beginning of a warm friendship which only ended with the death of that enthusiastic little lady who was so keen in her affections and appreciations, and whose delightful letters were as charming as any of her literary work. This warm-hearted authoress, who was effusively fond of those she admired, had taken a great fancy to Mr. Fields, whom she had known for some little time before she met the senior partner of the firm. From the time of this meeting, she maintained a strong and affectionate regard for Mr. Ticknor, who on his part never lost an opportunity of doing anything in his power for the plucky little woman, who, despite her invalidism, had such a wealth of joy and cheer to offer to all about her. Miss Mitford was deeply touched by the prompt recognition which her work received in America and she used frequently to remark: "It takes ten years to make a literary reputation in England, but America is wiser and bolder, and dares say at once, 'This is fine.'" She herself was untiring in her efforts to aid and encourage young writers and she did a vast amount for the struggling authors who were endeavoring to gain an impartial hearing in her own country.

On August 9, Mr. Ticknor writes that he has visited Miss Mitford, and about the same date she describes the visit to Mr. Fields to whom she is writing. She says:—

"Never, my dear friend, did I expect to like so well a man who came in your place, as I do like Mr. Ticknor. He is an admirable person, very like his cousin in mind and manners, unmistakably good. 'T is delightful to hear him talk of you, and to feel that the sort of elder brotherhood which a senior partner must exercise in a firm is in such hands. He was very kind to little Harry, and Harry likes him next to you. You know he had been stanch in resisting all the advances of Dear Mr. ——, who had asked him if he would not come to him, to which he had responded by a sturdy 'No!' He (Mr. Ticknor) came here on Saturday with the dear Bennochs (N.B. I love him better than ever) and the Kingsleys met him. Mr. Hawthorne was to have come, but could not leave Liverpool so soon, so that is a pleasure to come. He will tell you that all is arranged for printing with Colburn's successors, Hurst and Blackett, two separate works, the plays and dramatic scenes forming one, the stories to be headed by a long tale, of which I have always had the idea in my head, to form almost a novel. God grant me strength to do myself and my publishers justice in that story! This whole affair springs from the fancy which Mr. Bennoch has taken to have the plays printed in a collected form during my lifetime, for I had always felt that they would be so printed after my death, so that their coming out now seems a sort of anachronism. The one certain pleasure that I shall derive from this arrangement will be having my name and yours joined together in the American edition, for we reserve the early sheets.

"Nothing ever vexed me so much as the other book not being in your hands. That was Mr.——'s fault, for, stiff as Bentley is, Mr. Bennoch would have managed him. . . . Of a certainty my first strong interest in American poetry sprang from Dr. Holmes's exquisite little piece of scenery painting, which he delivered where his father had been educated. You sent me that, and thus made the friendship between Dr. Holmes and me.

"I suppose Mr. Ticknor tells you the book news? The most striking work for years is 'Haydon's Life.' I hope you have reprinted it, for it is sure, not only of a run, but of durable success. You know that the family wanted me to edit the book. I shrank from a task that required so much knowledge which could only be possessed by one living in the artist world now, to know who was dead and who was alive, and Mr. Tom Taylor has done it admirably. In his early days I used to be a sort of safety-valve to that ardent spirit, most like Benvenuto Cellini both in pen and tongue and person. Our dear Mr. Bennoch was the providence of his later years. . . .

"Make my love to all my dear friends at Boston and Cambridge. Tell Mrs. Sparks how dearly I should have liked to have been at her side on the Thursday. Tell Dr. Holmes that his kind approbation of 'Rienzi' is one of my encouragements in this new edition. I had a long talk about him with Mr. Ticknor, and rejoice to find him so young. Thank Mr. Whipple again and again for his kindness."

In his letter written at about this time Mr. Ticknor says: —

"I spent Friday and Saturday most delightfully: Friday with Mr. Tupper, who is a glorious fellow, and Saturday with Miss Mitford. I have not time to tell you what a charming time we had. Mr. Bennoch and his good wife accompanied me, and better company, always excepting my dearest Eme, I could not have had.

"On Sunday, I went to church half a day and spent the evening with a friend from Boston. Yesterday I was busy in business; met our neighbor Mr. Moses Williams in the evening.

"I have done very little business to-day. I went in the morning to see, with Mr. W., various objects of interest, and among others, the famous wine vaults: one covering eleven acres underground and containing 30,000 pipes of wine. It was truly one of the most remarkable sights that I have ever seen in London."

A few days later Mr. Ticknor writes of the interesting scenes in Paris which he had witnessed during his brief stay there: —

"As there was to be a great fête in honor of Napoleons I and III, on the 15th [of August], I concluded to come to Paris at once, and left on Saturday evening, expecting to arrive very early the next morning, but from some cause, I could not ascertain what it was, we were greatly delayed and did not reach here until one o'clock in the P.M., and then the stupid omnibus driver made blunders with a host of luggage, and among others (while I was seeking a

Hotel), carried·mine off. It took me two hours to
find it, so that it was three o'clock before I was fairly
in lodgings. I had great difficulty in finding a room
at all, for everybody has turned hither to see the
sights. I finally got a room, high up in 'Hotel Wind-
sor,' about the size of one of our smallest chambers.
I am thankful for this.

"Sunday was a great day in Paris. The military,
some 120,000, made a grand parade and were received
by the 'Emperor.' The streets were crowded with
people. I assure you, my dearest wife, it seemed very
little like the Sabbath. I was not in season to see the
display of military, but was told by some Boston
friends, that nothing could exceed it in splendor.
Carriages were not allowed to pass in the principal
streets. You cannot imagine anything more significant of the state of things in France, than the
unbounded enthusiasm that you witness among
the common people towards Louis Napoleon. The
country is prosperous, there is plenty of work and
'Strasburg beer,' and all is ascribed to the good
government of the Emperor.

"Short crops or a famine might change essentially
this state of things, and I think it would. But at
present he is very popular with the masses, and so
long as he can secure this, is he safe — and no longer.
I had a fine opportunity of seeing him and the Empress on Monday. I went with Mr. F. H. Walley,
Mr. Reynolds, and Mr. Russell, all of Boston, to see
the wonders at 'Champ de Mars.' After visiting
several places, we drove to the 'Champ de Mars' and
secured seats, so as to have a fine view of the perform-

ance, and for which we paid three francs, or sixty cents, each.

"There was a great variety of exhibitions, got up at the expense of the Government to gratify 'the people.' I suppose at least 300,000 persons were present, men, women, and children. (A full account of which I have sent you as contained in four numbers of 'Galignani' and in the programme of the day, by Mr. Reynolds of Roxbury.)

"In the course of the P.M. the Emperor appeared in an open carriage drawn by four elegant horses, accompanied by the Empress, and I was told, a son of Marshal Ney. They took a circuit around the entire field, and as they came up to the building where we were sitting, they halted and remained almost directly in front of us for some twenty minutes. So that I had an opportunity of looking upon Napoleon III to the full extent of my curiosity. He says he is a man of destiny, that he can't change his fate, and therefore he seems not alarmed at the attempts to take his life. He looks like a man regardless of consequences. At the time he was near me a person not of rank, standing near the carriage, was recognized by the Emperor, who at once gave him his hand and entered into conversation with him. This little incident raised a tremendous shout among the crowd. He evidently understands where his safety lies.

"In the evening was the grand illumination, and it far exceeded anything that it was possible to conceive. I never expect to see the like again, and am glad that I came to Paris if I see nothing else. Nothing described in the 'Arabian Nights' could exceed the brilliancy of 'Place Concord' and 'Champs Élysées' for hours. In fact all the streets were more or less illuminated, but here was the grand spectacle. The number of persons present cannot, of course, be estimated, but I believe 500,000 a moderate calculation. And yet perfect order prevailed in every respect. Everybody seemed happy. The only person I saw intoxicated, I am sorry to say, was an American, from New York.

"I had not a very good opportunity to see the fireworks, but as the masses began to disperse, I took a long walk and I could hardly believe what I saw to be a reality. Preserve the papers which I have sent, as I shall wish to see them; I thought it the best way to give you an idea of what I had seen.

"Yesterday I passed in the Louvre, or a good portion of it. It rained in the P.M. and evening. I went, however, to the circus with my friends, and was very much entertained. This morning we had the prospect of a charming day, but about eleven o'clock the clouds appeared and it commenced raining and continued till five o'clock. . . .

"I long for the comforts of home. There is much that is interesting to be seen in the Old World, but it is really hard work. . . . Two things are very essential to enjoy Paris — viz., a good knowledge of the language and plenty of money, and as I have neither I shall make a short visit."

On August 26, Mr. Ticknor writes home that he has decided to remain in England a fortnight longer than he had planned to do, as he had not quite completed his business, and also as he felt the need of a few days of rest and leisure at the end of the very busy weeks through which he had passed.

"I intend to visit a portion of England and Scotland after I leave London, which I am quite willing to do at any moment. It rains nearly all the time and when it does not rain you may almost cut the smoke with a knife. . . .

"On Monday (while still in Paris) I visited the Garden of Plants, Père la Chaise, an immense slaughter-house, such an establishment as is not known in America: I mean in magnitude. It was really a curiosity. I can tell you more of it than I have time to write. We then visited the Hôtel des Invalides, and with the aid of a five-franc piece we succeeded in getting admission to the Tomb of Napoleon. This was one of the most interesting sights I witnessed in Paris. Louis Napoleon has already expended some millions of dollars in carvings and beautifying the tomb, if such it may be called, for it is a large hall of most splendid finish as far as the work has proceeded, but it will not be completed for a long time. I saw the coffin in which repose the bones of *the* Napoleon, as he is properly called, and the same that was brought from St. Helena. This is to be placed in a sarcophagus, the most magnificent structure that you can possibly imagine, standing in a room below directly under the dome, with stairs leading from the upper room, so that visitors can examine the splendid workmanship of the whole structure. When complete there will be nothing in the whole world, probably, that can equal this in splendor and expense.

"I was hardly expecting to see this interesting room, as it is with some difficulty that a ticket of admission can be obtained, but the Boston gentlemen and myself thought proper to adopt that plan which in Europe rarely fails to accomplish the object, and I do not think it altogether confined to Europe. For money is a powerful advocate everywhere. Having seen this I was satisfied to leave Paris, although there is still much there that I should like to see, but it requires much time. Paris was never more gay than now, but no regard whatever is paid to the Sabbath. I was in hopes under the new Government there might be some improvement in this respect, but such is not the fact.

"I intend to get through with London if possible next week so as to leave early the week following. . . . I leave London before I leave Liverpool. I shall probably spend a few days with Hawthorne. He wishes me to do so. He is getting on finely."

The first of September finds Mr. Ticknor still in London and hard at work, taking only an occasional day off for recreation. He writes: —

"Yesterday I passed in sight-seeing. I was in company with Judge Washburn and lady, of Worcester, and several Boston gentlemen. In the morning we went to the Bank of England, having, through the politeness of Mr. Sturgis, tickets of admission to all the principal rooms. It was all quite new to me and I was very glad to witness the operation of this great institution. More than eight hundred persons are constantly employed in the various departments. I saw in one room over 70,000,000 pounds sterling. A snug little fortune for any one who might get possession of it.

"We next went to view Lord Elmere's Gallery of Paintings at the Bridgewater House. It is said to be the finest collection in England belonging to a private gallery. There are many very splendid pictures in the collection for which large sums of money have been paid.

"Next to the Royal Stables, to see the Queen's horses. Some of them were away, but there were in the stables about seventy. Ponies for the royal children, saddle-horses for the Queen and Prince Albert and their attendants, twenty-four elegant bays for ordinary coach purposes, eight magnificent blacks used only on state occasions; then the twelve beautiful creams. I think Tommy would have opened his eyes to have seen these elegant steeds. The carriages are, of course, very splendid. The state carriage built for George III is the most magnificent affair of the kind I ever saw. It weighs four tons, is eight feet wide, and is drawn by twelve horses. It is used only when the Queen opens or prorogues Parliament. The pony carriages are also very beautiful, such as Royalty only would presume to ride in.

"We next went to Westminster Abbey where we spent the remainder of the P.M. I had been over the Abbey before, but was very glad of the opportunity of doing so again. Many new monuments have been put up since I was there nine years since. In the evening I went to Vauxhall Gardens. This did not amount to much. Upon the whole, I passed a very pleasant day. To-day the same party have been to Hampton Court. I did not care to go, as I had matters of more importance for me to attend to. I am now very glad, for it must have been most uncomfortable there in the tremendous rain which has been falling nearly all day. I did not feel inclined to expose myself to another cold.

"The wet weather is doing great damage to the harvest. Grain will undoubtedly be very high this year, which must fall heavily on the poor. This we shall feel at home by way of $7 or $8 for flour. I see by the papers that the price has already gone up.

"I think if I were at liberty I could enjoy a month or two in Old England now very comfortably. I shall probably leave London early next week, as I wish, if possible, to go and see Mr. De Quincey, and also to spend a day or two in Liverpool.

"I find it much pleasanter at the Hotel than at private lodgings, although much more expensive. There are now at this house (Morley's Hotel) several Bostonians, and all persons that I have known for years. At breakfast we often get five or six at one table. This relieves from loneliness which one feels when away from home and friends. . . .

"My most trying duty now comes, to get something to take home to the children; although there seems to be everything, yet it is difficult to decide. I wish you had advised me on this point, but I must do the best I can. . . .

"I promised to go to see Mary Howitt, Mr. and
Mrs. Hall, and Miss Pardoe, but I fear I shall not
have time, as a day passes before you are aware of it.
The people in London begin the day so late that
much good time is lost."

VI

MEMORIES OF DE QUINCEY

HAWTHORNE had long been an admirer of De Quincey's writings. As far back as the days spent at Lenox, in 1850, he had sat down cozily by the evening lamp to read aloud the brown-covered volumes of Ticknor's American edition, to Mrs. Hawthorne, who in her letters described these happy times, which ensued after the children had been put to bed: "Now follows our long beautiful evening, which we richly enjoy. My husband has read aloud to me ever since he finished his book. 'David Copperfield,' he has read. I never knew such reading, it is better than any acting or opera. Now he reads De Quincey."

The picture of Hawthorne perusing with especial pleasure the pages of De Quincey is agreeably supplemented by that of the De Quincey family enthusiastically enjoying the work of Hawthorne. Indeed, some months before the latter embarked for England, a letter written by Miss De Quincey had expressed great enthusiasm for Hawthorne's productions. She wrote to a friend that they were "rabid admirers of his. There is no prose-writer of the present day," she continued, "in whom I have half the interest that I have in him. His style is in my mind so beautifully refined, and there is such exquisite pathos and quaint humor, and such an 'awfully' deep knowledge of human nature, — not that hard, unloving, detestable and (as it is purely one-sided or wrong-sided) false reading of it that one finds in Thackeray. He reminds me in many things of Charles Lamb, and of heaps of our rare old English humorists, with their deep, pathetic natures. . . . I cannot satisfy myself as to whether I like his sort of essays contained in the 'Twice-Told Tales' best, or his more finished works such as 'The Blithedale Romance.' Every touch he adds to any character gives a higher interest to it, so that I *should* like the longer ones best; but there is a concentration of excellence in the shorter things, and passages that strike in force like daggers in their beauty and truth, so I generally end by liking that best which I have read last. Will you tell him how much we love and admire his gracious nature? There are other stars in your firmament, all of whom we admire, some greatly; but he outshines them all by infinite degrees."

Not only did Hawthorne derive much satisfaction from the perusal of De Quincey's volumes as they appeared from the presses of his American publisher, but he reread them with pleasure on subsequent occasions, and selected eloquent passages to serve as models for his children to study for their music of style and smoothness and perfection of diction. And in 1854, he penned an indignant letter to his friend, Henry Bright, because he had failed to praise De Quincey's work more warmly in an article written for the "Westminster."

Thus it was, that shortly after Hawthorne's arrival in England a cordial invitation was received by him to visit the De Quincey family, in company with his friend Ticknor. At first it seemed likely that the two could carry out this plan together, before Ticknor took his departure for America, but when the appointed time arrived, Hawthorne was unable to accompany his publisher on the much-talked-of excursion. Ticknor, therefore, made the visit without him, returning with an interesting description of the fine old man and his agreeable daughters.

It was towards the middle of September, 1853, that De Quincey's American publisher journeyed to his "Cottage at Lasswade," in response to a most friendly invitation from Miss Margaret De Quincey, who had written soon after his arrival:—

"Your house has shown such a kindly spirit to my father that I take the liberty of addressing you as a friend. Mr. Bennoch has offered to get a note conveyed to you, as I very much wish to say that we hope Mr. Hawthorne and you still mean to visit Scotland, as our friend Mr. Fields meant to have done had he come over, and if so, that you will let us have the pleasure of seeing you.

"I am sorry to say our cottage is too small to offer you beds. If you can, however, come over from Edinburgh, I really cannot say how charmed we shall be to see you, and what I now more particularly write about is that Papa and I are both exceedingly anxious that I should be at home at the time you are in Edinburgh, which would not naturally be till about the last week in August, but I have made such arrangements as enable me to start off from wherever I am at once, provided I can learn what time you are to be there. If, therefore, you can let me know in time to do so, will you oblige me thus far; a single line to say when you will be in Edinburgh is all that is necessary. My address up to this day week is, The Viscount Valentia's, Bletchington Park, near Oxford; — from that time for about a week after, The Rev. Philip Serle's Rectory, near Oxford; — after which it will be better if you will be so kind as to address your note to my sister Florence at home, — Mavis Bush, Lasswade, near Edinburgh. As the remaining part of my time will be spent in a tour through Westmoreland, as yet I have no knowledge of where our letters may be sent, but my sister would be the first to know.

"Will you excuse all blunders, as I am writing in an enormous family and a perfect whirl of things to be thought and said and done, and I only hope the consequences may not be that I am totally non-understandable in this case."

Prior to this excursion to Lasswade, another cordial communication was received from Miss Margaret de Quincey, who had been ill during the intervening time; she wrote on this occasion: —

My dear Sir, — I write a short note to say that we hope you will dine with us whatever day you find you can come to us. Our dinner hour is five o'clock, and we shall hope for a single line to say what day we may expect you on. Any day will suit us. So you have only to mention the day in order that Papa and my sisters may be at home. It would give us very great pleasure if you could arrange to spend a day or two with us, but I should warn you that as a punishment for some of our sins, you may as well look for a soft stone to lie upon as a soft bed in our house, and I am afraid Hotels are too well conducted now to make even a far-travelled man like you put up in these days of luxury with our penitential beds.

Thank you for your kind expression of regret at my illness. I am much better, and am very glad that I recovered in time to get home before you came.

Papa is not here at present or he would join my sisters and me in kind regards and thanks for the notes which travelled safely home with me.

I remain,
Very faithfully yours,
M. DE QUINCEY.

Sept. 12, 1853,
MAVIS BUSH, LASSWADE.

Remember we have a bed such as it is. This is Papa's suggestion, who has just come in and so does join in all kind messages.

Despite the discouraging picture painted of the penitential aspect of the guest-chamber, De Quincey's American publisher was not deterred from the long talked-of visit which proved in every way enjoyable.

That he returned to the consulate with a satisfactory account of the household at Lasswade is evinced not only in his own letters but by those of Mrs. Hawthorne, who wrote to her father: "Mr. Ticknor has been to see Mr. De Quincey, and says he is a noble old man and eloquent, and wins hearts in personal intercourse. His three daughters Margaret, Florence, and Emily, are also very attractive and cultivated, and they are all most impatient to see Mr. Hawthorne."

Upon the night of his arrival at Lasswade Mr. Ticknor, after having bid good-night to his host, heard a light tap on his door, and Miss Emily de Quincey stood outside inquiring, "Can I do anything more for you?" To this Ticknor replied: "Yes, one thing more; I wish that you would bring me my youngest son and put him on my knee." With which modest request even his thoughtful and sympathetic hostess could not comply.

The town of Lasswade is but half a dozen miles from Edinburgh and is situated very picturesquely upon the river Esk, and the De Quincey cottage, "Mavis Bush" (dignified in later years in the County Directory as the "De Quincey Villa"), was situated more than a mile beyond the town. It was a snug little cottage facing the road, with its little garden behind and its outlook upon the lovely hill country. About it were many pleasant walks, the prettiest of which led to the river banks or wound through wooded pathways. The interior of the cottage was cozy and attractive, and the atmosphere of this home is best presented in De Quincey's own words:

"More pleasant it must be if I try to give you some clue to the motive, the how and the why of my residence in this place. My companions, as you know, are my three daughters, who, if it should be found that they had no other endowments from the bounty of nature, have this one, better perhaps than

all that I could ask for them from the most potent
fairies, viz., that they live in the most perfect har-
mony I have ever witnessed. Such a sound as that
of dissension in any shade or degree I have not once
heard issuing from their lips. And it gladdens me
beyond measure that all day long I hear from their
little drawing-room intermitting sounds of gaiety
and laughter, the most natural and spontaneous.
Three sisters more entirely loving each other, and
more unaffectedly drawing their daily pleasures
from sources that will always continue to lie within
their power — viz., books and music — I have not
either known or heard of.

"Our dwelling is a little cottage, containing eight
rooms only, one of which (the largest), on what in
London is called the first floor, is used as a drawing-
room, and one about half the size, on the ground
floor, a dining-room, but large enough for a party of
ten people at the utmost. Our garden is exactly
seven measured miles from the Scott Monument
in Princes Street, Edinburgh. Lasswade, to which
nominally we allocate ourselves, is in fact one mile
and a half distant; but it is the nearest town possessing a market and a regular post-office. . . . We keep
only two servants (female servants), a housemaid
and a cook, and with so narrow a command of labor,
we are unable to send for our letters, the journey to
and fro making a clear total of three miles' walking."

While picturing De Quincey as located for many
years at Lasswade it must be remembered that he
was only there when he chose to be. He always
maintained lodgings in Edinburgh, where he so-

journed whenever his restless spirit moved him, and
to which he made frequent journeys. His favorite
habit of accumulating masses of papers which were
piled up in various hired lodgings has been often
referred to; he was known to have been responsible
for the rental of as many as four sets of lodgings, all
running on simultaneously. Each one in turn having been "snowed up" by an accumulation of books
and papers, would be carefully locked up for further
reference.

De Quincey's love of children and power of winning their confidence was one of his finest characteristics. This was not confined to his association with
his own children, but extended to every class in the
community, and the most extraordinary babies with
the most impossible mothers were a sure passport to
his heart and at times to his last shilling.

His habits were so simple as to be almost ascetic
and he subsisted upon the lightest possible diet. His
digestive trouble and neuralgic suffering, which first
led to his taking opium, caused him early to lose his
teeth, and from the extreme delicacy of his system,
he could eat nothing less capable of mastication
than bread, so that article with a little soup or coffee
was apt to comprise his whole dinner.

In reference to his manner of dress his daughter
has said: —

"His dress, unfortunately, he neither cared for
himself, nor would he let others care for it. I say
unfortunately, because this carelessness gave rise
among punctilious people, unaccustomed to eccentric habits, to an impression of poverty for which

there was no foundation. It might be that a thought occurred to him in the midst of some of his irregular processes of dressing, or undressing (I should say some thought did generally strike him at that time), and he would stop with his coat just taken off, or not put on, without stockings at all, or with one off and one on, and becoming lost in what grew out of this thought, he would work for hours hardly even noticing the coffee which was his chief support at such times.

"In the midst of this absorbing work, would arrive visitors of whom there were many, probably from such a distance that they could not be turned back without sight of the object of their long pilgrimage; upon which my father, with the unaffected courtesy which was one of the great charms of his character, would appear at once rather than keep them waiting while he put on his stocking, or whatever might be wanting, or which was just as likely in the wrong place, giving rise to awed impressions of poverty with some, while those who could withdraw their unaccustomed eyes from the nakedness of the land, as expounded by his feet, might have seen in his surroundings signs of scrupulous neatness, sufficient comfort and refinement enough to reassure them on this point.

"His presence at home was the signal for a crowd of beggars, among whom, borrowed babies and drunken old women were sure of the largest share of the sympathy he refused to none."

De Quincey's greatest extravagance grew out of the morbid value he set upon his papers and their

not being disturbed; he was in the habit of accumulating these until in his own words he was "snowed
up," which meant that when matters reached such
an extremity that there was not a square inch of
room on the table to set a cup upon, and no possibility of making his bed for the weight of papers
gathered there; no chair which could be used for its
legitimate purpose, and the track from the door to
the fireplace, always kept open until the last, was
completely obliterated so that he had not even place
in which to set his foot, — then De Quincey locked
the door upon his paper treasures and turned elsewhere. At his death there were at least a half-dozen
such places "papered" by him and being maintained at no small expense.

Such a thing had been experienced as his actually
"papering" his family out of a house, but in later
years his daughters learned how to guard against
such a contingency.

De Quincey usually spent the evenings with his
family, who looked forward to these hours with
much pleasure. Upon the arrival of the newspaper
he would render the news in his own quaint manner,
questioning the various members of the group about
him, and illuminating the various subjects touched
upon with a wealth of memories, good stories, or humorous experiences, until the happiest flow of real
conversation sprang from the circumstances of the
moment.

He was not a tranquilizing companion for nervous
persons to live with, as those nights were the excep-
tions on which he did not set fire to something. It

was a common occurrence for one of his daughters to look up from her work and to say casually, "Papa, your hair is on fire!" To which he would respond calmly, "Is it, my love?" and a hand rubbing out the blaze was all the notice taken.

On one occasion, when the maid rushed in to announce that Mr. De Quincey's room was on fire, he hastened to the rescue of his already "snowed-up" apartment, refusing all suggestions that water be poured upon his treasured papers. Armed with a heavy rug he disappeared into the burning room determined to conquer without water or perish in the attempt, while the members of his affrighted household trembled for his safety outside the door, locked to prevent the abhorred water from being poured in. Presently, after occasional bursts of smoke and a very strong smell of fire, all were assured that the danger was over; the victor emerged triumphantly from his fight with the flames, and the dreaded element having been subdued for the evening all retired in a state of thankfulness.

De Quincey's manner to his three daughters was the perfection of chivalric respect as well as affection. He had an unfailing habit of turning courteously to them and explaining in his own choice diction any casually employed term from the "dead languages" which might lie outside the sphere of feminine acquirements. He was a man once seen, never to be forgotten: a small figure — five feet, three inches in height — and with a countenance remarkable for intellectual attractiveness. His features, though not regular, were aristocratically firm, and an air of delicate breeding pervaded his face. His forehead was unusually high, square and compact. At first sight his face appeared boyishly fresh and smooth with a sort of hectic glow upon it that contrasted remarkably with the evident appearances of age in the grizzled hair and eyes dim in aspect; this dimness, however, did not indicate any lack of sight, as to the end of his life he could read the smallest print without spectacles.

All were struck with his extreme sweetness and courtesy of manner, and Mr. Ticknor, like all the rest of his friends, was vividly impressed by his brilliant and lovable personality.

Even before England had come to realize the importance of De Quincey's work, America had hailed him as one of the foremost English classicists. There had been popular American reprints of certain individual pieces by this author, and Messrs. Ticknor and Fields had recognized the desirability of bringing out a set of his collected works.

Almost simultaneously with the suggestion presented by this American publishing-house, had come a similar demand from Mr. James Hogg, of Edinburgh, who had determined to give to his English market a complete set of De Quincey. The Boston edition of the works was not, however, to interfere with that projected at Edinburgh, which was to differ from the other in several respects. The latter was to be less complete in some ways, as it was to omit a number of the extracts included in the Boston edition, while other articles were to be cut down and condensed under De Quincey's personal supervision; on the

Thomas de Quincey.

other hand, for the American edition, Mr. Fields was himself to collect and classify the scattered articles, obtaining from their author any information that was necessary for their proper arrangement.

This first American edition of De Quincey's works was begun in 1851, and completed in 1855, in twenty volumes, while the first volume of the Edinburgh edition did not appear until 1853. In this, De Quincey's own work proved rather unsatisfactory; things were jumbled together and mixed up in a manner which in no way equaled Mr. Fields's systematic method, and in fact the American edition coming over to England in successive volumes proved De Quincey's greatest help in the task of editing his own complete works. In several instances the American publisher unearthed articles which the author would never have rediscovered for himself.

Mr. James T. Fields has published his recollections of his visit to the De Quincey home in 1852, when upon taking leave of Miss De Quincey he placed in her hands a check for part of the profits which were already accruing from the sale of the American edition. In writing of this visit Miss Mitford exclaims: "Did I also say that the last act of my excellent friend, before leaving England, was to carry to Mr. De Quincey, in Scotland, the author's profits of the seven volumes of his collected works, which he, Mr. Fields, had collected with so much care and pains, and edited himself? This piece of generosity, unprecedented in any publisher, English or American, gave great pleasure to the Opium-Eater."

De Quincey was much gratified by the success of

his American edition, though his pleasure in it was perhaps tempered a bit by the consciousness that his American publishers had so speedily accomplished without his aid that which he was struggling to do with equally commendable results for his Edinburgh publisher, Mr. Hogg, who found it a hard task to keep his friend's nose to the literary grindstone in the Edinburgh sanctum where the collected works were being compiled. It was a harassing and yet amusing business, and proved a long struggle between De Quincey and the hungry printing-presses which were subjected to various painful delays. The presses were kept waiting for numerous unexpected causes; sometimes De Quincey had "lumbago"; again he fell asleep at the wrong time, or was forced to postpone his work for other reasons. His notes of excuse, sent to his waiting publisher, were in themselves models of superfluous precision; he was often unhappy at the thought that the compositors, whose time was their fortune, might be standing idle through his fault, but in the end De Quincey did not fail his Edinburgh friend and the task was accomplished. In all monetary transactions the writer was most scrupulous and sadly feared to benefit at another's expense. De Quincey disliked checks, preferring a little cash, on account, to larger sums on paper. He had a special aversion for greasy, crumpled Scotch one-pound notes, and did his best to smooth and cleanse them before parting with them, and he washed and polished up his shillings before he generously bestowed them on his deserving, or more often undeserving, poor.

Many are not aware that in his later years De Quincey almost entirely overcame his craving for opium. With a weak constitution, shattered nerves, and an accompanying deep depression which at times carried him to the verge of suicide, it required no little strength to refrain from this indulgence. The last ten years of his life embraced a period of quiet and steady activity; he was well cared for and to a great extent abandoned his wandering propensities.

Through the years of labor over the English edition of the collected works, De Quincey was constantly amusing himself with fresh literary projects. Some of these alarmed Mr. Hogg by threatening interruption to the main work in hand. One project was a new history of England, in twelve volumes, and at the age of seventy, he longed to begin this huge task, which he thought he could finish in four years.

But in the autumn of 1859, after the thirteenth volume of the collected works had been issued, and the fourteenth and last was nearly ready for the press, De Quincey laid down his active pen forever. He passed away at 42 Lothian Street, his Edinburgh lodgings, on the 8th of December, at the age of seventy-four years and four months. Although this writer passed three quarters of his literary life in Edinburgh, he seemed in no way to have been affiliated with that place, nor is he apt to be regarded as an Edinburgh man; indeed so little is he generally associated with this city of his literary workshop, that very seldom do visitors seek out his humble

grave there. He was a man who belonged to the
universe of literature, and his real home was and
must remain ever in the realm of those numberless
appreciative readers who care for De Quincey's
work. And in this realm we are inclined to think his
countless American readers predominate. He was,
like Hawthorne, a dweller in the land of dreams for
a great portion of his life; he added real and permanent treasures to English literature, and from first to
last he was absolutely untouched by the vulgar desire for fame.

VII

AUTHOR AND PUBLISHER AT OLD CHESTER

ON August 22, prior to Ticknor's trip to Scotland, Hawthorne writes to his friend, then in London, in regard to his homeward-bound passage; he also consults him about a gold watch which he desires to purchase.

"I have engaged berth 37 for you, in steamer Niagara, to sail September 3d. . . . No. 37 is situated just about the same as the one you came over in.

"If you have time before leaving London, I wish you would buy a lady's watch, good and handsome, but not very expensive — sufficiently so, however, to ensure a faithful timekeeper. Are there any objections to Swiss watches? Ladies' watches, I believe, are not so costly as gentlemen's; and I should suppose that ten or twelve guineas might fetch a good one.

"Do Chapman and Hall mean to send me any copies of 'Tanglewood'? . . .

"Do try to spend two or three days here before sailing. I shall feel as if my last friend was leaving me when you go aboard. You had better come to the Rock Ferry Hotel, whence you can be transferred to the steamer. . . . Mrs. Hawthorne and the children will not excuse you if you do not come."

Ticknor's promptness in executing even the smallest commissions is evinced by the fact that two days

later, Hawthorne writes again in response to a letter
received from him, describing the variety of watches
which may be purchased for the price suggested.
Hawthorne inquires: —

"Could not the white-faced watch be bought with
the understanding that it might be exchanged for
a gold-faced one, in case the latter should be preferred? And you might select the gold-faced one, to
be sent if I return the white-face. Do you mean to
bring the watch, or send it? I don't care which."

The day following, the watch has been received
and Hawthorne writes back: —

"I like the watch much, and mean to keep it, if my
wife approves of it as I do. I am very glad you
bought it of Mr. Bennett, because his name gives
full assurance of its quality. Pay him; and I will fill
your pockets when you go home. I think I had better
not come to London yet."

The berth on the Niagara having been exchanged
for one on the America, which was to sail a fortnight
later, it was arranged that the departing friend
should stop over a few days in the new home, of
which the Hawthornes had just taken possession.

"You must not think of going elsewhere than to
our house," wrote the new consul, one week later.
"We got into it yesterday, and are just as well established as if we had been there a year. It is an
abundantly large house, and we want you to let our
American friends know from your own experience,
how comfortably we are situated. When you go to
Liverpool, drive to the consulate, and I will cross the
river with you; or, if I should not be at hand, you will

easily find the way alone. The boats go hourly from George's Dock. Can't you come before the 14th?"

Once more, the home passage is postponed; this time to October 1, and Hawthorne writes to his friend in London: —

"I don't believe you ever mean to go home at all. However, I am willing you should stay in England four years longer, at least; and so I have engaged a berth for you on the steamer for October 1st. In requital for my trouble, I shall expect you to spend a good deal of the intervening time with us. By the by, Julian wants to go home with you."

On September 9, Mr. Ticknor writes to his wife that he has decided to remain until the above-mentioned date, asserting: —

"Notwithstanding the positive manner in which I last wrote, I have, owing to your goodness in asking me not to hurry, and to Mr. Fields's account of matters at the store, in connection with urgent requests here, reversed my decision, and leave October 1st. . . .

"Hawthorne says he does n't believe I intend to go home at all, but he is willing that I should stay at least four years, that is, during his term.

"On Monday I visited the Newgate Prison, Old Bailey, and Christ Hospital, — in the morning. At eleven, went to Cambridge to see the colleges in company with Judge Washburn and lady, Walley, Russell, Dr. Dalton and brother, and returned at 7.30 in the evening. I passed a very pleasant day.

"The colleges at Cambridge are quite distinct from each other and are all on the most magnificent

scale. The architecture is very beautiful, some of
the buildings are very old. The painted windows,
statuary, etc., are great curiosities. We had hardly
time to see the different buildings, but I was glad
that I went.

"A little incident happened to us in the morning.
We purposed to have gone at eight o'clock and had
our breakfast early in order to be in season. We were
(that is Messrs. W., R., D., and myself) duly at the
station. On our arrival we found Judge W. and lady
waiting for us. The Judge had secured seats and we
soon occupied them. I found the hour had passed
and remarked that it was not usual for English
trains to be behindhand, when one of our party,
chanced to make an inquiry of one of the attendants in regard to some place on the route, when we
were informed that we were in the Colchester and
not the Cambridge train. We turned out directly,
had a good laugh at the Judge, and waited three
hours, but improved the time in visiting the
prisons. . . .

"I dined at Richmond on Wednesday with Mr.
Russell Sturgis, formerly of Jamaica Plain, but now
a partner of the house of Barings, and had a delightful time. You can conceive of nothing more beautiful than Richmond; its splendid parks, groves, rivers,
ponds and elegant residences, cannot, it seems, be
excelled either in nature or art.

"Yesterday I visited the Zoölogical Gardens in
the morning, and although we passed several hours,
we did not see all the objects of interest. In fact it
would take a week to accomplish this. Probably the

most extensive collection of wild animals to be found anywhere are to be found here. I thought what a treat it would be to our children if they could spend a day here.

"To-day I have been running about, without accomplishing much. I walked through the British Museum, but could not stop to see with much care. My friends Russell and Walley leave to-morrow for the North. I intended to have gone with them, but as I prolonged my stay I must attend to a little more business. I hope to meet them in Edinburgh."

A week later, he writes that he is starting on his trip to the North, having been detained several days by additional business; during this interim he has visited the Foundlings' Hospital which he describes in his letter.

In all his journeyings Ticknor made a special point of inspecting the public institutions, improving every opportunity of visiting the prisons, hospitals, and schools, and studying their methods of management. Thus, he hoped to take back to his own land many valuable suggestions which might with advantage be adopted in his own community; the interests of the city of Boston were ever in his mind, taking precedence of the interests of the "Old Corner."

If he had but a few days to remain in any foreign city, a brief view of its art and architecture did not suffice him, for he was ever conscious that these reflected but a certain phase of the condition of the community. Beyond these there was always something more that he desired to investigate, and he had an intense curiosity to know the truth about a city's life as displayed in its public institutions. In his earliest accounts of his experiences in Paris in 1844, when he describes the splendor of the July fête, then taking place, and the extent of all the grand illuminations and social functions, he writes that he has stood aghast at the record of vice in Paris as read by him from the inspection of the foundling hospitals, which each year sheltered such an appalling multitude of tiny outcasts; and while delighting in the beauty of artistic Paris, he deplored its wide moral degradation.

Above all, he was keenly interested in the school question, of which he made a study in every important city which he visited. For he believed most fervently that the future success of his own nation depended, not on the reformation of the criminal classes, the disciplining of the unruly, or the supplying of occupation to the unemployed, but in the conscientious training of its children to be efficient and righteous citizens. Especially he saw in the rightly directed education of the poor children gathered together in all the towns and cities of this land the great solution of the country's problems.

In the letter above referred to, he writes: — "I bade good-bye to London at two o'clock yesterday. I arrived here about 4.30 o'clock, intending to go farther, but found that I could not accomplish my object, therefore I have remained here till 10.30 to-day, when I go to Blenheim, Warwick, Stratford-on-Avon, and Kenilworth. I hope to be in Edinburgh to-morrow night. . . .

"Last Sunday I went in the morning to the Foundlings Hospital. It is an institution for receiving the children of women who have previously sustained a respectable character, and who are known to the trustees. There are now about 400 in the hospital, rather more than half girls. The services in the chapel were interesting: the singing performed by the children with the assistance of two male and two female singers. They sang from Handel and it was most beautifully performed. The children were dressed in the uniform of the Institution, and they all looked cheerful and happy. Immediately after service they all went to the dining-hall, marching in regular step. The tables were furnished with an ample supply of good roast beef, fine potatoes, bread and water. I have not seen more intelligent and good-looking countenances among any class of children.

" England with all her faults has some good things, yes, many good and praiseworthy institutions. In the afternoon I went to Richmond to dine with Mr. Bohn and had a very pleasant time."

In fulfillment of his promise, Ticknor returned from his trip to Edinburgh, to spend his last few days in England with the Hawthorne family, who welcomed him back with much affection and begged that he might remain longer with them. Of the pleasant excursions taken during this little visit, Hawthorne has himself left a charming account in his journal, and Mrs. Hawthorne records the same in her home letters.

She writes to her father on September 30: —

"Mr. Hawthorne and Mr. Ticknor had a fine excursion to Old Chester, and were so occupied with it that no time was left for Eaton Hall. Julian has been parading around the garden this morning, blowing a trumpet which papa brought him from Chester, and dragging after him a portentous wooden cannon, which would not help to gain the smallest battle. It is actually a sunny day! A very great joy it is to Rosebud to see the lovely little English robins come to pick up crumbs. They excite a peculiar love. They have great faith in man and come close to the window without fear. They have told the linnets and thrushes of our hospitality, and the linnets actually come, though with dread and trembling; and they carry off the largest crumbs for their families and neighbors. The English robin is very dear. . . .

"We are all going to Chester first on a Sunday, to attend the cathedral service with the children. How very singular that this dream of mine, like so many other dreams, is coming true! For I always wished earnestly that the children might go to church first in a grand old cathedral, so that their impression of social worship might be commensurate with its real sublimity. And behold, it will be so, — for they never yet have been to church. The echoes of those lofty vaults are scarcely ever silent, for an anthem is sung there every day. Afterwards, we shall go on a week-day to examine the old town, said to be older than Rome itself!"

On October 1, Hawthorne writes in his journal: —

"On Thursday I went with Mr. Ticknor to Chester

by railway. It is quite an indescribable old town,
and I feel at last as if I had had a glimpse of old
England. The wall encloses a large space within the
town, but there are numerous houses and streets
not included within its precincts. Some of the principal streets pass under the ancient gateways; and
at the side there are flights of steps, giving access to
the summit. Around the top of the whole wall, a
circuit of about two miles, there runs a walk, well
paved with flagstones, and broad enough for three
persons to walk abreast. . . . It is all very strange,
very quaint, very curious to see how the town has
overflowed its barrier, and how, like many institutions here, the ancient wall still exists, but is turned
to quite another purpose than what it was meant for,
— so far as it serves any purpose at all. There are
three or four towers in the course of the circuit; the
most interesting being one from the top of which
King Charles the First is said to have seen the rout
of his army by the Parliamentarians.

"We ascended the short flight of steps that led up
into the tower, where an old man pointed out the site
of the battle-field, now thickly studded with buildings, and told us what we had already learned from
the guide-book. After this we went to the cathedral,
which I will perhaps describe on some other occasion, when I shall have seen more of it, and to better
advantage. The cloisters gave us the strongest impression of antiquity; the stone arches being so worn
and blackened by time. Still an American must
always have imagined a better cathedral than this.
There were some immense windows of painted glass,

but all modern. In the chapter-house we found a coal fire burning in the grate, and a large heap of old books — the library of the cathedral — in a discreditable state of decay, — mildewed, rotten, neglected for years. The sexton told us that they were to be arranged and better ordered. Over the door inside hung two faded and tattered banners, being those of the Cheshire regiment."

Hawthorne continues his description of the day's exploration and dwells upon that characteristic feature of Chester, the "Rows": —

"At frequent intervals little narrow passages go winding in among the houses, which all along are closely conjoined, and seem to have no access or exit, except through the shops, or into these narrow passages where you can touch each side with your elbows, and the top with your hand. We penetrated into one or two of them, and they smelt anciently and disagreeably. At one of the doors stood a pale-faced but cheerful and good-natured woman, who told us that she had come to that house when first married, twenty-one years before, and had lived there ever since; and that she felt as if she had been buried through the best years of her life. She allowed us to peep into her kitchen and parlor, — small, dingy, dismal, but yet not wholly destitute of a home look. She said she had seen two or three coffins in a day, during cholera times, carried out of that narrow passage into which her door opened. These avenues put me in mind of those which run through ant-hills, or those which a mole makes underground. The fashion of Rows does not appear to be going out;

and, for aught I can see, it may last hundreds of years longer. When a house becomes so old as to be untenantable, it is rebuilt, and the new one is fashioned like the old, so far as regards the walk running through its front. Many of the shops are very good, and even elegant, and these Rows are the favorite places of business in Chester. Indeed, they have many advantages, the passengers being sheltered from the rain, and there being within the shops that dimmer light by which tradesmen like to exhibit their wares."

Hawthorne contrasts the comparatively modern Rows with those of great antiquity, — "with oaken frames visible on the exterior. The Row passing through these houses is railed with oak so old that it has turned black, and grown to be as hard as stone, which it might be mistaken for, if one did not see where the names and initials have been cut into it with knives, at some bygone period. Overhead crossbeams project through the ceiling so low as to almost hit the head. On the front of one of these buildings was the inscription, 'God's Providence is Mine Inheritance,' said to have been put there by the occupant of the house two hundred years ago, when the plague spared this one house only in the whole city. Not improbably the inscription has operated as a safeguard to prevent the demolition of the house hitherto; but a shopman of an adjacent dwelling told us that it was soon to be taken down."

The two friends next turned their attention to the finding of a dining-place which was not too highly flavored with antiquity.

"Here and there, about some of the streets through which the Rows do not run, we saw houses of very aged aspect, with steep, peaked gables. The front gable-end was supported on stone pillars, and the sidewalk passed beneath. Most of these old houses seemed to be taverns, — the 'Black Bear,' the 'Green Dragon,' and such names. We thought of dining in one of them, but, on inspection, they looked rather too dingy and close, and of questionable neatness. So we went to the Royal Hotel, where we probably fared just as badly at much more expense, and where there was a particularly gruff and crabbed old waiter, who, I suppose, thought himself free to display his surliness because we arrived on foot. For my part, I love to see John Bull show himself. I must go again and again to Chester, for I suppose there is not a more curious place in the world."

Hawthorne closes this entry in his journal with the announcement of his friend's departure which followed immediately after the trip to Chester: "Mr. Ticknor, who has been staying at Rock Park with us since Tuesday, has steamed away in the Canada this morning. His departure seems to make me feel more abroad, more dissevered from my native country, than before."

On the eve of Mr. Ticknor's departure for America Mrs. Hawthorne wrote the following of which he was to be the bearer to her father: —

MY DEAREST FATHER, — I was afraid that I should not have time to write to you by the Canada and Mr. Ticknor; but accidentally he has not

arrived from Chester so early as I expected, so I have
time to say a few words. We were all to go to Chester
together to-day; but the weather was so threatening
that the rest of us stayed behind, and only Mr.
Hawthorne and Mr. Ticknor went.

On Wednesday Mr. Henry Bright came over to
dine. He visited Miss Martineau at Ambleside, and
found her very entertaining, and in a very singular
state of doctrine, — for she now professes to believe
and declare that there is no God and no future life!
He says it is wholly impossible to argue with her,
because she is so opinionated and dogmatical, and
has such a peculiar advantage in putting down her
ear-trumpet when she does not choose to hear any
reply to her assertions. She has been making some
beautiful designs for the windows of her brother's
church in Liverpool, which are accepted and to be
painted thereupon; but she is at enmity with her
brother, and has no intercourse with him. . . .

The Queen's visit to Ireland is considered of great
moment. Ireland is reviving from various causes;
and one cause is the potato blight itself! The immense emigration has thinned the population, and
the Irish in America have sent really vast sums of
money to their friends, and this Mr. Dargan rises
up all at once like a savior to the land. It will be
deeply interesting to watch on the spot all these
progressive movements; and the "Times" is an extraordinary organ of expression for all good things.
It is very just generally, I think (it is not of much
importance what I think, however), and seems full
of humanity and wisdom.

Last week Mr. Hawthorne was invited to dine with the magistrate in West Derby, and he met there a gentleman who wishes to introduce him to the two sons of Burns, and to-morrow evening is the time appointed. I expect another dinner-party this evening, and must now go and dress. Mr. Ticknor came from London rich in gifts: to Julian, a superb book, called "The Country Year-Book," with a hundred and forty fine engravings; to Una, a green and gold morocco portfolio with "Una" in gilt letters upon it, and quires of notepaper and envelopes; to Rosebud, a real waxen doll; to Mr. Hawthorne, a pair of superfine razors, made to order in Sheffield, with ivory handles, and "N. Hawthorne" finely marked in the steel of the blades; and to me, a case of scissors made for me in Sheffield, with my name on the blade of each, and a very superb book of Flowers. . . .

VIII

HAWTHORNE'S LETTERS

THE first week in October found Ticknor in mid-Atlantic bound for home. He had taken leave of the Hawthorne household and of his many English friends, all of whom seemed to feel for him the warm affection which he invariably inspired in those with whom he came in contact. During this London visit he had accomplished much important business, had been forced to decline many of the invitations which were so cordially tendered him, and had as usual executed to a nicety every small errand and commission with which he had been entrusted by those friends who, in the olden time, were wont to ask so many favors of the foreign traveler.

In taking leave of the consul at Liverpool, Ticknor had, no doubt, been urged to suggest something that might be done for him in return for his recent kindnesses, and it is evident from Hawthorne's next letter, that the departing friend had expressed a wish for some gloves, some ale and an English cheese. The fact that this modest request was not complied with for over four months, must be attributed to the consul's artistic temperament and not to any lack of affection on his part.

LIVERPOOL, Oct. 8th, 1853.

DEAR TICK, — While I write this, you are tossing in mid-ocean; but I hope it will find you safely ensconced in your Paradise, at the Old Corner. We all miss you very much.

Should my tax-bill for Concord be presented to you, please pay it, — or refund the money to Mr. Ball, if he pays it. We forgot to draw up the power of attorney; but I will send it, if you will instruct me how.

I wish you would send me two or three copies of "Tanglewood"; for Chapman has sent only one — and I want to give it to one or two friends.

Mrs. Hawthorne will buy some of those gloves as soon as the weather permits her to cross the river. I am looking out for a good cheese and some ale. Any further orders we shall be happy to execute. . . . I dined with two of the sons of Burns, last Saturday, and got into great favor with them — partly by the affection which I showed for the whiskey-bottle. One of them (an old white-headed major) sang several of his father's songs.

Send Fields over as soon as possible.

N. H.

On November 25, the cheese is again referred to by Hawthorne: —

"Yours by the Niagara received; as also the newspapers. Mrs. Hawthorne has been scolding me daily, since you went away, for not buying the cheese; and I really meant to have sent one by this steamer; but have neglected it, such is the continual pressure and hurry and urgency of my business. When I have a moment to breathe, I will buy both the cheese and ale. I am almost worn out with hard work. In fact, you must have noticed how overburdened I was with consular engagements while you were here. But I think I shall live through it.

"What has become of Fields? He never writes; and your own notes are of the briefest. Can I do anything for you here? — or for any of my friends or yours?

"We are all as well as this abominable climate will let us be. You speak of the 'wretched climate' of New England. God forgive you! You ought to spend a November in England."

In his next letter, penned December 8, Hawthorne incloses a draft for an old gentleman whose funds had failed him and to whom he had given that financial assistance, which was so frequently bestowed by him upon his impecunious countrymen. The old gentleman is on his way back to Philadelphia, and the writer hopes that the draft will prove a good one, adding, "although my clerks (who have seen a thousand such cases) tell me it will never be paid. In that event, I shall lose not only this, but a much larger sum for his passage money. . . .

"I wish you would go to Mr. F. C. Butman, and learn what are the probabilities of William Lilley's draft on him being paid by said Lilley's friends. This fellow is the newly appointed consul to Pernambuco, and drew a bill on Butman for which I engaged to be responsible to Brown & Shipley, who advanced the money, — £50. It turns out that he had no funds in Butman's hands, nor any right whatever to draw on him. If I lose the money, he shall lose his consulship; although I don't know that he is worse than

many other of our foreign appointments, who are
(but don't whisper it) a set of swindlers generally.
They almost always get short of money here, and
never can raise a shilling without my indorsement;
for the Liverpool merchants seem to know their character of old. You must not take the above as true
to the letter; though it has a great deal more of truth
in it than I wish it had.

"I received an immense bale of newspapers by
the last steamer, and thank you heartily for them.

"I suppose Baring Brothers have already advised
you of my depositing £300 to your credit. If it had
been £3000, I would kick the office to the devil, and
come home again. I am sick of it, and long for my
hillside; and what I thought I never should long for
— my pen! When once a man is thoroughly im-
bued with ink, he can never wash out the stain.

"I am invited to dine with the mayor again, but
don't mean to go.

"Remember me to Fields, Whipple, Longfellow,
and friends generally. I was delighted with Whipple's
notice of 'Tanglewood.'"

Christmas found a token characteristic of New
England in the hands of the Hawthorne household;
one which the sender knew would appeal to the
children especially, for who can call himself a de-
scendant of the Pilgrims without pronouncing the
English apple "only a crab-apple." Mrs. Hawthorne
writes in regard to this remembrance:—

By this steamer Mr. Ticknor has sent us a Christmas present of a barrel of apples. I wish you could

see Rosebud with her bright cheeks and laughing
eyes. A lady thought her four years old, the other
day! Julian has to-day gone with his father to the
consulate. Una is in the drawing-room reading Miss
Edgeworth. Rose is on the back of my chair.

On Christmas night the bells chimed in the dawn,
beginning at twelve and continuing till daybreak.
I wish you could hear this chiming of bells. It is the
most joyful sound you can imagine,—the most hopeful, the most enlivening. I waked before light, and
thought I heard some ineffable music. I thought of
the song of the angels on that blessed morn; but
while listening, through a sudden opening in the air
or breeze blowing towards us, I found it was not the
angels, but the bells of Liverpool. One day when I
was driving through Liverpool with Una and Julian,
these bells suddenly broke forth on the occasion of a
marriage, and I could scarcely keep the children in
the carriage. They leaped up and down, and Una
declared she would be married in England if only
to hear the chime of the bells. The Mummers stood
at our gate on Christmas morning and sang in the
dawn, acting the part of the heavenly host. The
Old Year was tolled out and the New Year chimed
in, also, and again the Mummers sang at the gate.

The opening of the new year brings up once more
the good resolve to forward the long delayed cheese
homeward, and on January 6, Hawthorne writes in
closing a business communication: "I meant to have
sent you that cheese by to-morrow's steamer, but
have not had time to select a good one. You shall

have it by the next one — or else I will give you leave
to call me inattentive and unpunctual. The ale shall
follow in due course. We must let it ripen a little
first."

On February 3, however, the cheese is at last on its
way, and the sender writes: —

"I send a note from Una, thanking you, I presume, for your magnificent present of paper.

"I have been very busy lately with those shipwrecked vagabonds from San Francisco — having
had to clothe and feed them all on my own private
responsibility. Uncle Sam will pay me, I suppose,
and he will likewise pay a larger sum for their passage home than all their bodies and souls are worth. I
made the bargain myself; so you will readily conclude
it is a poor one. This responsibility, however, rests
on the shoulders of the officer commanding — not on
mine. . . .

"If you know of any American Gazetteer, cheap
and accurate, and of recent date, I wish you would
send me a copy per next dispatch. So many inquiries
are made of me with respect to American localities,
that I need something of the kind; but if not very
recently published, there is no use sending it. . . .

"I sent your cheese per last steamer. Sometime or
other, you shall have the ale.

"As usual, I had something else to say, but have
forgotten it."

In Hawthorne's next letter he acknowledges the
receipt of a book of verse, "Passion Flowers," by
Julia Ward Howe: —

DEAR TICK, — Thank you for the books and papers. Those are admirable poems of Mrs. Howe's, but . . . What a strange propensity it is in these scribbling women to make a show of their hearts, as well as their heads, upon your counter, for anybody to pry into that chooses! However, I, for one, am much obliged to the lady, and esteem her beyond all comparison the first of American poetesses. What does her husband think of it? . . .

Redding has published a list of the monied men of Massachusetts. I consider myself one of them, since you tell me I have $3000 safely invested. Send me the pamphlet; for I ought to be acquainted with the names of my brethren.

I think I asked you for a United States Gazetteer.

That must have been a glorious dinner at the Cornhill Coffee-House.

Fields's friend, Miss Glyn, is in Liverpool, and Bennoch has sent me a letter of introduction to her. I shall probably deliver it, although rather shy of actresses.

Hawthorne adds in a postscript: "Please to pay Driscoll's bill, and remember me to him. I wish I had got him to make me a consular dress; for it would have been first-rate to wear to a fancy-ball, to which I am invited to-night. Having nothing to wear, I shan't go."

During the latter part of March, Hawthorne forwards a long communication regarding the outcome of the affair with the San Francisco sufferers before referred to: —

DEAR TICKNOR, — I enclose a paragraph from the Marblehead "Advocate," defending me, in my official capacity, from a statement in the Portsmouth "Journal" relative to my conduct with regard to the San Francisco sufferers. If nothing further has been said of the affair, let it rest. It will not be worth while to rake up a forgotten slander. But I herewith send you the facts of the case to be used if necessary.

When Captain Watkins and Lieutenant Winder came to my office, I explained to them that I was not officially empowered to provide for sending the troops home, but I would telegraph to Mr. Buchanan, and ascertain whether he would take the direction of the affair, or sanction my proceedings in it. This appeared to me the most eligible course, because his larger powers would probably enable him to do everything that was necessary; and also because (not being empowered to pledge the Government credit, and my private means being very limited) I doubted whether it would be possible for me to charter a steamer or other vessel, without the minister's sanction.

Mr. Buchanan replied to my message, that he had no authority to take charge of the troops; neither did he offer any advice as to my own course; but he facilitated my operations by suggesting to Messrs. Baring Brothers, to open a credit with me in behalf of the San Francisco sufferers. I do not question the propriety of Mr. Buchanan's conduct, and am bound to presume that he could estimate the extent of his official powers better than I could do it for him.

Before Mr. Buchanan's answer was received, Captain Watkins had started for London, not by my request or advice, but solely for his own satisfaction. Meanwhile, I had given directions for supplying the troops with provisions and clothing, on my personal credit, and to the amount of about two thousand dollars — that being the extent of Lieutenant Winder's requisition. This was the only part of the business in which I used the services of my clerk; he being well acquainted with the quality and the prices of the articles required. Before the answer was received, too, I had begun to seek for means of transportation; and before noon of the day after the arrival of the troops, I had four propositions from shipowners ready for the commanding officer's consideration. Mr. Buchanan had nothing whatever to do with the matter; neither had Captain Watkins, who did not return from London until after the arrangements were made. Lieutenant Winder, as commanding officer of the detachment, signed the contract for the charter of the steamer, and I, as consul, appended my official certificate of his competency to do so.

I cannot imagine who is the author of the false statement to which I have referred. Certainly it could not have been either Captain Watkins, or Lieutenant Winder, from neither of whom did I hear a word of complaint or dissatisfaction; and after parting from me in perfect kindness, and with thanks for my services, they are not the men to attack me behind my back, on the other side of the Atlantic, and anonymously, through a newspaper. Yet no other person, except those two, is qualified to give any account of the matter.

The above comprises all that I need to say. You will observe that I was no more bound by my official instructions to take charge of these men, to feed and clothe them, or to send them home, than any private citizen would have been. But I should never dream of taking any credit to myself for my doings in the matter. I did nothing more than was virtually and morally, though not officially, incumbent on me. Any man of common sense and common feeling would have seen (as I saw) that his duty, in such a position as mine, must be measured by the peculiar exigency of the case and by his utmost capacity to deal with them and not by the narrow letter of his instructions, which were framed to meet only the ordinary routine of events. I therefore claim no praise. But on the other hand, I certainly deserve no censure; for my duty, on the largest interpretation of its limits, was as amply and as promptly performed as if I had been clothed with the fullest official powers for this identical contingency.

Truly yours,

NATH'L HAWTHORNE.

P.S. I was ready to sign the contract as principal, had the agent of the Cunard line preferred that course; but, instead of the Government credit, it would have involved merely my personal liability, which was very inadequate to the occasion. During the progress of the negotiation, if I mistake not, a despatch had been received by Lieutenant Winder from the Secretary of War, expressly authorizing

him to charter a steamer or other vessel for the
transportation of troops.

Do not make this public, unless circumstances
imperatively demand it. Otherwise, put it by.

N. H.

At the end of April, Hawthorne announces Mr.
Buchanan's arrival upon the scene and voices his
hope that it will not be necessary to print the letter
of explanation: —

DEAR TICKNOR, — I send a pamphlet which I
have been requested to forward to the Professor of
Mineralogy at Cambridge. I don't know who he is,
— so must leave it to you.

There is no news worth telling you. We are
expecting the arrival of the Collins steamer, which
is now several days behind her time. Mr. Buchanan
has been here since Tuesday in expectation of his
niece, who is supposed to be on board the steamer. I
had the old fellow to dine with me, and liked him
better than I expected; so I hope you have not found
it necessary to publish my letter on the San Francisco
business; for though I bear lightly on him, it would
undoubtedly have provoked a feud between us. But
he takes his wine like a true man, loves a good cigar,
and is doubtless as honest as nine diplomatists out of
ten.

My friend O'Sullivan and his family have been
staying with me this past fortnight, on their way to
Portugal.

The circular of the Secretary of the Treasury, to

which you allude, is, I suppose, the same about which I have already written you. It will seriously affect the emoluments of the office; but, if nothing happens, I shall get rather more than $20,000 out of it. The truth is, it is a devilish good office if those jackasses at Washington (of course, I do not include the President under this polite phrase) will but let it alone. They are now tinkering at a bill involving the whole subject of diplomatic and consular emoluments; and if they touch the Liverpool consulate at all, it will be to limit it by a salary. Now, with the inevitable expenses of a residence here, a salary of ten thousand dollars would hardly make it worth while to keep the office — and they would never think of giving more than six. But, I trust in God, Pierce will not let them meddle with me.

Before this reaches you, Fields will have sailed for England. I shall be rejoiced to see him, and shall make him come at once to my house. I wish I could hope to see you along with him.

That the publication of the explanatory letter did not take place is evinced by the contents of another letter that Hawthorne writes on May 5: "I am glad you did not find it necessary to publish my defense on the San Francisco business; for it is humiliating to be compelled to stand before the public in an attitude of defense. And, besides, I should have made several enemies — which it is not desirable to do, except in a case of necessity. But somebody must have lied most damnably."

On May 12, Hawthorne writes: —

"I thank you heartily for your kind exertions in regard to the invoice certificates. I can think of nothing to add to my arguments; except that, by dispensing with the certificates, a great injury is done to Americans (viz., myself and all other consuls in England, Scotland, and Ireland) for the sake of conferring a miserable little favor and facility on Englishmen and Canadians, who will never thank us for it, and who will abuse their opportunities to defraud the revenue, if they can. It is a piece of unmitigated folly, which old Gutherie ought to be ashamed of. If he knew the character of English merchants as well as I begin to know it, he would see the expediency of creating new checks against their malfeasances, instead of relaxing any old ones. I have been quite surprised to find that our respectable merchants have a higher moral standard than the same class over here. We Americans are the best people in the world, — but it is a poor world at that.

"I sent you a fortnight ago, a small pamphlet on Crystallography. Did I say that it was intended for the Professor of Mineralogy at Cambridge?

"It gratifies me much to see that you have been presented with an elegant silver tea-service. I hope to take a cup of tea from that silver tea-pot, some evening or other.

"My wife is pretty well, and the children quite hearty. As for myself I am afraid (from the compliments which I receive about my healthy aspect) that I am getting a little too John Bullish, and must diminish my allowance of roast beef, brown-stout, port and sherry. I never felt better in my life. England is certainly the country to eat in, and to drink in.

"Remember me to Colonel Miller, and thank him for his letter to the department about the invoice certificates, and also for the Salem 'Gazettes,' which, by the way, did not come per last steamer.

"I shall be rejoiced to see Fields, and will send him home in August according to your directions — if I can catch him."

The silver tea-service, to which Hawthorne refers, was a gift from the Roe Street Baptist Church, in token of the society's appreciation of Mr. Ticknor's services as Superintendent of the Sunday School for many years. The gift was an especially beautiful one, and an amusing accompaniment of the occasion was, that the presentation of the set, which was to have come as a genuine surprise to the recipient, was foreshadowed by his receiving a bill for it, some time before the arrival of the offering of love and friendship; this was the result of his being treasurer of the organization, in addition to his other office, and consequently handling all bills that came in to the parish.

June finds Hawthorne responding to a request from his publisher for more copy to be included in the "Mosses from the Old Manse." The consul writes: —

"You put me to my trumps by asking for additional matter for the 'Mosses'; for I considered myself exhausted on that score, long ago. Nevertheless, there is 'Feathertop' — which is almost as good as any of them. Let that go in. It has just occurred to me, moreover, that in the 'New England Magazine,' when published by Park Benjamin, many of the stories appeared which are now collected in the 'Twice-Told Tales'; and the publication of them was commenced with about ten or more pages of introductory matter, which, I think, will do very well to publish as an article in the 'Mosses.' It should be separated from all extraneous stuff (which if I recollect rightly, can be done easily enough), and may be called 'passages from a relinquished work' — or something of that kind. I believe the title was 'The Itinerant Storyteller.'

"There are other detached passages of mine scattered through Park Benjamin's volumes of that magazine; and Fields would readily recognize them. Let him do as he pleases about inserting any or all of them; — only being careful to put in nothing that he does not feel absolutely certain about. The beginning, and the conclusion, of the 'Itinerant Storyteller' are there, at an interval of some months, and are written quite up to the usual level of my scribblings. If I had the magazine at hand I could patch up an article in five minutes; and Fields can do it just as well, and without any trouble at all. If he should already have sailed, Whipple will doubtless do it. Do not put the patched-up article at the end of the volume, but somewhere about the middle, where it will not attract so much notice. . . .

"Yesterday I received a package, which appeared to be the one which you sent by the Andes. There being no bearer of dispatches to take charge of it, it had been sent to the Custom-House, and had lain there ever since, until inquiry was made on my part.

They have overhauled it, and made me pay duty on the books which it contained, and postage on the letters. Among other books, there was a Gazetteer, which I sent for so long ago that I had forgotten it, but am very glad to get it now. Also, Grace Greenwood's 'Haps and Mishaps,' which, it appears, she wishes to present to the Queen. I have forwarded it to Mr. Buchanan, who may hand it to Her Majesty, if he chooses to make such a fool of himself. . . .

"P.S. All that I now recollect of my articles in the 'New England Magazine' are, — 'The Storyteller' aforesaid, begun in an early October number, and concluded long afterwards, I think, under some other title; and a description of an evening at the mountain-house among the White Hills. These passages formed part of a work, the whole of which was never published. Do not print any more of it than will be sufficient to meet the exigency of the case; though really, as far as I can remember, it is no bad stuff."

A glance at the "Mosses from an Old Manse" will show the reader that Hawthorne's suggestion was promptly carried out, as the second volume contains the article entitled "Passages from a Relinquished Work," and following that, "Sketches from Memory," embodying the White Mountain episodes to which the writer had referred.

A fortnight later, Hawthorne expresses his disappointment that Fields has postponed his trip to England, but voices the hope of seeing him ere long, on the arrival of the favorite Niagara. He adds: —

"No package has come to hand by the America; but Mr. Beck told me that the bearer of dispatches

had charge of a box directed to me; and on inquiring what may have become of it, I find the Custom-
House officers have seized it. They opened it, and
it appears, have found various dutiable articles, and,
at the very bottom of the box, a quantity of cigars,'—
too large a quantity to pass free of duty, and too
small to be imported on paying duties. Nothing
less, I think, than one hundred pounds weight is
allowed to be entered. This is a very awkward
occurrence; for it is now impossible to get the box,
even by payment of fines and duties, without special
order from the Treasury in London; and it is by no
means certain that this can be obtained. As respects
the other articles, I shall do my best; for I understand from Mr. Beck that they were intended as
presents for some of Fields's friends in London and
elsewhere. As for the cigars, I have no hope of getting them out of limbo, and, indeed, do not think it
advisable to make any strong attempt to do so, lest it
should be supposed that I had some previous knowledge of an attempt to smuggle them. Even as the
case stands, my consular good name can hardly fail
to suffer some damage; and I am afraid the officers
will pay special attention to all packages directed to
me hereafter. It was an ill-advised affair; but perhaps, when Fields arrives, he may be able to make
such explanations as may facilitate the release of all
except the cigars. They are gone to Hell; and may
the Devil smoke them.

"My whole family (including my wife, and I believe, myself) are at this moment in the spasmodic
stage of whooping-cough. The children have it

pretty severely, but seem now to be on the mending-point. This climate (as I have said a thousand times) is most detestable. We still find it necessary to keep fires."

Four days later, the matter of the unfortunate box seems to have been pleasantly adjusted, for Hawthorne explains in another letter: —

"The affair of the confiscated box has turned out better than I expected. Judicious measures having been used on my part, the Custom-House people have given it up on payment of duties. I say nothing of what was paid on the cigars (that being my own affair); but for Fields's silver articles £2 4s. Nothing was demanded for the books. I thank you heartily for the cigars. They look first-rate, and no doubt will prove so, when I try them — which I have not yet been able to do, on account of the whooping-cough. I have put the silver things in my safe, and shall keep them there for the present, in expectation of Fields's arrival by the next steamer.

"If the bearer of dispatches had done his duty, the box might have been delivered at once, without trouble or expense; but he went away, leaving it in the hands of the officers. His name is 'Longbottom'; — and his bottom deserves to be kicked, be it long or short.

"We are getting through the whooping-cough pretty comfortably, but it will be a long while before the children are in rugged health again."

"One year yesterday since we sailed from America," writes Hawthorne, on July 7, 1854. "I was," he continues, "even more disappointed than before, at Fields's non-arrival by the last steamer. He must come. If he can't, you must. The whooping-cough is on the decline; and I intend, in the course of a week or so, to take my family into Wales or somewhere else, for change of air. If I could have one week of my Concord hillside, it would do us more good than all the English air that ever was breathed. But it will be many a long day yet before we see the old house again — perhaps never; for you seem to be in such a confounded mess there, that it quite sickens me to think of coming back. I find it impossible to read American newspapers (of whatever political party) without being ashamed of my country. No wonder, then, if Englishmen hate and despise us, taking their ideas of us and our institutions from such sources."

By the 20th of July it is plain that Fields is not to carry out his European plan, and Hawthorne refers playfully to that gentleman's disinclination to cross, on account of his tendency to extreme seasickness:—

DEAR TICKNOR, — I am very sorry to find that we are not to see Fields, this year. Enclosed are some letters that have been on hand for him this long while. Does he expect immunity from seasickness next year? Or are we to have a railway across? He had much better have come now; but since it is not to be so, I wish you might find it necessary to come over and make purchases for the holidays. I see Americans enough, Heaven knows — but nobody that I care about seeing. . . .

I have made a short but very pleasant tour in

North Wales, since I wrote last, and have also visited
the Isle of Man, which is the most interesting place
I have yet seen. Sophia and the children are now
staying there; and I shall go to them to-morrow and
remain until Monday. The health of my family (and
my own, indeed) required a change of air, and nothing
could be purer than the atmosphere of the Isle of
Man.

You talk of intolerably hot weather. Until the
past week, we have had constant fires, both at house
and office — and hardly comfortable at that. It is
fine weather now, however — quite warm enough for
comfort, and not a bit too warm for exercise; and if
English weather were all like this, England would
really be an earthly paradise. Unluckily, there is
not more than a week of such weather in the whole
year.

The silver tokens sent by Mr. Fields seem to have
been through various vicissitudes before reaching
their destination, for in the consul's next communication to the senior partner he says: —

"I sent Fields's silver things to London some time
ago, and considered that I had done with them; but
a day or so since, I received back a silver shovel and
pie-knife, for which no claimants could be found.
Finding them thus providentially returned, I was a
good deal inclined to confiscate them for the use and
ornament of the consular table; but have finally concluded to send them to Mrs. Bennoch and Mrs.
Craig (De Quincey's daughter) for whom Fields
writes me they were intended. I don't know the

locality of the latter lady, but will endeavor to find out.

"I observe that a bill for the remodeling of the Diplomatic and Consular service was reported in Congress, August 3, and referred to Committee of the Whole. I should suppose they could hardly have acted on it, in the brief remnant of the session; but if so, it cannot fail to have been most disastrous to my official interests. However, I am so sick and weary of this office, that I should hardly regret it if they were to abolish it altogether. What with brutal shipmasters, drunken sailors, vagrant Yankees, mad people, sick people, and dead people (for just now I have to attend to the removal of the bones of a man who has been dead these twenty years) it is full of damnable annoyances. . . . After all there are worse lives than that of an author — at least, when he is so fortunate in his publishers as I am. I suppose some persons would console themselves with the dignity of that office, and public and private dinners, and the excellent opportunity of playing the great man on a small scale; but this is to me a greater bore than all the rest; so that you see I have nothing to comfort myself with but the emoluments."

IX

HAWTHORNE'S LETTERS (CONTINUED)

TOWARD the close of September Hawthorne writes
to his publisher to forward him some typical examples of American literary work; these are for the edi-
fication of Monckton Milnes, who was a warm friend
of Ticknor, and whose generous hospitality both he
and Hawthorne had greatly enjoyed.

Richard Monckton Milnes, who was afterwards
Lord Houghton, was a Cambridge man and an intimate of Tennyson, Hallam, and other men of literary
mark; he was himself a poet and a warm enthusiast
in the cause of literature. During his Parliamentary
career, he was, in 1837, instrumental in passing
the Copyright Act. A more urbane and delightful
English gentleman it would have been hard to find.
He was of medium height, well-built, and with a
large and well-formed head and wavy dark hair.
His likeness to Longfellow was considered marked,
though he was not as handsome as his American
double.

Milnes was particularly fond of giving breakfasts
to companies of choice spirits, and as he was able to
draw from the best that England had to offer, and
was a truly tactful and gracious host, invitations to
his entertainments were highly prized. It was said
that to breakfast with Milnes meant to discount the
remaining meals of the day, but his guests always

S. A. Schoff Sc.

Aet. 36

Nathaniel Hawthorne

displayed a willingness to take this risk for the pleasure of sitting down at the hospitable board of this veritable "autocrat of the breakfast-table."

Hawthorne writes: —

"Mr. Monckton Milnes wants me to send him half a dozen good American books, which he has never read or heard of before. For the honor of my country, I should like to do it, but can think of only three which would be likely to come under his description — viz., 'Walden,' 'Passion Flowers,' and 'Up-Country Letters.' Possibly Mrs. Mowatt's 'Autobiography' might make a fourth; and Thoreau's former volume a fifth. You understand that these books must not be merely good, but must be original, with American characteristics, and not generally known in England. If you, or Fields, or anybody else, can produce any such, pray send them along. At any rate, send those I have mentioned; for my credit is pledged to supply the number Mr. Milnes asked for. Whittier's book is poor stuff. I like the man, but have no high opinion either of his poetry or prose. Send Lowell's 'Biglow Papers.' He is very little known in England, and I take that to be the best thing he has written. . . .

"You speak of another book from me. There is no prospect of that so long as I continue in office; but if the Consular Bill should pass at the next session, I shall soon be an author again. It proposes to allow no more than $7500 for the salary and all expenses of the office. No consul can live as a gentleman in English society, and carry on the office business, on these terms. But it would not cost me many pangs to resign. I hardly think, however, that the bill can pass during the short session."

Hawthorne's trials in becoming responsible for the return passages of the irresponsible were many and varied. He sympathized with the innumerable tales of woe which were presented to him and generally aided the applicants after listening to their pitiful appeals. The results of his charitable assistance of his countrymen in distress were varied; sometimes the persons returned his loan immediately; again they delayed until he almost lost belief in their integrity; and very frequently they never paid at all. The following letter cites one of the consul's usual perplexities. It also mentions the purchase of property in New York, and the shipment of one more cheese to Ticknor, who seems to have had a great fondness for this product of old England.

LIVERPOOL, December 8th, 1854.

DEAR TICK, — Here is another bad speculation of mine in becoming responsible for people's passages. Captain Gibson (the Dutch claimant) writes me that he is unable to pay a draft which he gave the Cunard agents; so they will come upon me. It is for £30, and I suppose the draft is in the hands of the agent in New York. Please to pay it (unless it be already sent over to Liverpool) and write to Captain J. W. Gibson, Washington, D.C., informing him of the fact. He is a man of honorable intentions, but is now in great difficulties, and I always had a presentiment that I might be left in the lurch.

I have determined to buy some real estate in

New York; not that I want it, but because I must either buy the property, or lend $3000 to O'Sullivan, who never would be able to pay me. He says this property will be a very good investment, and pays much more than the interest of the money. Half of the amount I shall be able to pay here; and for the other half (£300) I must draw on you. If business had not been so very bad, I could have paid the whole on this side of the water. I shall not draw before the first of January, and will give the bill as long a date as may be found practicable. It is marvellous what a difficulty a man finds in keeping his money, the instant he is known to have any. Friends and strangers settle on my poor little pile of gold, like flies on a lump of sugar. You must save what you can for me.

I want you to send the "Boy Hunters" for Julian. Mrs. Hawthorne wants a version of the Psalms separate from the rest of the Bible. There is no such edition to be found in England, except as altered and amended for the use of the English Church. Mrs. Hawthorne wants the Psalms pure and unadulterated. If not to be found separate, one of the American Bible Society's editions of the New Testament may be sent, with the Psalms annexed.

I send the cheese by this steamer and hope that (like General Washington) it is as good as it is great. Mrs. Hawthorne insists on your considering it her Christmas present, so you must accept it without a word. I meant to have sent you some special good ale, as mild as milk and strong as brandy, which is never found in the market, but has to be brewed purposely for the purchaser; but the sea-captain, who made me acquainted with the ale, is not now in port, and I don't know where nor how to get any. So you must wait till some other time.

Be good enough to put American postage stamps on the letters which I have marked paid, for I have left the key of my drawer at home, and cannot get at any postage stamps.

I shall look with great interest for the action of Congress as regards the Consular Bill. It will settle the point whether I am to remain here six months or nearly three years; and whether I am to have a comfortable property, or to content myself with the little which you have now in charge. Anyhow, it will not break my heart to be released from this office; and I am almost ready to begin authorship again.

Truly yours,

NATH'L HAWTHORNE.

News of the approaching marriage of Mr. Fields having reached Hawthorne he writes: "It would gratify me to hear some particulars about Fields and his matrimonial affairs. Are they coming out in the spring? I saw in a newspaper that Fields had lately published a volume of poems for private circulation among his friends. I don't want to press my friendship on any man; but I really thought I was one of them — one of the b-hoys — and ought to have received the poems."

Once more the fate of the silver pie-knife is referred to in a postscript: "I hope Fields's silver pie-knife has reached Mrs. Craig before this time. I wrote to

De Quincey about the mode of transmitting it, but
received no answer, till at last a letter came from
Miss De Quincey in Ireland. It seems the old gentleman has shut himself up in Edinburgh to follow his
literary avocations (and eat opium, I suppose), and
all the letters that go to Lasswade are sent first to
Ireland and then transmitted to him, unopened.
Miss De Quincey conjectured from the seal and post-
mark that the letter might be from me, and so wrote
to inquire the contents. A book, which you sent
him, still remains on hand; for his daughters hint
that he opens no letters or packages, in his present
mood."

Hawthorne's various outbursts in regard to his
having tired of his duties as consul, were but the
expression of a passing mood, for he repeatedly
acknowledged that he had not learned to know
England as he yet hoped to do, and stated that if
there was sufficient remuneration to make him comfortable financially, he looked forward to spending
a couple of years more on British soil. As has been
previously suggested, his natural impracticability in
money matters made him a mark for sharpers and
impostors, who begged for aid in order that they
might return to America, and gave plausible promises
of speedy reimbursement. Ticknor, upon the other
side, was invariably the one to discover that there
was to be no reimbursement from the "pathetic
cases," who had taxed Hawthorne's resources, as
well as his sympathies, and the publisher repeatedly
advised him against being too ready to advance
money without having first obtained due information

regarding the person begging for "just a temporary
loan."

In January, 1855, Hawthorne replies to a warning
concerning some risky expenditure: —

"I shall lose nothing by this investment; and as
to your advice not to lend any more money, I acknowledge it to be good, and shall follow it so far as
I can and ought. But when the friend of half my lifetime asks me to assist him, and when I have perfect
confidence in his honor, what is to be done? Shall I
prove myself to be one of the persons who have every
quality desirable in friendship, except that they invariably fail you at the pinch? I don't think I can
do that; but, luckily, I have fewer friends than most
men, and there are not a great many who can claim
anything of me on that score.

"As regards such cases as R—— and G——, my
official position makes it necessary that I should
sometimes risk money that way; but I can assure
you I exercise a great deal of discretion in the responsibilities which I assume. I have not been a year
and a half in this office without learning to say 'No,'
as peremptorily as most men.

"I enclose a letter to R——, which you will please
send to his direction, unless he has already depos-
ited funds for your draft and that of Mr. Cunard.
I also transmit the latter, which has been returned
by Cunard, and paid by me. If Mr. R—— neglects
to refund, he is the meanest scoundrel that ever
pretended to be a gentleman; for without my interference and assistance, he could have had no resource but starvation, or possibly a Liverpool work-

house. If he refuses to pay, himself, the fact of my aiding him, and of his extreme necessity at the time, should be stated to his brother, or nearest relative, who, in merest decency, cannot but pay the amount. But I still believe that he has a sense of honor in him."

Hawthorne leaves to his publisher the pleasant task of communicating with the relatives, or friends, of the various impecunious ones, whose sense of honor does not prove sufficient to impel them to refund without a delicate reminder, when they are once again safely within the borders of their native land, and there remains no record to prove how large a percentage of those "deserving" cases ever came up to the consul's high expectations.

In this same letter he remarks that he is willing to remain longer in office, and voices his habitual impatience with the increasing number of women writers: —

"I shall spend a year on the Continent, and then decide whether to go back to the Wayside, or to stay abroad and write books. But I had rather hold this office two years longer; for I have not seen half enough of England, and there is the germ of a new romance in my mind, which will be all the better for ripening slowly. Besides, America is now wholly given over to a d——d mob of scribbling women, and I should have no chance of success while the public taste is occupied with their trash — and should be ashamed of myself if I did succeed. What is the mystery of these innumerable editions of the 'Lamplighter,' and other books neither better nor worse? —

worse they could not be, and better they need not be, when they sell by the 100,000. . . .

"I meant to write Fields by this steamer, but fear I shall not have time. Please to convey to him my thanks for his slice of cake, and warmest congratulations on his marriage."

The following month finds Hawthorne in a softened mood towards the feminine "scribblers" (though hardly complimentary in his attitude towards the majority of them). After thanking Ticknor for a gift of the finest American apples and for a cheering account of his financial affairs, he says: —

"It gives me much pleasure to see that my affairs are in such good condition, and I feel truly obliged to you for your kind care. I hardly venture to hope that I shall do so well, this present year; but anyhow, with the assistance of my pen, I shall manage to live, even if my office should cease to be worth holding. I wish I could make a book calculated for schools. Can't you think of any?

"In my last, I recollect, I bestowed some vituperation on female authors. I have since been reading 'Ruth Hall'; and I must say I enjoyed it a good deal. The woman writes as if the Devil was in her; and that is the only condition under which a woman ever writes anything worth reading. Generally women write like emasculated men, and are only to be distinguished from male authors by greater feebleness and folly; but when they throw off the restraints of decency, and come before the public stark naked, as it were, — then their books are sure to possess character and value. Can you tell me anything about this Fanny Fern? If you meet her, I wish you would let her know how much I admire her. . . .

"I am going out to dine with the Mayor at the Town Hall, and expect to make a foolish speech to-night and wake up with a headache to-morrow morning. Luckily, the speeches at the Mayor's dinners are never reported. It is very difficult for an American to speak in public in a manner to suit both countries, just at this time, when there is a good deal of hostile feeling towards England, on your side of the water, and not a little on the part of England towards us. I shall be true to my country, and get along with John Bull as well as I can. The time will come, sooner or later, when the old fellow will look to us for his salvation. He is in more danger from his own allies, than we are either from him, or them. . . .

"If I really cannot pay the expenses of the office and live out of the salary, I shall go to Italy immediately, and perhaps come home in the autumn. The mere idea of this gives me a little touch of homesickness. I do love old Massachusetts, in spite of its ten thousand varieties of nonsense. . . .

"I wish you would come over — or Fields — or Whipple — or somebody that I care about. America begins to be dim in my remembrance, and my exile is not yet half over."

On May 11, 1855, Hawthorne suggests that it would gratify him to have his publisher take a trip to Concord in order to look over his property; he writes: —

DEAR TICKNOR, — I thank you for Kingsley's book, which I think a first-rate one; also on Julian's behalf, for the Australian adventures, which has just met his wishes. . . .

I want you to send me a copy of the Liturgy of King's Chapel, published by you. The New York "Inquirer" has not been sent for some weeks. Do you receive it?

I wish you would take a convenient opportunity to go to Concord, with Fields or Whipple, or some other friend, dine at the Middlesex Hotel, and take a look at my place, and charge the expenses to me. First, read over the lease which I gave Mr. Bull (a copy is in your keeping) and see whether he is complying with the terms of it, as respects the improvements to be made on the land in front of the house. It will be a great injury to me if he does not promptly fulfil the conditions as to setting out an orchard, etc.; and I have some reason to think that he has not, thus far, quite come up to the contract. Do not give yourself any extra trouble about this matter; but when you want a pleasure excursion, I should be glad to have you make it in that direction. . . .

I enclose a note drawn by Mr. W. E. T.—— in favor of Una and Julian in their infancy, by a friend. Dr. P—— invested it in this way; but perhaps it had better be in your hands, to be reinvested. This I must leave to your judgment.

This is the worst pen I ever wrote with.

Truly yours,

NATH'L HAWTHORNE.

I am nearly out of postage stamps. Please to send some more.

N. H.

"We intend to set out on our rambles about England, soon after the first of June," wrote Hawthorne on May 27. "I shall spend much of the summer away from Liverpool, but shall pay frequent visits to my consulate; and I rather think matters will go on about as well as if I were constantly on hand. At all events, I have a right to some recreation, for I have had very little hitherto.

"It is a very disagreeable office; but some amusing incidents happen occasionally; — for instance, I send home by this steamer a Doctor of Divinity who has been out here on a spree, and who was brought to my office, destitute, after a week's residence in a brothel! He shook in his shoes, I can tell you. Not knowing whether I should ever have another opportunity of preaching to a Doctor of Divinity (an Orthodox man, too), I laid it on without mercy; and he promised never to forget it. I don't think he ever will. You will probably see his name in the list of passengers, — but don't breathe a word about it. . . .

"I want some more postage stamps, but they will be of no use to me if Mr. Glyn declines to be the medium of conveying my letters. Our Government grows more intolerable every day. I wish it might be changed to a monarchy."

In August, 1855, Hawthorne writes in reference to the working of the new act which was to reduce the consular returns: —

"I shall probably soon send you some more bills on the Government — the last of the kind you are ever likely to receive from me. Business is not very brisk nowadays; but that does not concern me so much since the new act has come into operation. For my part, I should not care if the Liverpool trade were to dwindle down to absolutely nothing — leaving only the notarial business. I wish nobody any harm; but failures, shipwrecks, and all sorts of commercial disaster would have a direct tendency to fill my pockets; — whereas, a prosperous state of trade only gives me the more unpaid business to perform. So you see, I am somewhat in the situation of doctors and undertakers, who thrive by the misfortunes of their fellow-creatures. But success to Uncle Sam, say I, in spite of all the mischief the old rogue has done me."

During the first year of his consular duties Hawthorne had made the acquaintance of William Allingham, who had called upon him and presented him with a volume of his poems. He described the young man as "intelligent, dark, pleasing, and not at all John-Bullish." The young poet had said that he had been employed in the customs in Ireland, and was then going to London to establish a connection with some newspaper. He was already acquainted with a number of the literary people there and spoke of knowing Tennyson and Carlyle; he possessed pleasing manners and much independence of mind.

Hawthorne writes in regard to this young man's work on August 17, 1855: —

"I send some copies of Allingham's poems; and I wish you would have them distributed to people tinctured with poetry and such nonsense, — to edi-

tors of magazines or newspapers, — and to anybody
who will take the trouble to notice them. Will not
Fields give them a puff in the 'Transcript'? — it
used to be his organ in my literary days. Do ask
Whipple to take them into his gracious consideration. There is great merit in some of the pieces.
'Cross-Examination,' for instance, is wonderfully
pithy. I can't say I have read them all, for I dislike
poetry. But I know the author, and should be glad
to get him an American reputation, — which he
deserves as much as a good many whose works you
have published. I enclose a list of persons to whom
Allingham has already sent the poems. Please to
write 'With Author's compliments' on the title-
pages of those you distribute."

Hawthorne, although the friend of many poets,
could hardly be designated as the friend of poetry;
he took especial pleasure in denouncing all manner
of poetical productions, even though he thoroughly
enjoyed the best poetry and was ever ready to do the
poets themselves a good turn. And despite the fact
that he denounced them, the poets recognized in him
a fellow poet, and hailed him as one of them; they
sought him for sympathy, and brought him their
verses for criticism, feeling assured that he would
perceive both merits and defects with a discerning
eye and a responsive heart.

In connection with this attitude of Hawthorne
toward the poets, it is of interest to turn to an early
letter, penned from Concord, in 1845, by George
William Curtis, in which the writer voices his impressions of Emerson and Hawthorne; he says of

Emerson: — "I am glad that you treat him as a prophet rather than a poet. My feeling about the latter is very strong, and yet few contemporaries write verses which I love so much. I wish you might have seen Mr. Emerson and Mr. Hawthorne for the last year casually and at all times, as I have done, that I might know if you would not at last say, 'the wise Emerson, the poetic Hawthorne.' — I am going to show some of my verses to the latter. I do not dare to do so to the former, and I do it with some trembling, for I feel that he knows what is poetical, what is the power of the poet — and what the force of talented intuition."

Yet Hawthorne never could countenance the idea of being himself a poet, and when pressed too hard for sympathy, by the eloquent disciples of the poetic muse, his last resource seems to have been to consign them to his publishers for exploitation. And at their hands the poets fared exceeding well, as this firm invariably found a satisfactory market for their work, which was not apt to be the case with other publishers in this country. Indeed, poetry was not sought for with any especial interest by the other publishing-houses. This fact is attested by another communication from Mr. Curtis, who writes discouragingly to a rising poet, who desires to have a volume of verse brought out in New York. He says: —

"Poetry in New York never does well. Within a month I have spoken with the Harpers and Putnams about it, and although I had no proposals to make, they both said that they invariably declined everything.

"Your men, and the men for all printing poets, are Ticknor, Reed and Fields, of Boston, whose books of poetry sell well because they are theirs, and because they have such facilities for that peculiar sale. Mr. Fields wrote me that an edition of 1500 of Alexander Smith's book was sold the first week, and they have printed 2000 more. . . . You had better not publish with any New York men because they will not interest themselves enough to circulate the volume, — only Ticknor and Company do that."

On August 31, 1855, Hawthorne writes that his wife and daughters are about to start for Lisbon, where it is hoped the change of climate will prove beneficial to Mrs. Hawthorne.

DEAR TICKNOR, — Mrs. Hawthorne's health seems to have improved considerably; but she agrees with me that it is best to change the air before cold weather comes on; so she, Una, and Rosebud, are going to Lisbon, where the O'Sullivans are anxious to receive them. Julian will remain in England with me. They will sail from Southampton, probably towards the end of September; and we shall spend most of the intervening time either in London or the north of England. We expect to start for London next Tuesday. Very probably, I shall pay her a short visit before she returns from Lisbon.

I send three bills of exchange, to the aggregate amount, I think, of $2206.37 — which will be quite an important addition to my small accumulations. Don't you think I have property enough, now, to resign upon? I want to do so most damnably, but will try to hold on another year, unless the coming Congress makes the office worse than it now looks— I should n't wonder if it did.

A young gentleman of Liverpool wishes me to inquire if any of the Boston papers would like a correspondent here. He is a business man, of great intelligence, and of liberal and independent views in politics; he could give reliable information as to the actual state of the markets and fair conjectures as to what it is likely to be. He was employed last year, on the Washington 'Globe,' and gave good satisfaction. I don't know exactly what his price is; but I guess about $5 per letter, of a newspaper column — which is ridiculously low. Would you be kind enough to make a few inquiries among editors? He is not a penny-a-liner, but a man in business.

I feel a little homesick, now and then, but not to any great extent; and it is well for me that I don't, for it will be three years before I darken the doors of the Old Corner Store. I have gained a better acquaintance with my own countrymen since taking this office, than in all my previous life; and, to say the truth, I wish to get farther off, in the hope of liking them better. Two years on the Continent will perhaps revive my patriotism.

I made a convert to total abstinence yesterday. It was a sea-captain who has fallen into dissipated habits; I preached to him with such good effect that he asked me to draw up a pledge, which he signed on the spot, and declared that he felt himself a new man. On the strength of this good deed, I thought myself entitled to drink an extra glass or two of wine in the evening, and so have got a little bit of a headache. "Physician, heal thyself!"

Remember me to all friends. Tell Colonel Miller that I met Miss Cushman, a little while ago, at Windermere, and expect soon to see her in London.

A month later, having seen Mrs. Hawthorne and two of the children embark on their trip to Lisbon, Hawthorne writes that he and Julian have established themselves at Mrs. Blodgett's boarding-house, where they feel quite at home, after returning from a stay in London: —

"I have spent the last month almost entirely in London, and know it pretty well now; for I was never weary of rambling about, and peeping into all the odd holes and corners I could find. The last day I was there I called on Trübner, and found him so good a fellow that I was sorry not to have called sooner. I did not seek society; but I saw by chance one or two people that interested me, and who seemed glad to see me, — among others Leigh Hunt, whom I like very much, partly, perhaps, because he is half an American. I wish you could do him some of the good offices which you do for other English authors, by republishing his works. It is strange that he has not greater popularity on our side of the water, since he possesses many of the literary characteristics which we are quickest to recognize."

Leigh Hunt's charm and simplicity made a decided impression upon Hawthorne, who described him at some length in his sketches, and regretted that he had won from his countrymen insufficient appre-

ciation to place him eventually in the Poets' Corner
of Westminster Abbey. "He deserves this honor,"
Hawthorne declared, "if not for his verse (the value
of which I do not estimate, never having been able
to read it), yet for his delightful prose, his unmeas-
ured poetry, the inscrutable happiness of his touch,
working soft miracles by a life-process like the
growth of grass and flowers."

Hawthorne's first call upon Hunt is vividly set
forth by him:—

"A slatternly maidservant (doubtless a relic of Mrs.
Leigh Hunt's pitiful failure at housekeeping)
opened the door, and as the guests entered they
were immediately greeted by the presiding genius
of this forlorn and untidy home. He himself stood
in the entry, a beautiful and venerable old man,
buttoned to the chin in a black dress-coat, tall and
slender, with a countenance quietly alive all over,
and the gentlest and most naturally courteous manner. He ushered us into his little study, or parlor, or both, a very forlorn room, with poor paper,
hangings and carpet, few books, no pictures that I
remember, and an awful lack of upholstery. I touch
distinctly upon these blemishes and this nudity of
adornment, not that they would be worth mentioning
in a sketch of other remarkable persons, but because
Leigh Hunt was born with such a faculty for enjoying all beautiful things that it seemed as if Fortune
did him as much wrong in not supplying them, as in
withholding a sufficiency of vital breath from ordinary
men. . . . I have said that he was a beautiful old
man. In truth I never saw a finer countenance, either

as to the mould of features or the expression, nor any
that showed the play of feeling so perfectly without
the slightest theatrical emphasis. It was like a child's
face in this respect. . . . I have met no Englishman
whose manners seemed to me so agreeable, soft
rather than polished, wholly unconventional, the
natural growth of a kindly and sensitive disposition
without any reference to rule, or else obedient to
some rule so subtle that the nicest observer could
not detect the application of it."

Whatever may be the final verdict regarding
Leigh Hunt's poetry, his memorable lines penned
playfully to his friend Jane Carlyle will not soon be
forgotten: —

> "Jenny kissed me when we met,
> Jumping from the chair she sat in:
> Time, you thief! who love to get
> Sweets into your list, put that in!
> Say I'm weary, say I'm sad,
> Say that health and wealth have missed me,
> Say I'm growing old; but add, —
> Jenny kissed me!"

During their residence in Old Chelsea, Mrs. Leigh
Hunt was a very near neighbor of Mrs. Carlyle, whose
methods of household management were totally
different from those of her careless and shiftless
friend; Mrs. Hunt, it is said, proved a perpetual
thorn in the flesh of her neighbor by constantly
sending over to borrow kitchen utensils, or other
household necessities, of which she was generally in
need, until, at last, the long-suffering Mrs. Carlyle
quite lost her patience at a final demand for a coal-
scuttle.

The famous lines, above quoted, were supposed to
have described Mrs. Carlyle's delight at some unexpected good news brought her by Leigh Hunt, yet
who shall say, in view of the knowledge of some of
Mrs. Hunt's shortcomings in the housekeeping line,
that the immortalized "kiss" might not have ema-
nated from joy at the unlooked-for return of some
needed article *de cuisine*, possibly the "coal-scuttle"
itself.

At about this time Hawthorne writes to Ticknor:—

"Bennett told me that there is an illustrated edition of 'The Scarlet Letter' in preparation, in the
style of 'Evangeline,' with engravings by Vizetelly.
In fact, he told me as much as a year ago, but the
matter was to be kept secret, nor does he yet know
who is to publish it. He has seen some of the illustrations, and thought them good. I don't know when
it is to come out.

"I have little doubt that Congress will make such
changes for the worse in the law that I shall find it
advisable to resign. The sooner the better; money
cannot pay me for the irksomeness of this office, at
least only a very large amount can do it; and I really
think I should be glad to have Congress put the question of my remaining here at rest, by breaking down
the office altogether. This very morning I have been
bored to death by a woman; and every day I am
beset with complainants who I wish were all at the
Devil together. But I can get along well enough
with men, if the women would only let me alone.

"I want you to send me a copy of the 'House of
Seven Gables,' bound in dark calf, antique style.

"I had a letter from a German the other day, proposing to me to pay him for making a translation of my entire works, taking the chance of selling the copyright to the German booksellers!! I rather think the Germans are the meanest devils in the world; though the English deserve a pretty prominent place in that particular. After all the slander against Americans, there is no people worthy even to take a second place behind us, for liberality of idea and practice. The more I see of the rest of the world, the better I think of my own country (not that I like it very enthusiastically, either); and I thank God, England's day is past forever. I have such a conviction of the decline and fall of England that I am about as well satisfied as if it had already taken place. And yet I like John Bull, too."

A fortnight later he writes of Mrs. Hawthorne's arrival in Lisbon, and continues his whimsical thoughts concerning John Bull's Island: —

"I have this morning received Mrs. Hawthorne's first letter since her arrival in Lisbon. She and Rose suffered terribly from seasickness on the voyage, owing to the swell in the Bay of Biscay; but Rose was quite well before landing, and my wife was a great deal better. Her cough was already much alleviated, although the rainy season was not quite over. Una was not seasick at all; but she says she wanted you to walk the deck with her during the voyage. I feel confident that they will all derive great benefit from the change of climate.

"As for myself, I am living quietly at Mrs. Blodgett's among the sea-captains and transient

American tourists; and our talk is so very unlike what I hear among my English acquaintances that I could almost fancy myself back in America again.

"There is a strange idea, on this side of the water, that we are going to send a filibustering expedition against Ireland!! If we have any design of the kind, I go in for attacking England at once; and there is little (in the way of fortifications) to hinder an American fleet from sailing up the Mersey. I should like well to be superseded in my consular duties by the arrival of a Yankee Commodore, or General. The truth is, I love England so much that I want to annex it, and it is by no means beyond the scope of possibility that we may do so, though hardly in my time."

This letter closes with an urgent request for his publisher to make investigations at once in regard to some property which Hawthorne had purchased from his friend O'Sullivan; he wishes to find out immediately if there is any legal impediment, and begs Ticknor to have the affair skillfully and quietly arranged, as he does not doubt O'Sullivan's honor in the least, only his business qualifications.

John O'Sullivan had been appointed Minister to the Court of Portugal, and was on his way thither in 1854, when he stopped to make the visit to the Hawthornes previously mentioned. He had become acquainted with Hawthorne many years before, while editing the "Democratic Review," and later they had become close friends, so that he was spoken of as "Uncle John" in the Hawthorne family. O'Sullivan's enthusiasm for new projects and "magnificent ventures" was unbounded, and no amount of failures or financial misfortunes could in the least dampen his ardor. He was a man of exciting adventures, — from which he emerged unscathed and undismayed,—with sparkling eyes and with a lock of hair that fell gracefully over his forehead. He was courteous and affectionate, and possessed most winning manners which made him on the whole quite irresistible. He had a tremendous admiration for Hawthorne, and was always intent upon making him a multi-millionaire. This tendency was not on the whole beneficial to Hawthorne, who was persuaded to invest some ten thousand dollars, about the year 1858, in some remarkable copper mines, which were to bring him a marvelous return. This "return" proved, however, not unlike that from the vast "undiscovered country," from which no traveler has yet returned.

Mrs. Hawthorne's visit to the O'Sullivans in Lisbon proved most enjoyable, despite the fact that it was the first time she had experienced a lengthy separation from her husband; she remained there several months, participating in the splendors and diversions of the gay little court of Dom Pedro V and receiving innumerable social attentions.

Hawthorne's next communication penned November 9, 1855, contains another amusing outburst against England: —

"We have all been in commotion here, for a fortnight past, in expectation of a war; but the peaceful tenor of the last accounts from America have gone far towards quieting us. No man would be justified in wishing for war; but I trust America will not bate an inch of honor for the sake of avoiding it; and if it

does come, we have the fate of England in our hands.
If the Yankees were half so patriotic at home as we
on this side of the water, I rather think we should be
in for it. I HATE England; though I love some Englishmen, and like them generally, in fact. . . .

"Mrs. Hawthorne is delightfully situated with the
O'Sullivans (in Lisbon), and sees kings, princes,
dukes, and ambassadors as familiarly as I do Liverpool merchants. Nevertheless, she is homesick; and
I believe we should all be glad to return to the old
house at Wayside to-morrow. But I fear we shall
have outgrown that house before we get back, and I
shall at least be compelled to make some more additions to it, if not to build a new one. I sometimes
doubt whether this European residence will be good
for us in the long run. All of us will come back with
altered habits, accustomed to many things which we
shall not find at home; and as for the children
(though they imagine that they love America above
all the rest of the world), they will really belong on
this side of the water rather than on that. . . .

"I have received as yet no copy of 'Hiawatha'
from Longfellow or yourself; but Bogue has sent me
the English edition, and I like it very much. It
seems to me perfectly original — the annexation of a
new dominion to our poetical territories; and he
seems to have caught the measure and rhythm from
the sound of the wind among the forest boughs. I
believe it is not yet published here. As to its success
compared with his other writings, that must be a
matter of experiment, and I should deem it rather a
doubtful one. But, at any rate, it puts my estimate

of his originality a peg higher; and I love to see him
still on the ascent.

"I have requested Mr. Deane, the bearer of dispatches, to deliver into your care a shawl which was
left at our house some months ago by Miss Martha
Cochran, a friend of Mrs. Hawthorne's. I think
(but I am not certain) that she resides in Springfield,
and I believe Mr. Skinner, of Boston, married her
sister. Will you have the shawl disposed of so that it
may reach her. . . .

"I shall wait with much interest for the response
of Young America to the hostile demonstrations on
the part of England. If I mistake not, John Bull is
now heartily afraid of the consequences of what he
has done and will gladly seize any method of getting
out of the scrape. If we do not fight him now, I doubt
whether he will ever give us another chance. He begins to have some idea of what we are. There has
been a great change on both these points since I
came to England."

X

HAWTHORNE'S LETTERS (CONTINUED)

THE new year, 1856, finds Hawthorne in a rather depressed frame of mind; he is still leading a bachelor existence, as Mrs. Hawthorne has not returned from Portugal, and he appeals to his friend Ticknor to straighten out some complication which has arisen relative to the mail-bag. He also refers amusingly to the success of "Hiawatha" and the literary evils attendant upon its popularity.

"I don't understand this botheration about the bag. Colonel Lawrence wrote me that Secretary Macy allowed him to receive packages from this country through the medium of the Dispatch Bearers, and that the Dispatch Agent at Boston had promised him to deliver them, when forwarded in my bag. Did Glen ever make any such agreement? — and if so, why did he not stand to it? Tell Glen this, and let him ask an explanation of Colonel Lawrence. Meanwhile, the Assistant Secretary of State has written to me, laying the blame at my door. The Devil take him, and Glen, and Lawrence, and the Government, and everybody connected with it! I can justify myself (and shall do so) by quoting a letter of instructions from Buchanan, while Secretary of State, to one of my predecessors, — instructions which have never been revoked, and which have been acted on, up to this time. I shall continue

to send the bag, although hereafter I shall certainly
decline having anything to do with Colonel Lawrence's parcels. I shall be glad if you will let him
know the difficulty into which he has brought me.

"Julian thanks you very much for the two books.
I have read a part of Mrs. Ritchie's work, and am
much interested in it. I wish I was acquainted with
her. It gives me pleasure to hear of the great success
of 'Hiawatha.' On this side of the water, too, it is
received with greater favor, I think, than any of
Longfellow's former works, and has gained him admirers among some who have hitherto stood aloof.
Nevertheless, the following lines have been sent to
me:—

> "'Hiawatha! Hiawatha!
> Sweet Trochaic milk and water!
> Milk and water Mississippi
> Flowing o'er a bed of sugar! —
> Through three hundred Ticknor pages,
> With a murmur and a ripple,
> Flowing, flowing, ever flowing —
> Damn the river! — damn the poet!'

"Everybody seems to be seized with an irresistible impulse to write verses in this new measure. I
have received a lampoon on myself (in manuscript) of
as much as a hundred Hiawatha lines, some of them
very laughable. I would send you a copy, but have
already transmitted the verses to Mrs. Hawthorne.

"I still hear nothing from the President about my
leave of absence, and if it were granted, I could not
very well make use of it. My official responsibilities
are much heavier than under the old law. . . . I cannot express, nor can you conceive, the irksomeness of

my position, and how I long to get free from it. I
have no pleasure in anything — a cigar excepted.
Even liquor does not enliven me; so I very seldom
drink any, except at some of these stupid English
dinners. I have got to dine with the Mayor shortly,
— for the last time, I fervently hope; for my soul is
in peril already with the lies I have told at the
Mayor's dinner-table, in regard to the good feeling
of America towards England."

At a banquet, given in St. George's Hall, at about
this time, Mr. Hawthorne was one of the twenty invited guests to sit on an elevated dais. On this occasion Monckton Milnes gave the toast "Nathaniel
Hawthorne," and in an appreciative tribute declared
that the "'Scarlet Letter' struck to the hearts of all
who read it." This was rendered in an amended form
by a London reporter to read, "that the 'Scarlet Letter' *stuck* to the hearts of all who came in
contact with it."

By the last of February, Hawthorne's spirits
seem to have revived, and he writes to his publisher
in a lighter vein, in which he is pleased to have his
little fling at "Uncle Sam": —

"My health and spirits are considerably better
than in the earlier part of the winter. I begin to eat
and drink again. About the twentieth of March, I
mean to pay a visit to London, and shall probably
remain there twenty days — ten in the first quarter
of the year, and ten in the second; so that Uncle Sam
will not be able to grab my salary on plea of over-
absence. There is a pleasure in getting around such
a mean old scoundrel as Uncle Sam. . . .

"There is no news. The war talk has entirely died away; and I hope, on the American side of the water, we shall say nothing more about fighting, unless we really mean to come to the scratch. It is considered very doubtful here whether the conference at Paris will result in peace with Russia; and this is probably one of the reasons why the English tone is less hostile with regard to us."

A few weeks later, Hawthorne writes to acknowledge a splendidly bound set of his own books ordered as a gift for the King of Portugal, who had extended various royal courtesies to his family.

"The books are beautifully bound; and I have a greater respect for my own works than ever before — seeing them so finely dressed. I should like to give them to Mrs. Hawthorne, rather than to the King of Portugal.

"Mr. Dallas arrived two days ago. He seems to be a respectable old gentleman; but I should not take him to be an able diplomatist, and he certainly has a difficult business to handle. Buchanan is worth ten of him; and even he has made no great hand of it. Mr. D. is well provided as respects the female part of his establishment — seven ladies, I believe, to all of whom I had to be civil! Thank Heaven, I am not keeping house, and that there was no hospitality to be exercised.

"I intend to go up to London next Thursday, and spend two or three weeks, including the last ten days of March and the first ten days of April. By thus dividing my term of absence between two quarters of the year, I shall defeat Uncle Sam's shabby efforts to filch away my salary. During my stay in London, I will see your friends there, and some of my own, and hope to have an agreeable time. This has been a dreary winter, but I find myself in better health and spirits, now that it is over. But we still have wretchedly cold weather."

The London visit proved a great success, and Hawthorne, who returned in excellent spirits, was further cheered by the receipt of a most satisfactory accounting of his finances from his publisher, to whom he writes: —

"I staid in London exactly three weeks, and returned only last night, after having enjoyed myself gloriously — owing principally to Bennoch's kindness. I lived rather fast, to be sure; but that was not amiss, after such a slow winter. My health and spirits are much better than when I went away.

"I have not your letter by me, but am much pleased with the satisfactory summary you give of my affairs. If it becomes necessary to give up the consulate, before another winter, I shall do so without any apprehension as to my pecuniary prospects, though perhaps I may spend a little more than my income in travelling and residence abroad. But I think I can write a book or two that will set it all right. I need not say how much I feel indebted to you for your kind and careful stewardship of my affairs. I think all the better of mankind (and especially of publishers) for your sake.

"Fields writes me that, in case of a war between America and England, he is going to fight for the latter. I hope he will live to be tarred and feathered,

and that I may live to pour the first ladleful of tar on
the top of his head, and to clap the first handful of
feathers on the same spot. He is a traitor, and his
English friends know it; for they all speak of him as
one of themselves."

(This amusing onslaught was, of course, taken by
the one to whom it was addressed with the good-
natured indulgence that it was intended to arouse.)

"I heard from several people in London a strong
and confident assurance that Longfellow is coming
over this summer. Are there any grounds for this
report? If he cares about being lionized, let him
come now; for his reputation can never be higher
nor better. I wish he would come.

"I enclose a letter for Washington Irving, whose
present address I do not know. Please to direct and
send it.

"I wish you would send me two copies of Thoreau's books — 'Life in the Woods,' and the other
one, for I wish to give them to two persons here. . . .

"I saw (among about a thousand other noticeable
people) your author, Charles Reade, — a tall, stout-
ish, fair-haired, light-complexioned man, thirty
years old, or upwards. He did not make a very
strong impression on me. I like his books better than
himself; not that I saw any fault in him either. I tell
you this because you particularly wished me to see
him."

The last of April, 1856, finds Hawthorne deploring
the fact that neither of his publishers is coming to
England this season: —

"I am much disappointed to learn that there is

little prospect of seeing either you or Fields here this summer. It will be a long time yet before I shake hands with you, on your side of the water. To say the truth, the longer I stay away, the less I feel inclined to come back; and if it were not for my children, I question whether I should ever see America again. Not but what I love my country; but I can live more to my individual satisfaction elsewhere. I am happy to say that Julian does not share my feelings at all. He got a black eye, the other day, fighting with some English boys, who, he says, abused his country; but I believe the quarrel began with his telling them that it was his highest ambition to kill an Englishman! He is a sturdy little devil, and as strong as most boys two or three years older than himself. . . .

"I thank you for the poem — 'The Angel in the House' — which you sent me by last steamer. I thought it very good — always excepting the measure, which has somewhat of the lame-dromedary movement which poets nowadays seem so partial to.

"I forget whether I told you of my spending two or three days in the camp at Aldershot, and messing with the officers of the regiment there. I fraternized very strongly with them all, from the Colonel downwards; and I don't think there will be any war between England and America."

Hawthorne has described his visit to Aldershot Camp at length in his "Notes," setting forth his hospitable entertainment there and his impressions of the delightful Irish officers and their efforts to bestow upon Bennoch and himself every attention even to contributing suitable music by the band. He asserts: —

"Several of the elder officers were men who had been long in the army; and the Colonel — a bluff, hearty old soldier, with a profile like an eagle's head and beak — was a veteran of the Peninsula, and had a medal on his breast, with clasps, for three famous battles besides that of Waterloo.

"The regimental band played during dinner, and the Lieutenant-Colonel apologized to me for its not playing 'Hail Columbia,' the tune not coming within their musical accomplishments. It was no great matter, however; for I should not have distinguished it from any other tune; but, to do me what honor was possible, in the way of national airs, the band was ordered to play a series of Negro melodies, and I was entirely satisfied. It is really funny that the "wood-notes wild" of these poor black slaves should have been played in a foreign land as an honorable compliment to one of their white countrymen."

Hawthorne's acknowledgment that he could not distinguish "Hail Columbia" from any other tune offers an illustration of the fact that the majority of literary men are not in the least musical; this assertion has been verified by the statements of a great many writers, nearly all of whom are rather annoyed than otherwise by musical entertainments. This rule is not necessarily applicable to the poets, whose sense of rhythm is apt to respond to the appeal which music brings them. The poet listens as well as looks,

but the universe of the prose writer comes to him
invariably through his eyes, and is from them trans-
lated into his thoughts. The world of sound is usually an annoyance to the writer, whose Mecca is a
"quiet spot," and whose Paradise is one of "silence."

Hawthorne further describes his camp experiences:—

"After dinner we played whist, and then had some
broiled bones for supper, and finally went home to our
respective huts not much earlier than four o'clock.
But I don't wonder these gentlemen sit up as long as
they can keep their eyes open; for never was there
anything so utterly comfortless as their camp-beds.
They are really no worse than the bed of honor, —
no wider, no softer, no warmer, and affording not
nearly so sound sleep. Indeed, I got hardly any
sleep at all, and almost as soon as I closed my eyes,
the bugles sounded, and the drums beat reveille, and
from that moment the camp was all astir; so I pretty
soon uprose, and went to the mess-room for my
breakfast, feeling wonderfully fresh and well, considering what my night had been.

"Long before this, however, the whole regiment
and all the other regiments marched off to take part
in a general review, and Bennoch and I followed, as
soon as we had eaten a few mutton chops. It was a
bright sunshiny day, but with a strong east wind, as
piercing and pitiless as ever blew; and this wide,
undulating plain of Aldershot seemed just the place
where the east wind was at home. Still it acted on
the whole like an invigorating cordial; and whereas
in pleasanter circumstances I should have lain down

and gone to sleep, I now felt as if I could do without sleep for a month. . . .

"The most splendid effect of this parade was the gleam of the sun upon the long line of bayonets — the sheen of all that steel appearing like a wavering fringe of light upon the dark masses of the troops below. It was very fine. But I was glad when all was done, and I could go back to the mess-room, whither I carried an excellent appetite for luncheon. After this we walked about the camp, — looked at some of the model tents, inspected the arrangements and modes of living in the huts of the privates; and thus gained more and more adequate ideas of the vile uncomfortableness of a military life."

Hawthorne's attitude toward sight-seeing, especially when he chanced to attempt it by himself, is characteristically chronicled by him. He writes in his journal during this London visit: —

"Yesterday I went out at about twelve, and visited the British Museum, an exceedingly tiresome affair. It quite crushes a person to see so much at once, and I wandered from hall to hall with a weary and heavy heart, wishing (Heaven forgive me!) that the Elgin marbles and the frieze of the Parthenon were all burnt into lime, and that the granite Egyptian statues were hewn and squared into building-stones, and that the mummies had all turned to dust two thousand years ago; and, in fine, that all the material relics of so many successive ages had disappeared with the generations that produced them. The present is burdened too much with the past. We have not time, in our earthly existence, to appreciate

what is warm with life, and immediately around us;
yet we heap up these old shells, out of which human
life has long ago emerged, casting them off forever. I
do not see how future ages are to stagger onward
under all this dead weight, with the additions that
will be continually made to it."

During the first week in June he writes Ticknor:—

"Our relations with England seem to me to bear a
more pacific aspect than for many months past.
Frank Pierce never did a better thing than in recog-
nizing Walker's Government; it has brought John
Bull to his bearings, and with his customary growling
and grumbling, he is going to back out. Crampton
ought to have been dismissed more promptly; but it
is better late than never. Most people here think
that Dallas will be sent home, and, I believe, he is
himself very uneasy. I hope he will be sent home,
because it will be such a very foolish act on the part
of the British Government — and, moreover, he will
be no loss to anybody. But I am of the opinion that
they will let him stay.

"In ten days more, I hope to see Mrs. Hawthorne,
and, for that purpose, shall go to Southampton. We
shall spend, I think, a good part of the summer in
the southern part of England. Bennoch is going to
Germany with his wife in July, and he has most
kindly offered us his house at Blackheath, during
his absence. It will depend on Mrs. Hawthorne,
whether we avail ourselves of his kindness. We will,
on one condition; — that you will come over and be
our guest, during the two months that we should
keep the house. Why not?"

The long-looked-for arrival of Mrs. Hawthorne took place a couple of days after the inditing of the last communication, and on June 20 her return is cheerfully chronicled; even the political situation seems to have brightened at her approach and Hawthorne begs Ticknor to take a more hopeful view of the situation in America, to which distance lent a greater degree of enchantment than could be perceived by the senior partner dwelling in the heart of the political storms.

"Mrs. Hawthorne arrived at Southampton ten or twelve days ago, in good health and spirits, only a little tired with her voyages and travels. She has little or no cough left and earnestly wishes to spend another winter in England. We shall decide about this, after trying the effect of the climate upon her. For the present she is staying near Southampton; but we shall take Bennoch's house early in July. Are you not coming over to pay us a visit? If you will, Mrs. Hawthorne shall read you my journal containing a full and particular account of my visit to London — which would be worth a mint of money to you and me, if I could let you publish it.

"I saw Bennoch yesterday, on my way hither from Southampton. He is in good condition.

"Pray do not be so hopeless about our political concerns. We shall grow and flourish, in spite of the devil. Affairs do not look so very bad, at this distance, whatever they may seem to you who are in the midst of confusion. For my part, I keep a steadfast faith in the destinies of my own country, and will not be staggered, whatever happens.

"You see, I was right in my opinion that Dallas would not be sent home. We have gained a great triumph over England, and I begin to like her better now; for, I can assure you, Englishmen feel that they have given up forever the pretensions to superiority, and the haughty tone, which they have hitherto held towards us. We have gone through a crisis and come out right side up. Give Frank Pierce credit for this, at least; for it was his spirit that did it. . . .

"Thank you for the two De Quincey books."

Mr. Bennoch's offer of his attractive suburban house at Blackheath was gratefully accepted by Mrs. Hawthorne on her arrival, and the stay there proved a very agreeable one, as the surroundings were delightful and the Hawthorne family were the recipients of many attentions from persons of culture and distinction in that vicinity. "Here," writes Hawthorne, "we spent a month, comprising some of the happiest hours that I have known since we left our American home."

He pens the following from Liverpool, July 17, 1856: —

"I have been in the south of England and in London for nearly three weeks past, and have now established Mrs. Hawthorne and the children at Blackheath. They are delightfully situated, and if I could only spend my whole time there, I should ask nothing better for the next two months. I got into a new vein of society, on this last visit to London, and have seen a good many interesting people. It is much pleasanter than stagnating in this wretched hole; but I must come back hither, now and then, for the sake of appearances.

"After we leave Blackheath (if Mrs. Hawthorne's health continues good enough to allow of her staying in England), I think of taking a house or lodgings in Chester, for what further time we spend here. It is an interesting old town, and the air there is much better than in Liverpool, and I could attend to all my official duties without inconvenience. It is not quite certain as yet that I shall not resign in the autumn; but, if possible, I am inclined to stay the four years out.

"I saw your namesake, Mr. Ticknor, in London, at a breakfast. I heartily wish it had been yourself."

The breakfast referred to was one of the notable literary gatherings of Mr. Monckton Milnes, who had, as was his wont, assembled a most distinguished company. Hawthorne, who had been asked to be present shortly after ten o'clock, arrived in London upon the day in question at such an early hour that he decided to take a stroll between times; he therefore rambled over London Bridge, inspected the Guildhall, and then walked on until he found himself so far from his destination that he was obliged to take a half-hour's drive back in a cab. He found that it was nigh eleven o'clock, when at last he was ushered into the presence of his host, hostess and the assembled company, all of whom had been politely awaiting his arrival, a fact which evidently left his serenity untroubled.

The host and his wife greeted their tardy guest with great cordiality, and he soon found himself conversing with the Marquis of Lansdowne, and his two fellow-countrymen, George Ticknor and John G. Palfrey, who were of the party. Mr. Milnes then presented Hawthorne to Mrs. Browning, and he had the pleasure of conducting her into the breakfast-room, in the center of which stood an immense round table suggestive of King Arthur's court. About this hospitable board the guests arranged themselves informally, and Hawthorne found himself seated beside Mrs. Nightingale, whose daughter Florence was one of the group; these ladies, with Mrs. Browning, furnished the entire feminine element present, in addition to their hostess, while the men numbered something like a dozen.

Next to the host sat an impressive gentleman who instantly attracted Hawthorne's attention, and whom he soon discovered to be no other than Macaulay, a man he had long wished to see; having made this discovery he listened eagerly to the great man's remarks in order to make the most of this brief opportunity of listening to this world-famous conversationalist. But upon this occasion, Macaulay spoke little, doubtless because the conversation turned too persistently to American subjects, and Hawthorne was convinced that he was being robbed of his conversational treat, because the presence of Ticknor and Palfrey restrained Macaulay, who felt unable to "talk them down" upon American topics regarding which they were well-known authorities.

When, after breakfast, all adjourned to the host's extensive library to inspect his large collection of rare autographs, Hawthorne conversed at length

Concord, Oct. 11th 1861

Dear Fields,

Mrs. Hawthorne has now
in readiness to send to England a
certain trunk, of which she spoke
to you a long time ago. Will you
see that it is shipped aboard some
steamer, to sail soon. Mrs. Hawthorne thinks it best not to send
the key, but to allow the lock to
be forced by the Custom House
examiner. The trunk is to be con-
signed to Mr. Wilding, who, I suppose will take charge of it after
its arrival in Liverpool.

Truly Yours,
Nath'l Hawthorne

P.S. Mr. H. wishes the trunk
to go by one of the Cunard steamers
for Liverpool, one of the screw
steamers, if less expensive.

with Robert Browning, who told him of his special admiration for "The Blithedale Romance," which he preferred to all his other works.

Hawthorne was deeply touched by the delicate courtesy displayed by the Marquis of Lansdowne, who insisted that he should precede him in going in to breakfast, which Hawthorne did with great reluctance, exclaiming afterwards: "Heaven knows, it was in no humility that I would have trodden behind him. But he is a kind old man; and of beautiful deportment, for certainly there never can have been mortals in a position more advantageous for becoming so. I hope there will come a time when we shall be so; and I already know a few Americans whose noble and delicate manners may compare with any I have seen."

One does not feel surprised that even the shy Hawthorne enjoyed this "vein" of London society, and sighed to turn back from it to the routine of consular affairs at Liverpool.

One of the pleasantest excursions made at this time by Mr. and Mrs. Hawthorne was to Oxford, where they were entertained by Mr. Spiers, the ex-Mayor of the town; here they remained several days, and before taking their leave, the whole party which had enjoyed the royal hospitality of the host, was photographed on his lawn. At the end of this elaborate house-party Mrs. Hawthorne desired to present their entertainers with some token of appreciation, and at once penned the following note to her husband's publisher: —.

MY DEAR MR. TICKNOR, — We have been the objects of perfectly magnificent hospitality to a gentleman of Oxford, — former Mayor, now Alderman, — a gentleman of the kindest heart,—most liberal hand, — sagacious, sensible, and of indefatigable activity. We wish to make a delicate return in the way of a memorial, and I have suggested to Mr. Hawthorne a set of his own works, — very splendidly bound, — "Wonder Book" and all. Will you order this to be done as soon as possible — to send by the next steamer, if that is not too soon? This gentleman has abundance of innocent vanity and self-appreciation, and would be pleased at such a gift from N. Hawthorne, Author of "Scarlet Letter," etc.!! Mr. Hawthorne was asked at Stanton Harcourt whether he was the author of "The Red Letter A"?

Was not that funny?

In greatest haste with very kindest regards, dear Mr. Ticknor, I am

Truly yours,

S. HAWTHORNE.

Sept. 7th, 1856.

BLACKHEATH PARK.

P.S. We leave Blackheath in a few days for the North.

Mr. Hawthorne has been reading my note and put all those exclamations on the other side, and he says I must say to you that haste to send the volumes must not in the least impair the perfection of their binding; — also that it would please the gentleman to have his name in gilt Old-English letters

R. J. Spiers, Esq.:

somewhere on the outside. Now I have told you his name, pray burn my note, because I have said he was vain. . . . But we like and respect him very much.

Hawthorne has added these lines at the end of Mrs. Hawthorne's letter: —

"*To*

"*R. J. Spiers, Esq.*

"in black-letter, on side-cover.   N. H."

And on the last page of the same sheet he has added: —

DEAR TICKNOR, — If I were to send a set of my books to everybody who shows me kindness, it would exhaust an edition. However, you may do as Mrs. Hawthorne says. We had a very jolly time in Oxford.

Elsewhere Hawthorne offers a glimpse of the home of their liberal entertainer: —

"At six we went to dine with the hospitable ex-Mayor, across the wide, tree-bordered street; for his house is nearly opposite our lodgings. He is an intelligent and gentlemanly person, and was Mayor two years ago, and has done a great deal to make peace between the University and the town, heretofore bitterly inimical. His house is adorned with pictures and drawings and he has an especial taste for art.

"The dinner table was decorated with pieces of plate, vases, and other things, which were presented to him as tokens of public or friendly regard, and approbation of his action in the mayoralty. After dinner, too, he produced a large snuff-box, which had been given him on the same account; in fact, the inscription affirmed that it was one of five pieces of plate so presented. The vases were really splendid, — one of them two feet high, and richly ornamented. It will hold five or six bottles of wine, and he said that it had been filled and, I believe, sent round as a loving-cup at some of his entertainments. He cordially enjoys these things, and his genuine benevolence produces all this excellent hospitality."

One can imagine that this genial host, when once in receipt of Hawthorne's works, bound in "Boston's best," and ornamented with his name, might possibly have added one more appreciative token to his dinner display, and on occasion of some "Red Letter" banquet, have placed in the center of his silver trophies a literary pyramid. Hawthorne, no doubt, had such a mental vision, and chuckled inwardly as he dispatched his wife's enthusiastic epistle to Mr. Ticknor. He closes his own letter with the following: —

"I enclose a letter to E. P. Peabody, and I particularly wish that you will learn her present direction, and forward it without delay. She has taken it into her head that Mrs. Hawthorne is extremely ill; and, unless prevented seasonably, I shall expect to see her on this side of the water. This would be exceedingly awkward and inconvenient; moreover, Mrs. Hawthorne is better, at this moment, than at any time since the first six months of her residence in England. . . .

"The time I spent at Blackheath and its neighborhood was most delightful, and I shall be eternally obliged to Bennoch.

"The new bill makes no alteration of importance, as regards my consulate, — except that there may be a small allowance for office rent. Thank God, it will not be many months, at longest, before I am free."

A few weeks later the Hawthornes are settled at Southport, where they are about to take a house for three months on Mrs. Hawthorne's account. Hawthorne writes to his publisher: —

"We are now residing at Southport, a seashore place about twenty miles from Liverpool. The physicians have recommended the sea-air for Mrs. Hawthorne until December, or later; and I think we shall take a house for three months at Southport. Our vagrant life, for the last year or two, has brought me acquainted with a great variety of English scenes and modes of living. We shall know how to prize a home, if ever we get back to one; but I must confess, I am in no great hurry to return to America. To say the truth, it looks like an infernally disagreeable country from this side of the water."

In his next communication, after suggesting a trip to Paris for himself and wife, he follows up this reflection with the words: —

"The wise ones prophesy great commotions in France, and all over the Continent. Very likely there will not be a quiet spot to live in, just when we are ready to go hither. But there seems to be no stormier prospect anywhere than in our own country; and

I find myself less and less inclined to come back, with every budget of news that comes from thence. I sympathize with no party, but hate them all — Free-Soilers, Pro-Slavery men, and whatever else — all alike. In fact, I have no country, or only just enough of a one to be ashamed of; and I can tell you, an American finds it difficult to hold up his head, on this side of the water in these days. The English expect to see the Republic crumble to pieces, and are chuckling over the anticipation. This is all nonsense, of course; but it grinds me, nevertheless.

"I see Whipple has come out as a politician, on the Frémont side. It is a pity."

Hawthorne makes frequent references to Whipple, whose admirable literary judgment played so important a part in the fortunes of the house of Ticknor and Fields. Mr. Howells has said of him: —

"Most distinctly of that uncitified Boston was the critic Edwin P. Whipple, whose sympathies were indefinitely wider than his traditions. He was a most generous lover of all that was excellent in literature. He was certainly as friendly to what promised well in the younger men as he was to what was done well in their leaders; and there was no one writing in his day whose virtues failed of his recognition, though it might happen that his foibles would escape Whipple's censure; his point-of-view was solely and always that which enabled him to discern best qualities. I doubt if he had any theory of criticism except to find out what was good in an author and praise it; and he rather blamed what was ethically bad than what was æsthetically bad.

"He was a slight, short, ecclesiasticized figure in black; with a white neck-cloth and a silk hat of strict decorum, and between the two, a square face with square features, intensified in their regard by a pair of very large glasses, and the prominent, myopic eyes staring through them . . . he was the sort of man to be kept fondly in the memory of all who ever knew him."

XI

HAWTHORNE AND DELIA BACON

IN theory, Hawthorne objected to "women writers," deplored their increasing numbers, and in a
mood of extreme cynicism, evoked by some reflections upon their steadily increasing literary output,
he wrote to Ticknor that he considered "all ink-
stained women detestable."

So much for Hawthorne's theory! Meanwhile, an
admirable example of his practice in this regard may
be found in the Delia Bacon episode. Despite his
avowed detestation of "female scribblers," he, upon
very slight acquaintance with this writer, and without feeling himself in sympathy with her Baconian
theory, deliberately proceeded to finance the publication of her book, an expense he could ill afford, and
one for which he afterwards received but little gratitude, Miss Bacon being highly indignant with him
because he would not pen an introduction to the
book upon the exact lines which she demanded.

Having plunged into this venture in response to a
kindly impulse, Hawthorne proceeded to confess the
enormity of his offense to his friend on the other side
of the water, upon whose aid he knew he could depend. He wrote to Ticknor on November 6, 1856,
invoking his timely assistance: —

"I want you to help me through a business, which,
very likely, you will think me a fool for engaging in.

Miss Bacon some time ago applied to me for assistance in getting her book on Shakespeare published. On reading the work I found it to possess very great merit, though I don't at all believe in her theory as to the authorship of the plays; — however, as it was impossible to get it published otherwise, I have agreed with Parker & Son, of London, to publish it on my assuming the pecuniary responsibility and writing the introduction. Acting on Bennoch's advice, I shall put the book into Parker's hands, in print; and it is now being printed in London under Bennoch's supervision.

"One thousand copies will be printed; and of these I shall send you 500, with your name on the title-page. You must excuse the liberty, as there is no time to consult you beforehand; and you may be assured that it is not a work which you will have reason to be ashamed of. Parker, I suppose, will sell the volume at 10/6 or 12/. You must put it at such price as will best suit our market. No doubt, I shall lose something; but having tried to help this poor woman, I do not like to desert her without doing my utmost.

"The title is 'The Shakespeare Problem; by Delia Bacon.' Advertise it if you like; and I suppose you will receive the unbound sheets early in December — perhaps sooner. By the bye, Miss Bacon herself doss not know of my pecuniary responsibility; so say nothing of it to anybody.

"You sent me, some two months ago, the poem 'Betrothed.' I liked it very much, and want the 'Espousals,' which I see you have now published. No part of Miss Bacon's book has ever been published.

The article in ' Putnam's Magazine' does not make a portion of this work."

On January 2, Hawthorne forwards the title-page of this remarkable production. He writes: —

" I wish you all the good wishes of the season, and I hope I shall see you on this side of the water before the end of the year. . . . Julian, Una, and Rose have all received your kind presents of books, and are delighted with them.

" I send you the title-page of Miss Bacon's book, as transmitted to me by Bennoch.

The Shakespeare Problem Solved
By Delia Bacon
With a Preface by
Nathaniel Hawthorne
Boston
Ticknor, Fields & Co.
London
J. Parker & Son, West-Strand.

" I don't know how the printing gets on. Bennoch sent me about 150 pages, a week or two ago, and I have had nothing since. It will be an octavo volume of some 500 pages, I should judge. I am an utter disbeliever in Miss Bacon's theory, but am much impressed with the depth and acuteness of her criticism of Shakespeare. I think the book will sell, to a certain extent, in America, and will attract a good deal of notice from literary people on this side."

The next communication regarding the book in question is penned on January 31: —

"Miss Bacon's book is printed, I believe, with the exception of my preface, which does not yet exist, but, I hope, will be written to-morrow. To say the truth, the book is d—d hard reading, but it contains wonderfully good matter, nevertheless.

"I have had all sorts of trouble in my consulate, lately; — indeed I always do, but now more than ever. The Liverpool Philanthropists are aroused about the enormities on board our ships, and would like to have me run amuck with them against American shipmasters; and as I choose to take my own view of my own duty, they censure me pretty harshly.

"They will hardly succeed in crowding me off my track; but it is not to be denied that there is nothing in this world so much like Hell as the interior of an American ship. I have made repeated statements on this subject to our Government and, long ago, I wrote most earnestly to Charles Sumner to bring it before Congress. Had he busied himself about this, instead of Abolitionism, he would have done good service to his country and have escaped Brooks's cudgel. I offered to supply him with any amount of horrible facts; but he never noticed my letter.

"N. C. Peabody will present a small draft on you; and I want you to pay, when presented, a bill for a new pump at the Wayside. I wish I had a better house to live in when I come home. It will be necessary to repair and enlarge it; and I sometimes think it would be well to sell the place, and look out for a more inhabitable one. If I once begin to build, I shall spend more than I can afford. What do you think of this matter? The fact is, I do not take root anywhere, and never shall, unless I could establish myself in some old manor-house like those I see in England.

"I have written (some time ago) to Bridge to communicate to the President-elect my purpose of resigning, in the course of a few months; and I should not wonder if my successor were already fixed upon. Poor devil! I pity him, whoever he may be; especially as he will never get so much solid sweet comfort out of the office as I have. I cannot express to you the pleasure with which I anticipate my release.

"I presided, last night, at a meeting of American shipmasters, and made a speech!!! It is easy enough to speak when a man is cornered and *corned*, but I here make a vow never to raise my voice so as to be heard by more than six people, nor to speak more than a hundred words together, after quitting this consulate."

What Mr. Ticknor's views were in regard to the publication of the Delia Bacon book cannot be here recorded, as his portion of the correspondence with Hawthorne concerning this especial venture has vanished from the earth; none of his letters to Hawthorne, save his last brief messages sent to Mrs. Hawthorne prior to his death, have been preserved by those into whose keeping they fell.

One may rest assured, however, that he accepted the sponsorship thus thrust upon him, in regard to the Baconian theory, with the same kindly indulgence that he accorded all interests which his friends had at heart, and the fulfillment of which required his aid. A less sympathetic publisher might have strenuously objected to the production of the Delia Bacon title-page bearing his imprint without his permission; but whatever his response may have been, it was such as to give satisfaction to Hawthorne, whose feelings he was careful to spare on all occasions. Knowing his good taste in book-making, however, one cannot but feel that he experienced little satisfaction in the circulation of the clumsy octavo volume, of between five and six hundred pages, which could have been cut down to great advantage..

Hawthorne writes on February 13: —

"Miss Bacon's book is all in type, and I have written and sent off my preface. The title is as follows: —

The Shakespeare Problem Solved
By Delia Bacon
With a preface by Nathaniel Hawthorne
Author of the Scarlet Letter, etc.
Boston
Ticknor and Fields.

"I should think it time to advertise; though I don't know how soon your part of the edition will be sent you. It makes an octavo volume of between five and six hundred pages. Thank Heaven, I have done with it, except paying the printer, etc.

"Mrs. Hawthorne and all of us are well and my spirits begin to rise with the certainty that my official trials are within six months of termination. I have sent in my resignation, to take effect from August 31. Buchanan may choose to turn me out sooner; but I should suppose he would prefer taking the office on

my own terms, as the old fellow and I are very good
friends. The office-holders on this side of the water
are very uneasy about their prospects, and with good
reason, I think.

"Do, Do, DO come to England, this summer. I
shall take it amiss if neither you nor Fields come.
I expect to leave for the Continent in the course of
September, and, meanwhile, shall visit such parts of
Great Britain as I have not yet seen. In Italy, perhaps, I shall begin to be a literary man again; for I
feel symptoms already. It is a pity I cannot take advantage of my residence in England to publish something while I remain here, and to secure the English
copyright. But it is quite impossible."

Miss Bacon's eccentric personality made it difficult for Hawthorne to remain upon a harmonious
footing with this "gifted woman." By February 26,
the blow had fallen, or rather the author of "The
Shakespeare Problem Solved" and the writer of its
preface, had "fallen out." Miss Bacon had taken it
for granted that the friend who was willing to aid her
in the publication of her volume must of necessity
have accepted her theory implicitly. She demanded
from Hawthorne a declaration of faith, and she
elicited, instead, a declaration of independence.

Hawthorne wrote to the senior partner the details
of the controversy: —

"Miss Bacon and I, just at present, have come to a
deadlock. She thinks my Preface (which is already
in print) does less than justice to her book, and refuses to let the publication go forward, unless I make
it more favorable. Having already gone to the limit

of my conscience, I cannot comply with her wishes; and as Parker will not take the book without my Preface, I do not quite see how the difficulty is to be settled. Bennoch is trying to arrange it, and I suppose the lady will have to come down in her pretensions. Nothing will satisfy her, short of my expressing full belief in the correctness of her views.

"Since I last wrote, our house at Southport has been broken into and robbed of various articles of plate, clothing, etc. The thieves were put to flight by Julian, who was awakened by the noise, and frightened them by calling his mother. He takes to himself great credit for his valor on the occasion; but the truth is, neither he nor anybody else knew what had happened till the next morning. This is the second time I have been robbed since we came to England; the first time, they took all our silver forks and spoons, and these last robbers had to content themselves principally with electro-plate. The thieves have been discovered and committed for trial."

Hawthorne's reluctance to be responsible for any suffering on the part of his fellow-beings, made him veritably regretful when he learned of the capture of the thieves in question, against whom his servants were called upon to testify. He later described the episode in detail, and voiced his regret that the evidence was so strong against the offenders that it was plain they must pay the penalty of the law. He asserts: —

"The thieves were two young men, not over twenty, — James and John Macdonald, — terribly shabby, dirty, jailbird-like, yet intelligent of aspect, and one of them was handsome. . . . The seats within the bar were occupied by the witnesses, and around the great table sat some of the more respectable people of Southport; and without the bar were the commonalty in great numbers; for this is said to be the first burglary that had occurred here within the memory of man, and so it caused a great stir."

Hawthorne notes the futility of breaking up the very complete chain of evidence, of which he says: "There seemed to be a strong case against the prisoners. A boy attached to the railway testified to having seen them at Birchdale, on Wednesday afternoon, and directed them on their way to Southport; Peter Pickup recognized them as having applied to him for lodgings in the course of the evening; a pawnbroker swore to one of them as having offered my topcoat for sale, or pledge, in Liverpool; and my boots were found on the feet of one of them, — all this in addition to other circumstances of pregnant suspicion. So they were committed for trial at the Liverpool assizes, to be holden some time in the present month. I rather wished them to escape." Had the affair not been beyond the personal jurisdiction of Hawthorne, he would no doubt have viewed with satisfaction the prompt release of the two fellows, even though one had worn away his best topcoat, and he had seen the other one departing in his favorite boots.

The controversy with the author of "The Shakespeare Problem Solved" was also "solved" eventually. Miss Bacon's displeasure was finally dispelled by Mr. Bennoch's tactful management, and Haw-

thorne's preface was reluctantly accepted. The latter
wrote his publisher on the 13th of March: —

"Miss Bacon has accepted my Preface, after cutting out a few paragraphs of not much importance.
The last I heard of the matter, she and Bennoch were
engaged in a discussion about the title of the book;
but she is the most impracticable woman I ever had
to do with — a crooked stick. No doubt, your copies
will soon be forwarded, now.

"I am well pleased with the condition of my finances, as shown in your statement; and if I were
now at home, I should hardly think it worth my
while to be any richer. During my voyages and
travels, however, I shall spend a little more than my
income; but will make it up by subsequent industry
and economy. . . .

"Bridge called on Mr. Buchanan, on my behalf,
and advised him of my intention to resign. The old
fellow was very gracious and complimentary towards
me, and said that I might take my own time. I presume my resignation is already in his hands, to take
effect on the last day of August. It would not suit
my arrangements to hold the office any longer.

"We shall go to Paris, probably in the course of
September, and thence to Rome, via Marseilles, for
the winter. I doubt whether you see us on your side
of the water in less than two years from this coming
summer; and if it were not for the children (who pine
for America) I should consider myself a citizen of the
world, and perhaps never come home. At all events,
I feel no symptoms of homesickness as yet. There
are a few friends whom I should be most happy to

meet again, however; and you rejoice me much by holding out a prospect (though a faint one) of your coming to England this season."

On March 20, 1857, the "Shakespeare Problem" was fairly launched, and all devotees of the Baconian theory may well remember this important date, and place it as a prefix in their anti-Shakespearean notebooks. Hawthorne wrote: —

"Miss Bacon's book seems to be ready, at last, and I send you a copy which will enable you to secure the copyright (doubtless invaluable) in America. She cut some passages out of my Preface, but did not otherwise alter it. The book grew above a hundred pages beyond its original size, in passing through the press. I hope you will sell so many copies that I shall not, at any rate, be quite ruined.

"It will probably be published in London in the course of next week and half, and more of the edition will be transmitted to you as soon as possible.

"Please acknowledge the receipt of the copy now sent, in a note addressed to the purser of the steamer Asia, care E. Cunard, New York."

It was not until the latter part of April, that the expected cargo of the "500 copies" of the Baconian treatise finally reached these shores; an invading army in the literary field, destined to awaken a lasting controversy in realms previously considered impregnable.

Previous to their exportation Hawthorne wrote:—

"The 500 copies of Miss Bacon's book have been sent me, ready for exportation, but the steamer cannot take them on Saturday, being already full-freighted. I shall send them either by the New York steamer, next week, or the Boston steamer in a fortnight — probably the latter, as I suppose the delay makes little difference, and it may be more convenient to you to receive them in Boston. They are in sheets. The London retail price is 18/.

"You will know what to charge in America. The 1000 copies, as they come from the printer's (exclusive of binding), have cost £238 7s. 9d. 'A fool and his money are soon parted.' However, I do not repent me what I have done; nor will I, even if I lose by it.

"I enclose the items of a small amount paid by me for the relief of three Americans — a musician, a painter, and a teacher — who threw themselves on my tender mercies. I think it will be refunded, sooner or later. Mr. T—— (whose drafts you tell me are not yet paid) had been shipwrecked, and absolutely needed the money which I advanced. His father will unquestionably pay it. Did you ever collect £30, or thereabouts, from old Mr. R—— whom I sent home? I have strong faith that he is an honest man.

"I wonder what will become of all these vagabonds when I quit the consulate! I doubt whether they will find so good a friend in my successor; and yet I have never relieved anybody except when it would have been harsh and inhuman not to do it. The United States ought to make some provision for the relief of these people, in view of the propensity of our countrymen to stay abroad without means.

"I think I have your disease, just at present — a spring fever, making me restless, sleepless, appetite-

less, and wholly uncomfortable. I mean to take a
trip to York with Mrs. Hawthorne, to-morrow."

Ticknor's criticism of the first volume received had
reached Miss Bacon's literary godfather ere the arrival of the "500" ponderous copies, which apparently
could not have been packed aboard the previous
steamer without causing the cargo to be overloaded.

On April 24, Hawthorne penned his response to the
senior partner's remarks about the book: —

"The books will go by this steamer, and I shall
send therewith the necessary documents. The volume, as you say, is too big to meet with a ready sale.
I expect to make a loss, and the only question is as to
the more or less. With the exception of the unfavorable criticism in the 'Athenæum,' I know nothing of
its success in England.

"I enclose a critique of a volume of poems by Mrs.
Howe; and the writer (Mr. Bright of this town)
wished it to be sent to her. I read her play (and
thank you for it), but her genius does not appear to
be of the dramatic order. . . .

"I shall leave the consulate joyfully, but England with some regret; for it is a good country to
live in, and if I were rich enough, I doubt whether
I should ever leave it for a permanent residence
elsewhere.

"I have done some speechifying lately, having
been toasted on a public occasion. I don't in the
least admire my own oratory; but I do admire my
pluck in speaking at all. I rather wonder at my coming off so well, but the reporters mar my eloquence

most awfully. I am convinced that other orators write a fair copy of their speeches, and hand it to the reporters; and if I ever address an audience again, I mean to do the same.

"It is now just about four years, I think, since you and I went to Washington together. It was a time of much enjoyment. . . . I wish you would come across and accompany us to the Continent. Your edition of the Waverley Novels is very beautiful, and I agree with you that it has advantages over every other."

Hawthorne's regret that he had not wielded the blue pencil in connection with the "Baconian Theory," is voiced a month later, when he says: —

"Matters look dark, as regards Miss Bacon's book. I shall certainly not 'save my bacon' there. It was absurd in me to let her publish such a heavy volume; and, in fact, I never thought of authorizing the publication of such an immense mass, which is enough to swamp a ship of the line. However, this shall be the last of my benevolent follies, and I never will be kind to anybody again as long as I live.

"If there shall be an opportunity to send by our bag, as heretofore, I want an elegantly bound copy (in the same style as the King of Portugal's and Mr. Spiers,) of the "House of Seven Gables." If they cannot be sent by the bag, nor by any private conveyance, I do not want them. . . .

"Mrs. Hawthorne and I start on a trip to Lincolnshire, etc., to-morrow. Would to Heaven you were with us! I want to see somebody from the 'Corner.'"

On returning from this proposed trip, the writer touches upon it briefly, and gives further news of the Delia Bacon book: —

"Since my last, Mrs. Hawthorne and I have been on a very pleasant tour to some of the eastern counties of England, and returned only a day or two since. We went, among other places, to Boston, and really felt as if we were at home. There is a strong feeling of pride among the inhabitants in the greatness of and prosperity of our American Boston, which they consider as the daughter of their old town. There is going to be a celebration, this summer, in honor of John Cotton, the first minister of our Boston; and Americans will be in great demand on the occasion. Our Boston ought to send a special representative.

"I think Miss Bacon's book has fallen perfectly flat here. By the bye, Mr. William H. Smith has demanded of me a retraction of my remarks about him in the Preface; and it does appear that I did him injustice, so I shall give him a sugar-plum. If there had been any decent grounds for it, I would have tickled him still further, by way of keeping this unlucky book before the public eye.

"Mrs. Hawthorne's health is very good, indeed; and in two or three weeks, we shall set out for Scotland. I have already been there once; but it is invariably my experience that second visits to a place are more agreeable than the first. Everything that I see in my travels goes down into my journal; and I have now hundreds of pages, which I would publish if the least of them were not too spicy. But Mrs. Hawthorne excels me as a writer of travels. Her descriptions are the most perfect pictures that ever were put on paper; it is a pity they cannot be published, but neither she nor I would like to see her name on your list of female authors.

"I observe that the President is offering my office among his friends, and that nobody seems desirous of accepting it. In fact, it is not very well worth acceptance, under the law that took effect the first of January last; for that law cuts deeper than the former one into the fees that rightfully belong to the consul. I shall assert my right to these fees, and hold on to them, if possible. . . ."

In his "Recollections of a Gifted Woman," Hawthorne has described his one and only visit to the eccentric lady, whose book he financed, and whose lasting displeasure he won, while her remarkable production was going through the press.

"The only time I ever saw Miss Bacon was in London, where she had lodgings in Spring Street, Sussex Gardens, at the house of a grocer, a portly, middle-aged, civil, and friendly man, who, as well as his wife, appeared to feel a personal kindness towards their lodger. I was ushered up two (and I rather believe three) pair of stairs into a parlor somewhat humbly furnished, and told that Miss Bacon would soon come.

"There were a number of books on the table, and, looking into them, I found that every one had some reference, more or less immediate, to her Shakespearean theory. . . .

"I had expected (the more shame for me, having

no other ground of such expectation than that she was a literary woman) to see a very homely, uncouth, elderly personage, and was quite agreeably disappointed by her aspect. She was rather uncommonly tall, and had a striking and expressive face, dark hair, dark eyes, which shone with an inward light as soon as she began to speak, and by and by a color came into her cheeks and made her look almost young. Not that she really was so; she must have been beyond middle-age: and there was no unkindness in coming to that conclusion, because, making allowance for years and ill-health, I could suppose her to have been handsome and exceedingly attractive once.

"Though wholly estranged from society, there was little or no restraint in her manner: lonely people are generally glad to give utterance to their pent-up ideas, and often bubble over with them as freely as children with their new-found syllables. I cannot tell how it came about, but we immediately found ourselves taking a friendly and familiar tone together and we began to talk as if we had known one another a very long while. A little preliminary correspondence had, indeed, smoothed the way, and we had a definite topic in the contemplated publication of her book.

"She was very communicative about her theory, and would have been much more so had I desired it; but, being conscious within myself of a sturdy unbelief, I deemed it fair and honest rather to repress than draw her out upon the subject. Unquestionably she was a monomaniac; these overmastering ideas about the authorship of Shakespeare's plays, and the deep political philosophy concealed beneath the sur-

face of them, had completely thrown her off her balance; but at the same time they had wonderfully developed her intellect, and made her what she could
not otherwise have become. It was a very singular
phenomenon: a system of philosophy growing up in
this woman's mind without her volition,—contrary,
in fact, to the determined resistance of her volition,
— and substituting itself in the place of everything
that originally grew there. To have based such a
system on fancy, and unconsciously elaborated it
for herself, was almost as wonderful as really to have
found it in the plays. But in a certain sense she did
actually find it there.

"Shakespeare has surface beneath surface, to an
immeasurable depth, adapted to the plummet-line of
every reader; his works present many phases of truth,
each with a scope large enough to fill a contemplative
mind. Whatever you seek in him you will surely discover, provided you seek truth. There is no exhaust-
ing the various interpretations of his symbols; and a
thousand years hence, a world of new readers will
possess a whole library of new books, as we ourselves
do, in these volumes old already. I had half a mind
to suggest to Miss Bacon this explanation of her
theory, but forbore, because (as I could readily perceive) she had as princely a spirit as Queen Elizabeth
herself, and would at once have motioned me from
the room."

In her subsequent conversation with Hawthorne,
Miss Bacon informed him that she never walked out;
she suffered much from ill-health, yet she was perfectly happy. She frankly confessed that she could

no longer bear the society of those who did not express some sympathy with her views, and this sympathy she found so rarely that she had practically secluded herself from the world. Firm in her belief that she had a high mission to perform and adequate powers for its accomplishment, she also had faith that her ends were to be furthered by special interpositions of Providence. Hawthorne's expressions of interest in what appealed to him as a very remarkable piece of literature, seemed to its author a happy indication of the workings of Providence in this particular instance.

Hawthorne describes the withdrawal of her favor from himself, remarking: —

"In consequence of some advice which I fancied it my duty to tender as being the only confidant whom she now had in the world, I fell under Miss Bacon's most severe and passionate displeasure, and was cast off by her in the twinkling of an eye. It was a misfortune to which her friends were always particularly liable; but I think that none of them ever loved or even respected her most ingenuous and noble, but likewise most sensitive and tumultuous, character, the less for it.

"At that time her book was passing through the press. Without prejudice to her literary ability, it must be allowed that Miss Bacon was wholly unfit to prepare her own work for publication, because, among many other reasons, she was too thoroughly in earnest to know what to leave out. Every leaf and line was sacred, for all had been written under so deep a conviction of truth as to assume, in her eyes, the aspect of inspiration. A practised book-maker, with entire control of her materials, would have shaped out a duodecimo volume full of eloquent and ingenious dissertation, — criticisms which quite take the color and pungency out of other people's critical remarks on Shakespeare, — philosophic truths which she imagined herself to have found at the roots of his conceptions, and which certainly come from no inconsiderable depth somewhere.

"There was a great amount of rubbish, which any competent editor would have shovelled out of the way. But Miss Bacon thrust the whole bulk of inspiration and nonsense into the press in a lump, and there tumbled out a ponderous octavo volume, which fell with a dead thump at the feet of the public, and has never been picked up. A few persons turned over one or two of the leaves, as it lay there, and essayed to kick the volume deeper into the mud; for they were the hack critics of the minor periodical press in London, than whom, I suppose, though excellent fellows in their way, there are no gentlemen in the world less sensible of sanctity in a book, or less likely to recognize an author's heart in it, or more utterly careless about bruising, if they do recognize it. It is their trade. They could not do otherwise. I never thought of blaming them. It was not for such an Englishman as one of these to get beyond the idea that an assault was meditated on England's greatest poet.

"From the scholars and critics of her own country, indeed, Miss Bacon might have looked for a worthier appreciation, because many of the best of them have higher cultivation and finer and deeper sensibilities than all but the very profoundest and brightest of Englishmen. But they are not a courageous body of men; they dare not think a truth that has an odor of absurdity, lest they should feel themselves bound to speak it out. If any American ever wrote a word in her behalf, Miss Bacon never knew it, nor did I. Our journalists at once republished some of the most brutal vituperations of the English press, thus pelting their poor countrywoman with stolen mud, without even waiting to know whether the ignominy was deserved. And they never have known it, to this day, nor ever will."

Had Hawthorne lived a few years longer he would have had the satisfaction of seeing his protégée's production viewed in a manner more gratifying to his desire for literary justice, although he would no doubt have stood aghast at the body of converts destined to uphold this theory, which he had launched out of sympathy for the eccentric author, while disavowing his belief in her Baconian gospel. Had he foreseen this result, perchance he might have hesitated, yet it is doubtful if he would have done so, as he was strong in his conviction that any one who sets the public studying the works of Shakespeare more intently, confers a lasting benefit upon mankind.

The closing chapter of Miss Bacon's life showed but a deepening of the gloom which shrouded this unfortunate and disappointed woman of lonely destiny. After some time, Hawthorne heard from the Mayor at Stratford-on-Avon, that the poor lady, who had hovered about the grave of Shakespeare, and threatened to disturb the stone guarding his

sepulchre, in order to seek the supposed proofs of
her theory contained therein, was "afflicted with insanity," and in her lucid intervals had made repeated
references to the American consul who had aided her
enterprise.

Miss Bacon survived the publication of her work
only two years, and its reception by the press and
public served only to increase her melancholy and to
convince her of the failure of her strange "mission."
Her sponsor lost money on his friendly venture, and
it was evident that neither author nor publisher
gained anything by the bringing-forth of this much-
debated book. But though Hawthorne had no con-
ception of how much fire his clumsy octavo volume
was destined to kindle, he never in the least regretted
lending his timely aid to one whose enthusiasm he
regarded solely as a tribute to Shakespeare's genius,
for which he himself possessed such fervent admiration.

XII

HAWTHORNE'S LETTERS (CONTINUED)

AFTER his return from his second trip to Scotland, Hawthorne writes to his publisher recalling the fact that four years have elapsed since they together set foot on British soil: —

LIVERPOOL, July 17th, 1857.

DEAR TICKNOR, — It is four years yesterday since you and we arrived together in Liverpool. The time has passed not unprofitably, nor unpleasantly, but I am not sorry it is gone. An official life is a hard one, though some people seem to think differently.

We have just returned from a very interesting tour of nearly three weeks in Scotland. It was my second visit.

Either to-morrow or Monday we are going to Manchester, and shall make that our abode during the rest of the time of my continuance in office. This will give us an excellent opportunity to see the Arts' Exhibition at our leisure, during six weeks.

I shall be glad to have those bound volumes of the "Seven Gables" and "Scarlet Letter"; as they will be sent me from London the day after the arrival of the steamer. There was no letter or note from you by last steamer. I hope you were enjoying yourself on a spree somewhere; for nothing else would reconcile me to a gap in your correspondence.

'Tis a great disappointment that I am not to see either you or Fields, or any of my friends, this season. I dreamed of seeing Fields, the other night, and he had grown so old that I hardly knew him; and I myself looked so very old that he did not recognize me at all.

In good earnest the cares and toils of office have given me a long shove onward towards old age during these past four years. Italy may perhaps revive me a little. I never felt better in my life, however, than during my late tour to Scotland. It suits my constitution, to be idle and enjoy myself. I wish I were a little richer; and I doubt whether you would ever advertise another book by the "author of the Scarlet Letter." Still, I thank God for bringing me through this consular business so well.

Mrs. Hawthorne received great vigor on our Scotland journey; I have no further fears of her health.

Sincerely yours,

NATH^L HAWTHORNE.

Having later visited the Arts' Exhibition, Hawthorne writes: —

"Nothing is more depressing to me than the sight of a great many pictures together; it is like having innumerable books open before you at once, and being able to read only a sentence or two in each. They bedazzle one another with cross-lights. There never should be more than one picture in a room, nor more than one picture to be studied in one day. Galleries of pictures are surely the greatest absurdities that ever were contrived, there being no excuse for them, except that it is the only way in which pictures can be made generally available and accessible."

It was during the above-mentioned trip to Scotland that Hawthorne made his second visit to Abbotsford, his especial admiration for Sir Walter leading him thither with ever-keen interest; there he wrote his name in the visitors' book, which lay upon the table, in the drawer of which Scott was said to have found the forgotten manuscript of "Waverley"; afterwards he lingered in Sir Walter's study, where he again gazed thoughtfully upon the clothes of the author of "Waverley," and noticed how the sleeve of the old green coat was well worn at the cuff; a minute circumstance which, more than all else, brought Sir Walter very near to the author of "The Scarlet Letter," whose own cuffs frequently showed kindred shabbiness. After inspecting the library and drawing-room, Hawthorne was disappointed not to enter the dining-room, in which Scott died, but this apartment was not then on exhibition. Within the armory he placed his finger upon the trigger of Rob Roy's gun, looked on the pistols of Napoleon, as well as the sword of Montrose and other interesting relics. Yet he asserted that, after all, the atmosphere of Abbotsford failed to inspire him with awe, it having too much of the character of a museum, and he exclaims:—

"I do abhor this mode of making pilgrimages to the shrines of departed great men. There is certainly something wrong in it, for it seldom, or never, produces (in me at least) the right feeling. It is an odd truth, too, that a house is forever after spoiled and ruined as a home by having been the abode of a great man. His spirit haunts it, as it were, with a malevolent effect, and takes hearth and hall away from the nominal possessors, giving all the world the right to enter there because he had such intimate relations with all the world."

In this reflection, Hawthorne has pithily embodied the reason for that universal trait exhibited by "all the world," namely, the strong conviction that it is both their right and bounden duty to enter into, and take possession of, the private, personal history of every great man, — not only have such, presumably, given their fellow-mortals *carte blanche* to enter freely into their outward habitations, but also to penetrate to their souls' inner shrines, without so much as saying "by your leave." This is one of the penalties of genius!

Towards the close of July, 1857, Hawthorne begins to look for news of his successor; he writes on the last day of the month: —

"Nothing important has happened lately; except that I have removed with my family from Southport to Manchester, where we shall probably remain until September. I sometimes feel as if I should like to have a home once more, and to be permanently settled from year's end to year's end; but that time is still far ahead. I wish I had a better house to come home to at last. What should you think of the expediency of investing some money in a place not very far from Boston, which I might occupy, if I liked it, after my return; or which I might sell again without loss, if it did not suit me as a residence?

"And yet I don't quite like to think of giving up Concord; for my place there has many conveniences well adapted to my taste—especially the hill and wood behind the house, where I can take refuge from intruders at any moment; a privilege which I intend to use pretty extensively. I have received, and been civil to, at least 10,000 visitors since I came to England; and I never wish to be civil to anybody again.

"I have engaged Miss Ada Shepard (a graduate of Mr. Mann's College at Antioch) to take charge of my children while we remain on the Continent. She is recommended to me in the highest way, as respects acquirements and character; and it is essential to have some such person in order to give Mrs. Hawthorne the leisure and freedom which her health requires. I have tried English governesses, and find them ignorant and inefficient. Miss Shepard is to receive no salary, but only her expenses; and if she should apply to you for her passage (as I shall advise her to do), you will oblige me by accepting her draft. I do not limit the amount, presuming she will only do what is right. She is to cross, probably to Havre, in a sailing vessel, and will join us in Paris. As she wishes to perfect herself in the French pronunciation, she will perhaps reach Paris some time before our arrival, which I hope will be in the latter part of September.

"I hear nothing about my successor, and begin to be rather anxious; not that the office gives me any trouble in the way I manage it at present, for I take my pleasure whenever and wherever I like, and get as well paid for it as if I slaved at the desk. But all my arrangements are made for quitting England, and I wish to be in Rome early in October.

A month later, he is still in the dark about the arrival of his successor, and voices his impatience in an outburst against "Uncle Sam," which he knows his friend Ticknor will read with an amused smile, realizing full well that Hawthorne is not slighting his duties of office even if he is able to enjoy a few more hours of leisure and recreation than formerly.

"No news yet of my successor; not even of his appointment. I have been well enough contented to wait hitherto, because I live at Uncle Sam's expense, and do him very little service — the old scoundrel! But it is getting late in the season, and I ought to be in Italy in a little more than a month. I shall write again to the Department by the next steamer, and shall press as earnestly for a dismissal as most people do for an appointment. If I should be kept here through the winter, it would delay my return to America another year; for I must spend two seasons on the Continent, at any rate.

"We are still living at Manchester, and I pass back and forth two or three times a week."

By the end of September the new consul is at last on his way to England, and Hawthorne writes with satisfaction: —

"I had a letter from the new Consul per last steamer. He is to leave New York to-morrow, and nobody will pray for his safe passage and speedy arrival more sincerely than I shall. You may be sure I shall lend him no money nor back him up with any responsibility; indeed, he will immediately find himself in possession of funds (not his own, to be sure) that will put him beyond the necessity of fleecing anybody but Uncle Sam. To that I have no objection, provided his own conscience will permit him."

A fortnight later, he sends the announcement of the new consul's arrival: —

"Here I am writing you one more scribble from the old place. Mr. Tucker arrived by the Baltic, but could not take the office immediately, his exequatur not being out. He will come in on Monday, and then I shall draw freer breath than for many days past. Mr. Wilding being ill, and Mr. Pearce so nervous that he can hardly speak or stand, I have had a heavy burthen on my shoulders; but a man never knows what he can do till he is put to it.

"Mr. Wilding's illness has most seriously inconvenienced me by the delay of my accounts; for they are of a peculiar class, and it has been necessary to instruct another person how to make them up without aid or advice from him; and he held all the clues in his hands. However, this difficulty is in a fair way to be surmounted; and I shall soon know how I stand with the Treasury Department.

"Wilding has run a narrow chance for his life, which was at one time despaired of. He is now on the road to recovery; and Mr. Tucker has promised to give him the place of vice-consul, which will be vacated by Mr. Pearce, who retires with me.

"The new consul will be very popular with the shipmasters and American residents; a bluff, jolly, good-natured gentleman, fond of society and an excellent companion — wholly unlike me in every possible respect . . . . We have met in a most agreeable way, and seem to like one another vastly.

"I have long heard rumors from the knowing ones of the terrible crisis that was coming in the finances of the United States. Very likely some of my investments may suffer; for the trouble seems to come down like an avalanche. If there were any ready cash to be had, I should think it would be a first-rate time to buy a place to live in; but I leave everything to your judgment, being sure that you have done, and will do, all for the best. Mrs. Hawthorne and the children are at Leamington, and our new American governess has joined them there. She seems to prove entirely satisfactory."

At the close of this letter the writer adds in postscript: "Old Cass has sent me a dispatch, referring to mine, and bearing testimony to the 'prudence and efficiency' of my official conduct."

Hawthorne's plans having been considerably delayed, the first week in November finds him still in England, but making preparations for his trip to the Continent. He replies to his publisher's query in regard to the issue of a new book: —

"We are going to London early next week, and I suppose we shall have to remain there a fortnight, and perhaps more, before it will be possible for me to leave England. I expected to have been in Rome before this date, but should be well enough contented to be in London, if this wet autumnal weather were not so unfavorable to Mrs. Hawthorne's health. She continues pretty well, however, and I hope will not suffer seriously from the delay.

"I understand that Mr. Alcott (of whom I bought the Wayside) has bought a piece of land adjacent to mine, and two old houses on it. I remember the situation as a very pretty one; and I do not doubt that those two old houses might be converted into a domicile that would just suit me. If he should swamp himself by his expenditures on this place, I should be very glad to take it off his hands; and it seems highly probable (judging from the character of the man) that he will ultimately be glad to have me do so. The matter may be ripe by the time we get back to America; but I should feel much more inclined to come home if I had the prospect of a more convenient house to come to. You would oblige me by having an eye to this.

"As regards the announcement of a book, I am not quite ready for it yet. If I could be perfectly quiet for a few months, I have no doubt that something would result; but I shall have so much to see while I remain in Europe that I think I must confine myself to keeping a journal. Unless I return home next summer, however, I shall make a serious effort to produce something.

"I heard from Bennoch a few days ago, but have not seen him for a long while. The commercial men seem to be in almost as much trouble here as on your side of the water."

The business reverses experienced at this time by the warm-hearted and widely beloved Bennoch, occasioned deep regret among his friends, who feared

that he could not rally from his misfortunes, but with
courage undaunted, that talented gentleman determined to regain his former position; a task which he
accomplished successfully.

Not until January, did the Hawthorne family reach
the Continent; then Hawthorne writes from Paris,
sending later tidings of their mutual friend Bennoch:

"We stayed at Leamington till the beginning of
November, and have been ever since in London,
where all the children had the measles, and Mrs.
Hawthorne suffered a good deal from illness. However, we saw and enjoyed a good deal, in spite of difficulties and troubles!

"I have seen our poor friend Bennoch several
times, and find him still the same warm-hearted and
excellent fellow that he was during his prosperity.
Nevertheless, he feels his misfortunes very sensibly,
though he bears them like a man. I do not know (nor
I think, does he) what he means to do, after the business shall be finally wound up. I advised him to
think of going to America, where he has so many
friends; for, you know, it is almost a hopeless business
for a ruined man ever to recover himself in England.
He spent the evening with us, last Monday, and bade
me tell Fields and yourself that he is not dead yet,
though beaten down.

"We reached Paris last night, by way of Boulogne.
The weather is terribly cold, and we find it difficult
to keep ourselves' from freezing by these wretched
little wood-fires. Indeed, I find how English I have
grown, in five years past, by antipathy to French
fires, and everything else that is French."

Three months later, Hawthorne writes from Rome that he is suffering from the effects of the climate there, which does not suit him, and that after another month they will go to Florence for the summer, returning to Rome for one more winter. He remarks:—

"I doubt greatly whether I shall be able to settle down to serious literary labor as long as I remain abroad; at all events, not in Italy. In England, if not interrupted by other avocations, I could have worked to good purpose.

"We find living in Rome quite as expensive, in most particulars, as it was in England. Rent is a good deal dearer; and nothing is cheaper except maccaroni, figs, bad cigars, and sour wine. Rome struck me very disagreeably at first, but rather improves upon acquaintance, and has a sort of fascination which will make me reluctant to take final leave of it. I wish I were a little more patriotic; but to confess the truth I had rather be a sojourner in any other country than return to my own. The United States are fit for many excellent purposes, but they certainly are not fit to live in.

"Miss Lander, a lady from my native town, has made an excellent bust of me, of which I will enclose a photograph, if I can get one. Even Mrs. Hawthorne is delighted with it, and, as a work of art, it has received the highest praise from all the sculptors here, including Gibson, the English sculptor, who stands at the head of the profession. Miss Bremer declares it to be the finest modelled bust she ever saw. I tell you this in the hope that you and Fields may do what may be in your power to bring Miss

Lander's name favorably before the public; for she is coming back to America (for the summer only) and might be greatly benefitted by receiving commissions for busts, etc. She is a very nice person, and I like her exceedingly. If you happen to see her, she will give you the latest and most authentic news of me and mine."

The bust to which Hawthorne refers so enthusiastically, did not prove in the end as satisfactory as the writer at first considered it. While it was in the clay it was pronounced a very good likeness, but during the process of putting it into marble some changes were made in it, at the suggestion of an American friend, who, in the absence of the sculptress, took the liberty of directing the marble-cutters to make certain alterations in the lower part of the face. The result was not to enhance the likeness, as those familiar with the work are doubtless aware. The bust, which, in its present state, has been said by certain critics to look like a combination of Daniel Webster and George Washington, is now in the possession of the Concord Library.

XIII

THE MARBLE FAUN

DESPITE his prophecy that he would write nothing in Italy, Hawthorne was destined to produce there the romance, which some think his masterpiece, and which he himself regarded as one of his best pieces of work. Whatever may be the ultimate position assigned it among Hawthorne's works, it is probable that the "Romance of Monte-Beni" is the most widely read of all his books, owing to the fascination of its theme and to its extensive circulation in Rome in the Tauchnitz edition.

Although "The Marble Faun" was finished in England, and a great part of it rewritten there, yet the work belonged to Italy, and will ever stand as an immortal tribute to that sunny land, by an immortal romanticist. This book was not completed until the spring of 1860, but it had begun to take shape in its creator's mind two years before, even while he was expressing to his publisher doubts of his ability to write anything in Italy beyond his notebooks.

Hawthorne had from his earliest days delved into the mediæval history of Italy, and he arrived there prepared to appreciate to the fullest extent all that this historic, poetic, and artistic land had to offer; this was one of the happiest periods of his life, and one filled with the most delightful social and artistic intercourse. He had, at this time, laid aside the many duties and restrictions of office, and had entered on an existence best suited to his own temperament, one in which he could gaze out upon a world filled with a wealth of beauty and interest, and could have leisure to contemplate, and to reflect upon the meaning of this enchanting moving picture.

Even before leaving England, Hawthorne had probably begun to put together certain fragments, which, like magnets, were ever after drawing to themselves other kindred bits of fact and fiction that were ultimately to make up the final unit.

One morning, early in the spring, Mr. and Mrs. Hawthorne chanced to enter the church of the Capuchins, where they saw, lying dead, the monk, who later appears in the pages of the romance. Hawthorne was vividly impressed by the appearance of this monk, and his description of the episode shows how immediately his lively imagination had seized upon this subject, and had begun to endow it with additional traits and weird suggestiveness.

"This poor monk, had perhaps died of apoplexy; for his face did not look pale, but had almost, or quite, the natural flush of life, though the feet were of such yellow, waxy hue. His gray eyebrows were very thick, and my wife had a fancy that she saw him contort them. A good many people were standing round the bier; and one woman knelt and kissed the dead monk's beads. By and by, as we moved round from chapel to chapel, still with our eyes turning often to the dead monk, we saw some blood oozing from his nostrils! Perhaps his murderer — or his doctor — had just then come into the church and

drawn nigh the bier; at all events, it was about as
queer a thing as I ever witnessed. We soon came
away and left him lying there, a sight which I shall
never forget."

One learns from Hawthorne's notebooks and letters how keenly sensitive he was to the merits of the
sculptor's art. No masterpiece of the painters could
rival in his mind the highest achievement of the
sculptor, and it was in response to this instinctive
enthusiasm for a wonderful statue, that the Faun of
Praxiteles became the center of his growing theme.

On April 22, 1858, Hawthorne visited the sculp-
ture galleries of the Capitol, where he stood before
this masterpiece for the first time; he says of this experience: "I looked at the Faun of Praxiteles, and
was sensible of a peculiar charm in it; a sylvan
beauty and homeliness, friendly and wild at once.
The lengthened, but not preposterous ears, and the
little tail, which we infer, have an exquisite effect,
and make the spectator smile in his very heart. This
race of fauns was the most delightful of all that antiquity imagined. It seems to me that a story with all
sorts of fun and pathos in it might be contrived on
the idea of their species having become intermin-
gled with the human race; a family with the faun
blood in them, having prolonged itself from the
classic era till our own days. The tail might have
disappeared, by dint of constant intermarriage with
ordinary mortals; but the pretty hairy ears should
occasionally reappear in members of the family; and
the moral instincts and intellectual characteristics
of the faun might be picturesquely brought out,

without detriment to the human interest of the story. Fancy this combination in the person of a young lady!"

Gradually, the original idea of making the Faun the center of his story, grew and developed into the final form given to his readers, in which Hawthorne presents the longest and most elaborate of all of his works. He attributed its length to the fact that he had not the heart to cancel his many descriptions of Roman and Florentine scenes, which it had given him so much pleasure to pen, and thousands of grateful readers are glad that he refrained from doing so.

It was his intention to finish this romance in Rome, but the serious illness of his daughter Una upset his plans, and he made up his mind to rewrite and complete this work in England, where he had intended to give it its finishing touches, in order to secure his English copyright in that country before sailing for America.

In March, 1859, Hawthorne announces that he has almost finished the work which has filled his mind for the past year. This would have been completed during his stay in Italy, had not the writer been distracted by the illness of his daughter, whose recovery was for a long time despaired of. Hawthorne, who was abnormally sensitive to the suffering of any persons near him, seemed to surrender his own vitality during this period of suspense, and never afterwards quite rebounded from its effect upon his constitution; he was never of a sanguine temperament, and at the first ap-

proach of illness, he foresaw the worst, and his vivid
imagination constructed scores of pictures which
were blacker than night.

On March 4, however, prior to his daughter's illness, he writes to his publisher in comparatively
good spirits, though protesting against the climate
which has somewhat affected his health: —

"This Roman climate is really terrible, and nobody
can be sure of life or health from one day to another.
The utmost caution is requisite in regard to diet
and exposure to air; and after all the care that can
be taken, there is a lurking poison in the atmosphere that will be likely enough to do your business.
I never knew that I had either bowels or lungs till
I came to Rome; but I have found it out now to my
cost. For the present, however, we are all pretty
well, and are rejoicing in the prospect of leaving this
pestilential city on the 15th of next month.

"It is our calculation to set sail from Liverpool
in the course of July next — probably by the steamer
of the first of that month. My wife's brother is to
leave the Wayside, in season for us to get into it
immediately. . . .

"I feel in somewhat better spirits to come home,
because I think I see how an addition can be made
to the house, which need not be enormously expensive, and yet will afford us the necessary space. I
want a drawing-room, two bed-chambers, and two
chambers for servants, in addition to what we now
have; and these, if I mistake not, I can get by adding
on a wing to the southern end of the house. I should
be very reluctant to leave Concord, or to live any-

where else than by my own hillside; that one spot
(always excepting the old 'Corner Store') is the
only locality that attaches me to my native land.
I am tied to it by one of my heartstrings, all the rest
of which have long ago broken loose.

"I told you, in my last, that I had written a Romance. It still requires a good deal of revision,
trimming off of exuberances, and filling up vacant
spaces; but I think it will be all right in a month or
two after I arrive. I shall do my best upon it, you
may be sure; for I feel that I shall come before the
public, after so long an interval, with all the uncer-
tainties of a new author. If I were only rich enough,
I do not believe I should ever publish another book,
though I might continue to write them for my own
occupation and amusement. But with a wing of a
house to build, and my girls to educate, and Julian
to send to Cambridge, I see little prospect of the
'dolce far niente,' as long as there shall be any faculty left in me. I have another Romance ready to
be written, as soon as this one is off the stocks.

"General Pierce has been spending the winter in
Naples, where he is still detained on account of his
wife's health; so that I have not yet met him, and
very likely our meeting may be deferred till we both
are home again. There are said to be fifteen hundred Americans now in Rome.

"We are now in the height of the Carnival, and
the young people find it great fun. To say the truth,
so do I; but I suppose I should have enjoyed it better at twenty. The Prince of Wales is here, and
seems to take vast delight in pelting and being

pelted, along the Corso. The poor fellow will not
have many such merry times, in his future life.

"Do you hear anything of Bennoch? I have received only one letter from him, since leaving England, and have hardly the heart to write to him, for
I greatly fear that there is no possibility of his ever
retrieving his fortunes. It is a great pity. . . . It
seems but a week or two now, before I shall shake
hands with you in America."

Hawthorne's plan for a speedy departure was
completely changed by the dangerous illness of his
elder daughter, previously referred to. For over three
months Una was critically ill with Roman fever,
which she had contracted while on a sketching expedition with her governess, Miss Shepard. These
two delighted to sketch the various picturesque
ruins, and although the edict had been issued that
they should always be within doors at six o'clock,
they were, on one evening, tempted to overstay their
time, at the Palace of the Cæsars, in order to finish a
certain drawing. A few days later, Una was attacked
by chills and fever, and the disease continued to become more and more severe until she became so ill
that her life was despaired of; she was convalescent
when Hawthorne wrote to his publisher on May 23
from Rome: —

"It is a very long while, I believe, since I have
written, and certainly very long since I heard from
you. Meanwhile, we have suffered a great deal of
trouble and anxiety from Una's illness; and, at one
period, we had scarcely no hope of ever taking her

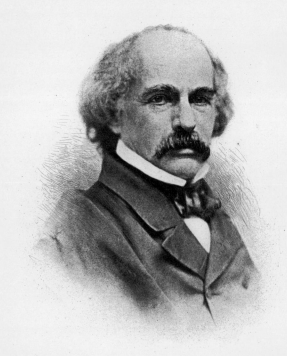

Nathaniel Hawthorne.

out of Rome. Indeed, the physician did not encourage us to think that she would live even from one day to another. She has been restored to us, however, and, for several weeks past, has steadily and rapidly gained strength; and the Doctor now assures us that she will be stronger and healthier than ever before in her life. God's providence and a good constitution (for I attribute little efficacy to homœopathic remedies) have brought her through. Had it been otherwise, I doubt whether we should ever have the heart to come home without her.

"It has been necessary for us to remain in Rome longer than we intended while Una was getting strong enough to travel. The Doctor now says she may safely set out, but advises us to spend some little time on the seashore. We shall, therefore, take the railway to Civita Vecchia (forty miles from Rome), where we mean to spend ten days or a fortnight. . . . You will see us before the end of the summer.

"Rome is very quiet, and the war on the frontier of Sardinia causes us no inconvenience here. We shall go a little nearer the seat of hostilities, at Leghorn, but we have no apprehension of difficulty or disturbance. The rush of strangers from Italy, however, has been very great, and I imagine lodgings will be very cheap here next season.

"Remember me kindly to all my friends. I shall be delighted to see you all again; but I will fairly own that it is not altogether agreeable to think of coming back, after so long an absence as mine. I am afraid I have lost my country by staying away too long.

"I enclose (to save postage) a letter from Una to her Aunt. You can read it if you please, as it gives some account of her illness; and then please enclose it to Miss Elizabeth M. Hawthorne, care of John Dike, Esq., Salem.

"General Pierce spent a month or two here, and left for Vienna, some weeks ago. I suppose he will be in Paris by this time. He has not decided whether to return home this year. Mr. Motley and family are still here, and will start for Paris next week. Our friend, C. G. Thompson, is about returning to Boston with his family. He has wonderfully improved since his residence here, and is now a very exquisite artist, but, I fear, not a very successful one. He deserves success, and I wish you, and Fields, and Whipple, and other kind-hearted people, would make some little flourish of trumpets on his return. A few paragraphs in the newspapers would be efficacious in giving him a fresh start, and a little popular sunshine is what he needs to make him flower out.

"We leave Rome the 25th — that is, the day after to-morrow."

In order to prepare the new romance for the English market and to secure its English copyright, Hawthorne decided to remain another year in England. He stayed for a while at Whitby, which was a moderately agreeable watering-place in which to find the needed seclusion; but the surroundings there did not prove satisfactory, and he soon removed to Redcar, which though not far distant, was far more secluded. The stay at Whitby undoubtedly supplied him with the name of Hilda, as he was just then in an undecided state regarding the names of his characters, and at Whitby were the remains of an abbey built in past ages by St. Hilda.

At Redcar, where Hawthorne remained three or four months, he kept steadily at his task, varying his work each day by walks with members of his family, and lonely rambles along the sandy coast which stretched away for some miles to the northward.

On November 8, 1859, Mrs. Hawthorne writes from Leamington: "My husband to-day finished his book, 'The Romance of Monte Beni.'" She furthermore remarks: "As usual, he thinks the book good for nothing, and based upon a very foolish idea which nobody will like or accept. But I am used to such opinions, and understand why he feels oppressed with disgust of what has so long occupied him. The true judgment of the work was his first idea of it, when it seemed to him worth the doing. He has regularly despised each one of his books immediately upon finishing it. My enthusiasm is too much his own music, as it were. It needs the reverberation of the impartial mind to reassure him that he has not been guilty of a *bêtise*. Mr. Hawthorne has no idea of portraying me as Hilda. Whatever resemblance one sees is accidental."

It was just at this time that considerable stir was taking place in regard to the old matter of the ill-treatment of sailors on board American vessels, and Henry Bright, who was intensely interested in the matter, brought out a pamphlet upon the subject.

Hawthorne's aid was invoked and he was himself prepared to write an article of protest, which, however, he did not produce, although he endeavored by his dispatches to Congress and by his letters to private individuals to bring about the needed reform. As usual, he appealed promptly to his friend Ticknor to lend his influence in this direction, and the following communication from Bright notes the fact that Mr. Ticknor was one of those to bring the matter to the attention of Congress: —

West Derby, Liverpool, July 29, 1859.

MY DEAR HAWTHORNE, — A letter is waiting for you at Whitby, where I supposed you were. Monckton Milnes is bringing on the ship-cruelty question in the House on the 2d of August, and he wishes you very much to send him a few lines relative to the matter. Do please write him at 16, Upper Brook Street, and tell him, if you will kindly do so, that the evils are very real and the law quite inoperative. Mr. Ticknor, Mr. Jay, and Charles Morton are going to try what your Congress can do; and on this side, Mr. Milnes will move an address to the Queen, "praying her to enter into negotiations with the Government of the United States for the purpose of preventing the gross cruelties practised on merchant seamen engaged in the traffic between this country and the United States, and for bringing the offenders to justice." To this I hope no objection can be raised, either on this side or on yours. Please do not lose a post in writing to Milnes, or it may be too late. Tuesday is the day.

I am already longing to be with you all again, and must certainly come to see you if you will let me.

Ever yours,

H. A. BRIGHT.

Owing to the exertions of Mr. Bright, the subject was discussed in the House, on the motion of Lord Houghton. The evil in time abated itself, chiefly owing to the decay of the commerce which had given rise to it. That Hawthorne complied promptly with Mr. Bright's request is testified to in another letter penned by the latter in which he says: — "Thank you most heartily for writing to Monckton Milnes on the cruelty question. You no doubt saw the papers of the 4th of August with an account of the debate in them, and how Mr. Milnes quoted us both. I do hope your people (I mean the people who were yours — you are an Englishman now) will help our Government in getting something done."

In October, Hawthorne left Redcar and took up his abode at Leamington, occupying a different house from the one in Lansdowne Circus, described in his notebook. Here, with the exception of two brief trips to London, he remained until March, 1860, when the romance was finally completed.

On the 6th of October, he writes to his publisher:

DEAR TICKNOR, — I was very glad to receive your note of the 20th September, and a little ashamed for not having written for so long a time. But I am never a very good correspondent; and for nearly three months past I have been constantly occupied with my book, which required more work to be done upon it than I supposed. I am now, I think, within a fortnight of finishing it. There will be three English volumes, or two of yours, each perhaps as big as the "Seven Gables." Mrs. Hawthorne (the only person who has read it) speaks very much in its favor; but I sometimes suspect she has a partiality for the author. I have not yet decided upon the title.

Smith & Elder have signed an agreement to publish the book, and pay me £600 on the assignment of the copyright. It will, I suppose, certainly be ready for the press in the course of this month (at furthest by the end of it), and these £600 will preclude the necessity of your remitting any money through the Barings. By-the-by, speaking of money matters, I should like to have some brief estimate of how much property I possess. If I find that I can prudently do it, I should be glad to spend some money before leaving England, in books and other matters.

"We have been spending the summer, since the middle of July, at Redcar, a little watering-place on the shore of the German Ocean. It was the most secluded spot I ever met with, and therefore very favorable to literary labor. We had not a single visitor or caller while we were there. This suited Mrs. Hawthorne as well as myself; for she was quite worn out with her anxiety and watching, during Una's illness. Her health now is considerably improved; and Una herself as plump and rosy as any

English girl. We are all very well, considering what some of us have gone through.

You will see us probably by the end of June next. I must confess that I have outlived all feeling of homesickness; but still there are some friends whom I shall rejoice to see again — and none more than yourself — I doubt whether I shall ever again be contented to live long in one place, after the constant changes of residence for nearly seven years past. I am much troubled about our house in Concord; it is not big enough for us, and is hardly worth repairing and enlarging.

I think we may probably spend the winter here at Leamington, as it is a very pleasant town, with many conveniences for transitory residents. You had better, however, continue to send your letters (when you write any, which I hope will be oftener than of late) through the Barings. I have received but one letter from you since we left Rome.

I write with a horrible pen; as you see; but such as it is, it has served me to write my whole book with.

Believe me most sincerely yours,

NATH. HAWTHORNE.

By the first of December the book is going through the press, and its author writes regarding its tardy appearance; he also discusses the much debated title, regarding which it seems impossible to come to an agreement.

"I finished the Romance some weeks ago; and Smith & Elder wrote me that it was in the printers' hands, and would pass speedily through the press.

Since then, I have heard nothing about the matter, and I cannot account for the delay, except on the supposition that they mean to put off the publication till spring. This, indeed, seems to me the most eligible course; because it would be quite impossible to make arrangements for the simultaneous publication on your side of the water, supposing the book to appear in this country at Christmas.

"By Fields's advice, I gave the book the title of 'The Romance of Monte Beni'; but as Smith & Elder thought it not a captivating name, I sent them several others to choose from. I do not know which they will select; but their choice need not govern yours, and, if you wish to announce the book, I should like to have you call it 'Saint Hilda's Shrine.' We can change the title afterwards, should it appear advisable.

"The publication of the Romance being deferred, I cannot call upon Smith & Elder to pay over the £600; so that you would oblige me by lodging £200, or thereabouts, with the Barings.

"I had a letter from Fields, about a week ago. He is still in Paris, and seems to have given up the idea of spending the winter in Italy.

"We hear from Bennoch occasionally, and are in hopes of seeing him in the course of a few days.

"When we were at Marseilles, last June, I left three trunks in charge of our consul there, to be transmitted to the United States, direct to your care. They contained clothing, books, and curiosities, and works of art which we collected in Rome. I gave directions to have them sent to Boston; but

it is possible, if no vessel offered for that port, that
they might go to New York. In either case, no
doubt, you would be notified of their arrival. If
they have been received, I wish you would let me
know; and if not, you would greatly oblige me by
writing to our consul at Marseilles on that subject.
His name is Derbé, I think, or some such French
name; but you would find it in a Blue-Book or
United States Register.

"Please to pay any bills that come to you, certi-
fied by Mrs. Horace Mann, for repairs on the house
at Concord. I wish I had a better house, and I should
enjoy far greater pleasure in the idea of coming
home. As the case stands I have hardly any other
anticipation so pleasant as that of seeing you at the
old 'Corner Store.'"

On December 22, Hawthorne continues to dis-
cuss the title of his forthcoming work and suggests
"The Marble Faun," which from this time on, he
maintained was his preference, although his English
publishers would not accept it. He writes: —

"I have received the proof-sheets of the Romance
as far as the commencement of the second volume.
They were going at the rate of fifty pages a day; and
I was afraid they would get the book out, on this
side of the water, before Christmas, without waiting
for you to get it through the press and publish it
simultaneously. So I suggested that there was no
occasion for haste, inasmuch as I should remain in
England till next summer. The printing has since
gone on much more leisurely.

"The exact middle of the work is at the 10th chapter (called the 'Pedigree of Monte Beni') of the second volume; and you must commence the second volume with that chapter.

"The publishers propose to call the Romance 'The Transformation; or the Romance of Monte Beni,' but this title did not suit me, and I rejected it. I think I shall call it 'The Marble Faun'; and unless I write you to the contrary, I wish you would prefix that title on the title-page."

A month later, the work of getting the volumes through the press was nearly at an end, and the title was still under discussion; Smith & Elder did not take kindly to the preference of the author, whose judgment might well have been relied upon in this respect, as Hawthorne was particularly happy in his choice of titles. Indeed, these may be regarded as models to be studied by other writers, few of whom succeed in selecting titles so pleasing to the ear, suggestive to the imagination, and so truly significant of the motive of the works for which they stand.

Hawthorne writes on January 26: —

DEAR TICKNOR, — Your letter arrived yesterday, and was very welcome, after so long a silence. The printers are now nearly at the end of the third volume of the Romance, but I presume the publishers will not think of bringing it out at present. I wrote to Smith & Elder, not long since, to remind them of the necessity of a simultaneous publication on both sides of the water. They replied that they had already sent you the proof-sheets of the first volume, and would duly forward the remainder, and would also let you know the time of publication here. . . .

I cannot think of a better title than 'The Marble Faun'; and I hope you will call it so: — 'The Marble Faun, or the Romance of Monte Beni.' Smith & Elder do not seem to be decided yet on this point; but I am well assured that the above title will suit the American public better than any which these English booksellers are likely to substitute for it; nor is there any reason, that I know of, why the book should not have two titles in two countries.

We are passing rather a dull winter here; for the cloudy, chill, rainy weather leaves us little inclination to make excursions, and, besides, Mrs. Hawthorne's health is not so good in this damp atmosphere as it was in Rome. I shall really be glad to get home, although I do not doubt that I shall be tortured with lifelong wishes to cross the sea again. I fear I have lost the capacity of living contentedly in any one place. . . . Bennoch sent his remembrances to us, at Christmas, in the shape of a barrel of oysters; since which I have not seen or heard from him.

I will write again, when I hear anything definite about the Publication of the Romance.

Affectionately yours,
NATH^L HAWTHORNE.

On February 3, Hawthorne writes in distress that his English publishers are obdurate: —

"Smith & Elder are determined to take a title out of their own heads, though they affirm that it was originally suggested by me, 'Transformation'; I beseech you not to be influenced by their bad example. Call it 'The Marble Faun; a Romance of Monte Beni.' If you are in any doubt about it, ask Whipple to read the book, and choose or make a title for it; but do not let it be 'Transformation.'

"Give copies to Whipple, Hillard, Longfellow, and others whom you know to be friends of the author. Give one to Elizabeth Peabody; send one to my sister, care of John Dike, Esq., Salem; also one to David Roberts, Esq., Counsellor at Law, Salem, and to William B. Pike, Esq., Collector, Salem. I can think of no others at this moment. Of course, General Pierce is to have one; Lowell, too. In short, you know pretty well who are the persons whom I should like to please, and who would be gratified by a presentation copy."

On February 10, Hawthorne writes apologetically in regard to the tardy arrival of his volume in America: —

"I am surprised that the first volume of the Romance had not sooner reached you. Smith & Elder told me they had sent it as early as the 6th of January. I should have objected to their publishing so early as the 28th inst., but they did not give me notice of their design until after they had sent off the 3d volume, and made all their arrangements. I fear you will be pressed for time; but if you bring out your edition before the importation of any copies of the English one, it will save the copyright. This will give you a whole week or more, in March. Moreover, if your first edition consists only of a single copy, it will guard the copyright as well as if it were ten thousand. If the whole work should not be ready, you could publish the first volume.

"I am fully determined not to retain their absurd title of 'Transformation.' Let it be 'The Marble Faun; a Romance of Monte Beni,' unless Whipple (if he will do me the kindness to set his wits to work upon the matter) should think better.

"If you have an opportunity, by any person going to Rome, I wish you would send William W. Story a copy. If I could bring any public notice upon his sculptural productions (which are shamefully neglected), I should feel that I had done a good thing.

"Fields means to come home in the same steamer with me; and it is my purpose to sail in the latter part of June. I long to be at home, and yet I can hardly anticipate much pleasure in returning when I consider the miserable confusion in which you are involved. I go for a dissolution of the Union; and on that ground, I hope the Abolitionists will push matters to extremity.

"I should be very glad to send you an article for the 'Atlantic Monthly,' but see little chance of being able to do it at present. I have lost the habit of writing magazine articles, and it would take me a long while, and very favorable circumstances, to get into a proper fix for such compositions. I have many proposals from magazines on this side of the water, but shall certainly decline them all, and listen to nobody but yourself. It is possible that some good idea may occur to me, and, if so, I will do my best to take advantage of it.

"I have come to the conclusion that New England is the healthiest country in the world. Everybody here has one sort of sickness or another, throat-complaints being the most prevalent. Mrs. Hawthorne has been confined to her bed for some weeks past, by a severe access of her old bronchial complaint. The Doctor speaks favorably of her case; but I shall be rejoiced when we leave England.

"As soon as Mrs. H. is able to move, I intend to take my family to Blackheath, or somewhere else in the neighborhood of London, there to remain till time of sailing.

"All the advantages of residing in England are concentrated in London. Leave out that, and I would rather be in America — that is to say, if the Presidential elections and all other political turmoil could be done away with — and if I could but be deprived of my political rights, and left to my individual freedom. The sweetest thing connected with foreign residence is, that you have no rights and no duties, and can live your own life without interference of any kind. I shall never again be so free as I have been in England and Italy."

A month later, March 9, 1860, Hawthorne acknowledges the remittances received from his American publisher on the much-debated volume, of which he says: —

"I am sorry you have been so much hurried about the book. It came out in London at the time appointed, and seems to have gone off pretty well, for Smith and Elder wrote me, some days ago, that their edition was nearly exhausted, and that they were about printing another. As everybody complains that the mysteries of the story are not sufficiently accounted for, I intend to add a few pages to the concluding chapter, in order to make things a little clearer. The additional matter, when written, shall be sent you in manuscript.

"I think there would have been no danger, in a legal point of view, in changing the title of the Romance; and I therefore hope you will have called it 'The Marble Faun.' But, after all, it is of no essential consequence.

"I thank you for the number of 'The Atlantic,' which seems to me a good one; also for the newspapers. The only American papers that I have seen, for nearly a year, are those which you have sent me; but I shall see enough of them in a few months more.

"I have a letter from Fields this morning dated at Rome on the 2d of this month. He purposes leaving Rome in a few days, and will probably be here early in April, at farthest. I have engaged passages for him and my own family at one of three dates, — June 2d, 16th, or 30th, — most probably we shall sail on the 16th; but if he chooses to come at an earlier date, it will be in his power. For my part, I absolutely long to be at home, and if an earlier voyage would be comfortable, I should certainly prefer it. I shall enjoy nothing till I have touched my native soil again."

"I went up to London, the other day, and found Bennoch in good trim. He says that the past year has been very favorable to him in his business relations; and I hope we shall yet see him as prosperous as formerly."

On April 6, Hawthorne writes from Bath of the receipt of the first copies of his American edition:—

"I have received the three copies of 'The Marble Faun'; and I wish, whenever you print the concluding pages (which I transmitted several weeks ago), you would send me another copy, if you can find means so to do. I want it for Bennoch. Your edition is certainly much handsomer than the English one — at exactly a fifth the price!

"I have been much gratified by the kind feeling and generous praise contained in the notices you sent me. After so long an absence and silence, I like to be praised too much. It sounds like a welcome back among my friends. But, in fact, if I have written anything well, it should be this Romance; for I have never thought or felt more deeply, or taken more pains. So far as I can judge, its success in England has been good. Smith & Elder published their second edition a week or two ago, and I daily receive notes of congratulation and requests for autographs — which latter annoyance seems to be the great and ultimate result of literary reputation. I scarcely thought that these fat-brained Englishmen would have taken so wild a fiction in such good part. To say the truth, some of them do grumble awfully; for it is not every man who knows how to read a Romance; and if I were not myself the author, I doubt whether I should like this one.

"It is very long since I heard anything of Fields—

not since February, I think, while he was still in
Rome. Where can he be? If I leave England without him, you need never expect to see him again; for
he certainly will not return, unless in somebody's
custody. You had better stop his supplies, after the
middle of June. For my part, I already begin to
count the days that intervene between now and
departure, and we are all restless and feverish with
the thought of home. I cannot promise to be contented when I get there, after becoming habituated
to such constant change; but I mean to try to settle
down into a respectable character, and have serious thoughts of going to meeting every Sunday fore-
noon.

"If you happen to hear of a puppy-dog, of a large
good breed, I should like to get such a one.

"I find myself respectably off, as to funds, and
I shall begin to make an addition of two or three
rooms to my house as soon as we get back. It was
small enough, in all conscience, when we left it; and
now the children (who used to be bundled together
in one room) will require separate apartments. I
really don't see how we are to live in it; but we all
have an attachment for the spot, and have looked
upon it always as our ultimate home; so that, poor
as it is, I should prefer it to a better one. . . ."

On the 19th of April, Hawthorne forwarded one
more communication in reference to the much-
talked-of Romance. His letter is dated from Bath,
and in it the writer indulges in one of his many little
pleasantries put forth at the expense of the British
public: —

DEAR TICKNOR, — Yours of the 3d inst. has come to hand, and also the newspapers, and the "Atlantic" for May, for all of which I thank you. This number promises to be particularly good, both as regards poetry and prose.

I am glad that the Romance has gone off so well. Here, it may also be called a successful affair; Smith & Elder having got out their third edition, and perhaps more by this time; for the good opinion of the "Times" has great weight with John Bull.

Just now, however, the English public cares very little for any American except John Heenan, the prize-fighter. You cannot imagine the interest that is felt in the battle, nor their surprise at Heenan's standing up so sturdily against their champion. No moral or intellectual triumph, that we could possibly win, would inspire them with half the respect, or half the mortification, that the loss of this fight would have caused them. It is, indeed, a great pity that it was left undecided — that is, provided (as there were ten chances to one) the event had turned out favorably for our side. You see, having lived so long among Englishmen, I have grown to be almost as great a fool as themselves.

I still hear nothing from Fields, nor do I know how to direct to him. Unless he turns up soon, I shall have to relinquish the stateroom which I took for him and his wife in the steamer of the 16th June. My own purpose to sail at that date is decided, and I long for the time to come. All my homesickness has fallen on me at once, and even Julian is scarcely more impatient than myself.

I shall pay a parting visit to London in the course of next month, where I mean to pass a quiet week or two, leaving Mrs. Hawthorne and the children here. Mrs. Hawthorne has been very well, till a few days ago, when she caught a cold by sitting down in the open air, and is now confined to her bed. In my opinion, America is the healthiest and safest country to live in, in the world. There are more delightful atmospheres, perhaps, than that of New England, but none that has so little mischief in it. I look upon it as quite a Paradise, but am afraid I may change my opinion, after a few months' trial. But I shall do my best to live contentedly at home.

I don't know whether I remembered to ask you to send a copy of "The Marble Faun" to General Pierce; but, of course, you will have done it.

Your friend,

NATHᴸ HAWTHORNE.

Although the "Transformation" was received with great eagerness by the British public, a general disappointment prevailed because of its vague conclusion. Most of the English reviewers voiced this feeling, and there was a widespread demand for an "explanation."

Hawthorne, who was keenly sensitive to critical estimates of his work, and ever ready to think slightingly of his productions, was rather depressed by the attitude of the English critics, and in a half-ironic mood, he penned the brief chapter which is now appended to the book.

Even his friend Bright joined the chorus of questioners, and exclaimed in a letter to the author: —

"I have finished *the* book, and am, I think, more angry at your tantalizing cruelty than either 'Athenæum' or 'Saturday Review.' I want to know a hundred things you do not tell me, — who Miriam was, what was the crime in which she was concerned and of which all Europe knew, what was in the packet, what became of Hilda, whether Miriam married Donatello, whether Donatello got his head cut off, etc. Of course, you'll say I ought to *guess;* well, if I do guess, it is but a guess, and I want to *know*.

"Yesterday I wrote a review of you in the 'Examiner,' and in spite of my natural indignation, I hope you will not altogether dislike what I have said. In other respects I admire 'Monte Beni' more than I can tell you; and I suppose no one will now visit Rome without a copy in his hand. Nowhere are descriptions to be found so beautiful, so true, and so pathetic."

The middle of May found Hawthorne in London, where he remained some ten days in the enjoyment of his friends, staying with John Lothrop Motley (the historian), and spending much time with his devoted friend Henry Bright, with whom he visited Cambridge before returning to join his family at Bath. Shortly afterwards the Hawthornes set out for Liverpool, and before many days had elapsed they were once again upon the Atlantic, homeward bound.

XIV

HAWTHORNE AGAIN AT HOME

THE uncertainty concerning the whereabouts of Mr. Fields was dispelled ere the day of embarkation arrived, and the junior partner appeared in due season to make one of the homeward-bound party, so that Hawthorne was not without the society of a publisher on either the outward or the homeward trip. The voyage home was a calm and delightful one, and Hawthorne was brimful of life and spirits; he rallied Fields upon his unfortunate tendency to seasickness and amused him with fanciful tales of the viands he himself was able to consume. While Fields counted the days off in increasing gratitude, Hawthorne exulted in the sea and wished that the voyage might be indefinitely prolonged.

The end of June, 1860, found the Hawthorne family once more settled at the Wayside, where the long-talked-of repairs were soon under way, proving a satisfaction and also an added anxiety, as, like all repairs, they turned out a far greater expense than had been anticipated.

On June 28, Hawthorne writes in regard to a plan for his immediate entertainment among his literary friends, and voices his usual antipathy to anything like a banquet in his honor.

DEAR TICKNOR, — We arrived here safely, and are established in our little house, and as comfortable as can be imagined.

Mr. Emerson has just called, and says he will not be able to come to your dinner, if it is to take place as soon as Monday, — inasmuch as he is to go over to Ohio for a week. It would also be more convenient for me to come to Boston some little time hence. Could the dinner be put off a week or so?

In a great hurry,

Your friend,

NATHᴸ HAWTHORNE.

P.S. Act as you think best about the dinner. I shall be ready at any moment — only pray don't let it take the form of a banquet in my honor! You will think me vain for apprehending any such thing.

N. H.

By the end of September the expense account for the improvements has begun to worry the owner of the Wayside. He writes anxiously: —

DEAR TICKNOR,

or DEAR FIELDS: —

I am in need of $50; and the case being urgent I wish you would send it by the Concord expressman (Adams) so that I may get it Friday evening. Would it not be practicable, hereafter, to give me a credit to some moderate amount in the bank in this place; so that I need not be continually bothering you for money?

Una seems entirely well; her case having yielded

at once to the incantations of a certain electrical witch. This doctress says that the crisis was a most fortunate one, and that without it she would have been subject to a life-long disease.

Your friend,

NATH^L HAWTHORNE.

The response to Hawthorne's request having been at once complied with he writes a few days later: —

DEAR TICKNOR, — Five hundred dollars is just the sum to begin with.

Una, I am happy to say, appears perfectly well. From henceforth, forever, I shall recommend medical electricity for all diseases. Driscoll had better try it. Mrs. Rollins, of Cambridge, is the doctress.

I am glad that you took a little time for recreation, and I only wish I could have been with you.

Your friend,

NATH^L HAWTHORNE.

P.S. My house begins to make a good appearance.

The end of the month brings still greater demands for the enlargement of the family treasury in order to defray the necessary expenses for building. The anxious author writes: —

" I have a bill for timber and other building materials to pay, amounting to $484, or thereabouts; and I wish you would send me another check for $500, available at the Concord Bank. I have still some of the former $500 remaining, but want to reserve it to draw upon at need. I should like this money in a day or two, if convenient.

"I have a bad cold, which I caught in coming home, last Saturday."

The next communication is penned on behalf of a needy friend, and goes to prove that it is not only within the walls of a consulate that the man who "must have a small loan" turns up.

DEAR TICKNOR, — I have given B—— an order on you for $50. Pay it, and I promise you not to trouble you again on his account. It is impossible not to assist an old acquaintance in distress — for once, at least.

Your friend,
NATH^L HAWTHORNE.

P.S. Do not write me about this; for I do not wish my wife to know how I throw away money.

A few days prior to this note he writes: —

DEAR TICKNOR, — We bought a carpet at Chipman's, Hanover Street, price $32.23. The bill will probably be sent you; and if the amount is as above stated, you would oblige me by paying it. I enclose a bill for marble fireplaces; and shall take the liberty to tell the dealer to call on you for payment. If ever I can repay for all this trouble by taking charge of your business, you may command me; but I doubt whether you would be quite as well satisfied with my administration as I am with yours.

Your friend, (in haste)
NATH^L HAWTHORNE.

At the end of the first week in December the house-repairing department is still calling for "more." He writes: —

" I find that my cash balance at the bank is getting very low; and as I have some immediate payments to make on account of the new house, I wish you would give me another credit for $500.

"I find the weather terribly cold this morning — colder than I have known it for eight years."

The day following he says: —

"The study-table is all right; and I am writing this note at it in my new study.

" Business is now so dull that I should think you might find time to come and smoke a cigar with me in this comfortable room. The rest of the tower is not yet finished.

" I told some marble manufacturers, whose names I have forgotten, to send you their bill for fireplaces, — sixty dollars or thereabouts.

" Is there going to be a general smash?"

Rumors of the "hard times," which affected the book trade, as it did all other business interests, reached Hawthorne rather vaguely, and he realized, to only a very limited extent, the many perplexities which beset his friend in his dealing with authors and publishers across the seas, in addition to his business responsibilities at home.

Extracts from a letter written in 1860, to Mr. Ticknor's son Howard, then in London, set forth some of the trials which were the portion of the man whose honorable treatment of English authors and publishers did not always elicit equally fair treatment in return. Ticknor herein states clearly his intention to pursue a course of absolute fairness towards other American publishers, enjoining his son not to make any overtures towards authors whose works are already upon the lists of other American houses.

Boston, October 16, 1860.

My DEAR SON, — Before you receive this you will have received my letter of last Friday touching the matter of the "Odd People." I repeat that I think R—— & Co. are very much to blame in this business. This delay in sending us the casts has caused the whole trouble, and has cost us, to say the least, all the profits of this book. The buying advanced sheets is at an end unless we can have the advantage of time more than has been allowed us in the past year. The year past has been most unfortunate for us in regard to reprints. I had much rather take my chance and pay nothing than to "swamp" $3000 on books from which we get nothing. I shall wait for an explanation from R—— before I make up my mind fully, in regard to that house. But my present impressions are not much in favor of that house. I shall write them, also Mayne Reid, by this mail. I see by the English papers that the "Book of Animals," for which we have paid $——, has been published in London; — we have the casts of the illustrations, but the book has not appeared. You will see at once that we cannot pay for "early sheets," if we do not receive them. In fact, for the present we must hold off, as the ——s are evidently resolved to print whatever we get that is popular. Mr. Fields is in New York, but has made no arrangement with them, and I think they are not disposed to make any terms. They think we are paying too much to English authors and are bound to put a stop to it. This, of course, is for you and nobody else.

I hope you got Mr. Fields's letter in time to countermand your order for Miss Procter's poem. You know that Appleton published her first volume and they will publish this, but will not pay any such price as £40, — so they say; . . . if the sheets come to us I shall at once send them to D. A. & Co., and let them pay what they please, which will probably be about £10; the balance, if you are bound by your offer, we shall pocket as loss.

You must not make an offer for any book if any publisher in this country has published the previous book by the same author: I mean exclusively. If different publishers have published, then the objection is withdrawn. This matter you well understood, as it was very fully discussed by us last winter. Leaving out Tennyson, we have hardly made a dollar on our reprints for the past twelve months, and this, as you may suppose, is not very satisfactory. We cannot pay to English authors and publishers as much as we have done, unless we can have more protection than they have given us in advance sheets. This, as you will remember, I explained to Mr. Fields when he was in Europe. He is now convinced that I was right, and says we must hold on. This business has cost us some "thousands," and the result is not different from what I anticipated.

I think, notwithstanding, that we can pay for good
English works, if they can be sent us promptly; —
but not if they are to be sent a week or so before publication in England. This business must be more de-
finitely understood. You will find it necessary to be
very guarded in your bargains with English publishers; I mean, to make your agreements very specific.
I write thus, for I feel that our arrangements for the
past year have not been profitable, but I hope better
things for the year to come. In regard to C. Pat-
more's new Poem, — we shall remit him the amount
direct.

Your work in regard to the plates for "Scott" is
capital. . . . I send by this mail the November number of the "North American."

I hope to hear in regard to Mary Howitt, as we can
do nothing, as at present advised, in regard to her
translation. We are entirely in the dark as to this
book. The city at present is all excitement. Politics
and the "Prince" take the public. . . .

Your affectionate father,
W. D. TICKNOR.

While his friend faced the problems and vexations
which in war-times were gathering thick and fast,
and was endeavouring to straighten out the tangled
threads attached to foreign literary projects, Hawthorne rejoiced in the completion of his harassing and
irritating repairs. He had long desired a tower in
which to do his writing, and now he had attained his
wish. The villa which he had occupied at Montaüto
had possessed one, which was the prototype of that

of Monte Beni. During the brief stay in this ancient edifice Hawthorne had delighted in the picturesque tower, with its ghost, its historic memories, and its owls. Here it had been Hawthorne's custom to ascend every evening with his family and to sit watching the stars till bedtime. Not far away from this romantic point of vantage was that other tower associated with Mrs. Browning's "Aurora Leigh."

The tower at the Wayside possessed neither the gloom nor the wild picturesqueness of its historic predecessor, but it was none the less a tower, though it was reached by a narrow wooden staircase which ascended abruptly through the floor.

When finished, the tower-room was about twenty feet square, and its four gables commanded a delightful view, which, if it failed to rival the outlook of the Italian villa, was yet a lovely bit of fair New England. This study had five windows, one of which faced the hill which was Hawthorne's favorite resort in leisure hours. The tower-room contained closets for books, and a high desk at which the author sometimes wrote standing, though this innovation appealed to him but slightly, and has been referred to by a member of his household in the following terms: "It was suggested by a relative, whose intellect, strength of will, and appetite for theories were of equally splendid proportions, that my father only needed a high desk at which to stand, when writing, to be restored to all his pristine vigor. With his usual tolerance of possible wisdom, he permitted such a desk to be arranged in the tower-study at the Wayside; but with his inexorable contempt for mistakes of judgment, he never, after a brief trial, used it for writing."

Hawthorne continued as of old, to write upon his simple desk of walnut wood, at which he plied the gold pen which he always used, leaving the new upright desk standing like an unwarranted intruder in its deserted corner of the tower-room. He wrote principally in the morning, with great absorption and regularity, and continued this practice until failing health caused him to labor less steadily. Hawthorne could best carry on a train of thought while walking, which he enjoyed doing in the fresh air when practicable, and when during periods of meditation he could not walk out of doors, he moved back and forth in his room, sturdily alert, his hands clasped behind him, quietly thinking, his head bent forward, or suddenly lifted upward, with a light in his gray eyes.

In Springtime and in autumn, Hawthorne's new study was very pleasant, but it was far too hot in summer, and in the winter-time its guardian stove rendered the atmosphere almost unbearable, so that the tower at Concord possessed certain drawbacks, though it lacked the ghostly inhabitants of its Italian prototype. Hawthorne, however, spent several hours daily in his tower, when it was possible to do so, and it was here that he penned the "Old Home," "Septimius Felton," and "Dr. Grimshawe."

When the additions were finally completed, the owner of the Wayside was surprised to find that the total expense had mounted to four times the original

Fields, Hawthorne, and Ticknor

estimate. With the following cheerful reflections he closes the year 1860: —

DEAR TICKNOR, — My building expenses will amount to about $550 dollars more than I have hitherto paid; and I shall have to draw upon your inexhaustible resources for that amount. This will make the cost of my additions somewhat more than $2000, — the original estimate having been only $500. Well, I suppose I am fortunate in getting off so cheap; but if I had known how much it was to cost me, I think I should have sold the old house and bought a better one.

I shall want some money soon for other expenses; so you may as well send me a check for $600, or $700, if convenient.

Are times so terribly bad as people say? I have left off reading newspapers and only know by hearsay that the Union is falling asunder.

I want to see you very much, but cannot conveniently leave home at this season; — the first train starting so early, and the second so late.

Your friend,

NATH^L HAWTHORNE.

About this time, Messrs. Ticknor and Fields brought out a complete edition of Walter Scott's works, and Hawthorne received a beautifully bound set from his publishers, in which the owner of the Wayside took great pleasure; he began at once to read the volumes aloud to the members of his family, who all regarded this experience as one of special privilege.

Lockhart's "Life of Sir Walter Scott" was one of Hawthorne's favorite books, and when this "Household Edition" appeared from the presses of Messrs. Ticknor and Fields, he was much gratified by the discovery that Mr. Fields had dedicated the edition to him. He wrote an enthusiastic letter of acknowledgment in which he paid his publisher a hearty compliment, asserting: "My literary success, whatever it has been, or may be, is the result of my connection with you. Somehow or other you smote the rock of public sympathy on my behalf, and a stream gushed forth in sufficient quantity to quench my thirst, though not to drown me. I think no author can ever have had publisher that he valued as I do mine."

Hawthorne's suggestions offered to Mr. Fields, after the re-reading of Scott's "Life," as to desirable additions to the last volume, are of particular interest, in view of the fact that he had repeatedly expressed violent opposition to the publishing of biographical data about himself. In this instance, Hawthorne calls for more intimate details, the rendering of which he had been wont to deplore in biographical work, and demands *more* personal items, in the name of "privileged posterity." After advising his publishers to insert in the last volume of Scott's "Life" an explanation of all that had been previously left vague, and insisting that the name of the lady with whom Scott was in love should be supplied, he adds: —

"It is desirable, too, to know what have been the fortunes and final catastrophes of his family and intimate friends since his death, down to as recent a

period as the death of Lockhart. All such matter
would make your edition more valuable; and I see
no reason why *you* should be bound by the defer-
ence to living connections of the family, that may
prevent the English publishers from inserting these
particulars.

"We stand in the light of posterity to them, and
have the privileges of posterity. . . . I should be glad
to know something of the personal character and
life of his eldest son, and whether (as I have heard)
he was ashamed of his father for being a literary
man. In short, fifty pages devoted to such elucida-
tion would make the edition unique."

Shortly after the arrival of Scott's works, Hawthorne writes Ticknor of his satisfaction in possessing the set, and in the same communication
touches upon the death of Driscoll, the tailor, who
had in times past furnished him with a variety
of garments: —

"Here is the bill sent me by poor Driscoll's ad-
ministrators, in which I find an error of $8. I be-
spoke two pairs of check pantaloons; but by some
mistake, only one pair was sent, and I afterwards
countermanded the other pair. Mr. Devereux will
remember the circumstances.

"Please not to forget that I have a payment to
make on or before the fifth (5th) of the coming
month, and should like a cheque for 300 or 400
dollars, in season for it. If I escape absolute beg-
gary, I shall thank Heaven and you. What will be
the use of having a house, if it costs me all my means
of living in it?

"Mrs. Hawthorne was completely delighted with the beautiful set of Waverley Novels; and I myself took very great pleasure in arranging them on the shelf. As soon as I have money to spare, I am going to spend it filling up some bookcases."

A fortnight later, Hawthorne declares that his literary work does not progress very rapidly in his tower-room.

DEAR TICKNOR, — I suppose the enclosed bill, or one similar to it, will be sent you; and you will much oblige me by paying it.

You have not yet been to see us; and I have hardly the heart to ask you, till our place shall look a little less dreary. The melting of the snow discloses so much rubbish to be removed, in the vicinity of the house, that I fear we shall not have a decent lawn for several months to come. Within doors, we are getting arranged by slow degrees.

I spend two or three hours a day in my sky-parlor, and duly spread a quire of paper on my desk; but no very important result has followed, thus far. Perhaps, however, I shall have a new Romance ready, by the time New England becomes a separate nation—a consummation I rather hope for than otherwise.

Your friend,

NATH^L HAWTHORNE.

By the middle of May, the repairs on the house were actually completed, but whatever satisfaction should have come with this accomplishment, was banished by the persistent rumors of the war, which constantly invaded the peaceful habitation of the writer of romances, penetrating even to the tower-room, and causing Hawthorne to explain in his next letter: —

"The war continues to interrupt my literary industry; and I am afraid it will be long before Romances are in request again, even if I could write one. I wish I could turn my hand to any useful labor. If I were younger, I would volunteer; but as the case stands, I shall keep quiet till the enemy gets within a mile of my own house.

"The house, by the by, is finished and painted, and really makes a very pretty appearance. It is odd, however, that I have never felt so earnest a desire to go back to England as now that I have irrevocably planted myself at home."

On May 26, Hawthorne writes cheerfully in regard to the return of some of his various loans: —

"Bridge has sent me $545, — being $500 principal and $45 interest on his note; so please to endorse this amount on the note. It comes unexpectedly, but not inopportunely; for I have a payment of about that amount to make soon.

"B——writes me that he has got a place as watchman at the Navy Yard which will keep him from starving. He would like to have his watch again, and I shall either send or bring it to you shortly. He must have it without refunding the $20, for he can be in no condition, at present, to pay debts.

"I think my health is rather better than it has

been for some time past; but I doubt whether I shall ever again be so well as I used to be in England. If I had established myself by the seashore instead of in this inland town, perhaps it would have been better; but I have fastened myself down by taking a house on my back. It is folly for a mortal man to do anything more than pitch a tent.

"I wish they would push on the war a little more briskly. The excitement had an invigorating effect on me for a time, but it begins to lose its influence. But it is rather unreasonable to wish my countrymen to kill one another for the sake of refreshing my palled spirits; so I shall pray for peace."

About this time, Hawthorne turned his attention to the beginning of "Dr. Grimshawe," but in all his efforts to concentrate upon his work, he seemed constantly to hear the echoes from afar, which cried out and seemed to mock his attempts at fiction, and to call to him that this was the day of cold, cruel facts.

In March, 1862, his health being rather precarious, it was decided that he should take a trip southward, accompanied by his friend Ticknor, and that he should have a chance to see for himself those conditions upon which all general interest was at this time focused, while benefitting from this change of scene and climate. He wrote from Concord, March 3, 1862: —

DEAR TICKNOR: — The magazines make a splendid addition to my book-shelves. I sincerely thank you for them.

I suppose Thursday holds good for our time of

starting. I have forgotten at what hour we are to
leave Boston, and will thank you to let me know.

Truly yours,

NATH⁺ HAWTHORNE.

This trip proved decidedly beneficial to Hawthorne, who returned in improved health and spirits,
and promptly set forth his experiences in his most
characteristic manner, in an article entitled "Chiefly
About War-Matters," which was published in the
"Atlantic Monthly" for July of that year. Its
opening words most admirably express the point of
view of the writer as he reflects upon the war and
its effect upon a literary recluse like himself:—

"There is no remoteness of life, and no hermeti-
cally sealed seclusion except, possibly, that of the
grave, into which the disturbing influences of this
war do not penetrate. Of course, the general heart-
quake of the country long ago knocked at my cottage door, and compelled me reluctantly to suspend
the contemplation of certain fantasies, to which,
according to my harmless custom, I was endeavoring to give a sufficiently life-like aspect, to admit of
their figuring in a Romance.

"As I make no pretensions to state-craft, or soldier-
ship, and could promote the common weal neither
by valor nor counsel, it seemed at first a pity that I
should be debarred from such unsubstantial business as I had contrived for myself, since nothing
more genuine was to be substituted for it. But I
magnanimously considered that there is a kind of
treason in insulating one's self from the universal

fear and sorrow and thinking one's idle thoughts in
the dread time of civil war; and could a man be so
cold and hard-hearted, he would better deserve to
be sent to Fort Warren than many who have found
their way thither on the score of violent, but mis-
directed sympathies. . . . So I gave myself up to
reading newspapers and listening to the click of the
telegraph, like other people; until, after a great
many months of such pastime, it grew so abomin-
ably irksome that I determined to look a little more
closely at matters with my own eyes. Accordingly
we set out — a friend and myself — towards Washington, while it was still the long, dreary January
of our Northern year, though March in name; nor
were we unwilling to clip a little margin off the five
months' winter, during which there is nothing genial
in New England save the fireside."

XV

WASHINGTON IN 1862

"IT was a clear, frosty morning when we started," wrote Hawthorne. "The sun shone brightly on snow-covered hills in the neighborhood of Boston, and burnished the surface of frozen ponds; and the wintry weather kept along with us while we trundled through Worcester and Springfield, and all those old familiar towns, and through the village-cities of Connecticut. In New York the streets were afloat with liquid mud and slosh. Over New Jersey there was still a thin covering of snow, with the face of Nature visible through the rents in her white shroud, though with little or no symptoms of reviving life. But when we reached Philadelphia the air was mild and balmy; there was but a patch or two of dingy winter here and there, and the bare, brown fields about the city were ready to be green. We had met the spring halfway, in her slow progress from the South; and if we kept onward at the same pace, and could get through the Rebel lines, we should soon come to fresh grass, fruit-blossoms, green-peas, strawberries, and all such delights of early summer."

The "pace" set by Hawthorne was a somewhat more leisurely one than that which his friend had planned that they should follow. Ticknor was eager to reach Washington before the many thousand troops assembled there had crossed the Potomac, but owing to his friend's reluctance to be hurried, they did not arrive at the capital until after the troops had gone.

Mr. Ticknor wrote from the Continental Hotel, Philadelphia, to his wife: —

"We are thus far on our journey without accident. Our ride to New York was not fatiguing; arrived at the Fifth Avenue Hotel at 5 o'clock with great appetites, I assure you, for after a moderate breakfast and a ride of 240 miles, one has a right to be hungry and so I think we did full justice to the half-past-five o'clock dinner.

"We passed a pleasant evening at a literary club where we met some very agreeable gentlemen — getting home at 11. Instead of leaving the next morning for Philadelphia, we concluded to take the train at 2 P.M. for this city, arriving at 7½, somewhat tired, for we had done a deal of walking in the morning, — but after a good night's rest, I feel none the worse for it. The weather has been delightful. To-day is a lovely spring day. There is no snow here; now and then a little ice may be seen, but the streets are dry and clean.

"I hoped to have been in Washington last night, but Mr. Hawthorne is not disposed to travel nights. He says he is on a trip for pleasure and intends 'to take it easy.' He is in good spirits and appears to enjoy himself. He has no care. He leaves the entire business part with me. If he wants a pair of gloves I pay for them; as I do all bills for joint accounts. He says this is the only way he can travel with comfort, and it is no trouble to me. He is hoping for exciting times in Washington this week, and it is generally believed that an important move is about to be made. I hope it may occur while I am in Washington. If there shall be any reasonable prospects of this, I shall remain rather than go farther. . . .

"I have been reading (yesterday) the new tax bill, as proposed, and in many parts it seems so absurd that I shall see what I can do with our 'delegation' to expose its absurdities. I do not think that A.H.R. is a man equal to the times as a M.C. The bill, as it now stands, will impose a heavy 'tax on knowledge,' — directly and indirectly, — which is certainly a most unwise thing to do. Give the people every facility for acquiring knowledge, and you will have good citizens. I mean useful knowledge; — put the tax on other things, liquors, wines, cigars, rich dresses, luxuries of every sort, but not on the means by which the people are educated. I should like to be a Member of Congress long enough to make a speech on this subject; — but as it is not necessary to make it now, I leave the question for the present.

"We shall leave for Washington early to-morrow; the only discomfort I have had is my coat. It is a perfect 'unfit,' and I made a mistake in not taking my frock. It is very strange that Devereux could have made such a blunder."

As the friends journeyed toward the capital, the signs and rumors of war increased, and everywhere military life became the pervading interest; a guard seemed to hold every station along the railroad, and on the hillsides they saw collections of weather-beaten tents and fortifications with muzzles of cannon protruding from the ramparts.

Hawthorne describes this military pervasiveness in his usual whimsical vein.

"Our stopping-places were thronged with soldiers, some of whom came through the cars, asking for newspapers that contained accounts of the battle between the Merrimack and Monitor, which had been fought the day before. A railway train met us, conveying a regiment out of Washington to some unknown point; and reaching the capital, we filed out of the station between lines of soldiers, with shouldered muskets, putting us in mind of similar spectacles at the gates of European cities. It was not without sorrow that we saw the free circulation of a nation's life-blood (at the very heart, moreover) clogged with such strictures as these, which have caused chronic diseases in almost all countries save our own.

"Will the time ever come again, in America, when we may live half a score of years without once seeing the likeness of a soldier, except it be in the festal march of a company on its summer tour? Not in this generation, I fear, nor in the next, nor till the Millennium; and even that blessed epoch, as the prophecies seem to intimate, will advance to the sound of the trumpet.

"One terrible idea occurs, in reference to this matter. Even supposing the war should end tomorrow, and the army melt into the mass of the population within the year, what an incalculable preponderance will there be of military titles and

pretensions for at least half a century to come!
Every country-neighborhood will have its general or
two, its three or four colonels, half a dozen majors,
and captains without end, — besides non-commis-
sioned officers and privates, more than the recruit-
ing officers ever knew of; — all with their campaign
stories, which will become the staple of fireside
talk forever more. Military merit, or rather, since
that is not so readily estimated, military notoriety,
will be the measure to all claims to civil distinction. One bullet-headed general will succeed another in the Presidential chair; and veterans will
hold the offices at home and abroad, and sit in Congress and state legislatures, and fill all the avenues
of public life.

"And yet I do not speak deprecatingly, since, very
likely, it may substitute something more real and
genuine, instead of the many shams on which men
have heretofore founded their claims to public regard; but it behooves civilians to consider their
wretched prospects in the future, and assume the
military button before it is too late."

Hawthorne's disinclination to hurry proved rather
a disappointment to his friend, who voices his regret
in his next letter from Washington: —

"As I wrote from Philadelphia, Mr. Hawthorne
was not disposed to hurry, although I told him I was
anxious to reach Washington and thought we ought
not to delay our journey on the way. We left Philadelphia on Monday morning, passed two hours in
Baltimore, and reached Washington at 6½ in the

evening, just in time to miss the grand view of the Army, as from 12 o'clock Sunday evening to 4 on Monday, some 60,000 crossed the Potomac, and they, with probably a much larger number on the other side of the river, had moved forward, — and in consequence it has been impossible for a civilian, unless he had official business, to obtain a pass to cross the river. If I could have obtained one I should have seen Manassas before this. But I shall succeed in a day or two, if I make up my mind to stay long enough to take this trip.

"I was, of course, a good deal disappointed in finding the 'bird had flown,' and had we left as we purposed we should have been here in just the right time, or had we come directly through on Saturday. The moving of the troops, their wagons, etc., is said to have been a very grand sight. They say Washington seems like Sunday compared with what it has been the past year, but there are many thousands of soldiers in and around Washington now, and the city is to me more lively now than I have ever seen it before. I have been among the camps, which has occupied most of the mornings. I shall hardly care to go again unless I cross the river.

"I have been twice to the Capitol, but there is little of interest going on in Congress at present. Yesterday morning we called on the President, quite early, with Mr. Train, of Massachusetts, who was charged with the duty of presenting to the President a whip, manufactured by the American Whip Company, of Pittsfield. I dare say you will see some account of it in the 'Journal,' as Perley was present.

"Last evening I went to Mr. and Mrs. Samuel Hooper's weekly reception. It was not a very brilliant affair. The number present was not very large; — Lord Lyons, and Fanny Kemble, Governor Andrew, and Caleb Cushing were among the number, however. I spent two hours with Mr. Rice in the evening; at 10 we made the call and got home at 11½. I pass considerable time at Willard's, where you meet everybody in the morning and evening. There is great fault found with McClellan and what will be the result I don't know. He has many enemies out of Congress as well as in that body."

A brief extract from Hawthorne's picturesque description of their impression of Washington at this time, and of the call upon President Lincoln, from which, at the time of printing, Mr. Fields thought it wise to eliminate the personal description of the President, forms an interesting supplement to Ticknor's brief résumé of their doings: —

"We were not in time to see Washington as a camp. On the very day of our arrival sixty thousand men had crossed the Potomac on their march towards Manassas; and almost with their first step into the Virginia mud, the phantasmagory of a countless host and impregnable ramparts, before which they had so long remained quiescent, dissolved quite away. It was as if General McClellan had thrust his sword into a gigantic enemy, and, beholding him suddenly collapse, had discovered to himself and the world that he had merely punctured an enormously swollen bladder. There are instances of a similar character in old romances, where great armies are long kept at bay by the arts of necromancers, who build airy towers and battlements, and muster warriors of terrible aspect, and thus feign a defense of seeming impregnability, until some bolder champion of the besiegers dashes forward to try an encounter with the foremost foeman, and finds him melt in the death-grapple. With such heroic adventure let the march upon Manassas be hereafter reckoned. . . .

"The troops being gone, we had better leisure and opportunity to look into other matters. It is natural enough to suppose that the centre and heart of Washington is the Capitol; and certainly in its outward aspects, the world has not many statelier or more beautiful edifices, nor any, I should suppose, more skilfully adapted to legislative purposes, and to all accompanying needs."

After describing Secretary Seward, Hawthorne continues: —

"Of course, there was one other personage, in the class of statesmen, whom I should have been truly mortified to leave Washington without seeing; since (temporarily, at least, and by force of circumstance) he was the man of men. But a private grief had built up a barrier about him, impeding the customary free intercourse of Americans with their chief magistrate; so that I might have come away without a glimpse of his very remarkable physiognomy, save for a semi-official opportunity of which I was glad to take advantage. The fact is, we were invited to annex ourselves, as supernumeraries, to a deputation that was about to wait upon the President, from a Massachusetts whip-factory, with a present of a splendid whip.

"Our immediate party consisted only of four or five (including Major Ben Perley Poore, with his notebook and pencil), but we were soon joined by several other persons, who seemed to have been lounging about the precincts of the White House, under the spacious porch, or within the hall, and who swarmed in with us to take the chances of a presentation."

It is, indeed, a most amusing picture which Hawthorne conjures up for us, of this incongruous group approaching the towering form of Lincoln; in front, the gentleman from Massachusetts with his imposing presentation whip, and following humbly in his train the modest author of "The Scarlet Letter," who writes: —

"Nine ò'clock had been appointed as the time for receiving the deputation; and we were punctual to the moment; but not so the President, who sent us word that he was eating his breakfast, and would come as soon as he could. His appetite, we were glad to think, must have been a pretty fair one; for we waited half an hour in one of the ante-chambers, and then we were ushered into a reception-room, in one corner of which sat the Secretaries of War and of the Treasury, expecting, like ourselves, the termination of the Presidential breakfast. During this interval there were several additions to this group, one or two of whom were in working garb, so that we formed a very miscellaneous collection of people,

mostly unknown to each other, and without any
common sponsor, but all with an equal right to look
our head servant in the face. By and by there was
a little stir on the staircase and in the passageway,
and . . ."

At this point the editor of the "Atlantic Monthly"
thought it wise to omit the writer's portrait of
the chief magistrate, and Hawthorne acquiesced
reluctantly, declaring that the editor had ruled out
his most important passage, and one possessing real
historical value. Nine years later, Mr. Fields inserted the tabooed description in his volume of
reminiscences, where it long stood, a disjointed
fragment, to be in later years once more connected
with its preceding paragraph. In this pen-portrait,
Hawthorne embodies the vivid impression which
Lincoln made upon him, as he and his friend, for
the first time, stood in the presence of this great and
eccentric figure.

"In lounged a tall, loose-jointed figure, of an exaggerated Yankee port and demeanor, whom (as
being about the homeliest man I ever saw, yet by no
means repulsive or disagreeable) it was impossible
not to recognize as Uncle Abe.

"Unquestionably, Western man though he be,
and Kentuckian by birth, President Lincoln is the
essential representative of all Yankees, and the veritable specimen, physically, of what the world seems
determined to regard as our characteristic qualities.
It is the strangest and yet the fittest thing, in the
jumble of human vicissitudes, that he, out of so
many millions, unlooked for, unselected by any in-

telligible process that could be based upon his genuine qualities, unknown to those who chose him, and
unsuspected of what endowments may adapt him
for his tremendous responsibility, should have
found the way open for him to fling his lank personality into the chair of state, — where, I presume,
it was his first impulse to throw his legs on the coun-
cil-table, and tell the Cabinet Ministers a story.
There is no describing his lengthy awkwardness, nor
the uncouthness of his movements; and yet it seems
as if I had been in the habit of seeing him daily,
and had shaken hands with him a thousand times
in some village street; so true was he to the aspect of
the pattern American, though with a certain extravagance which, possibly, I exaggerated still further by
the delightful eagerness with which I took it in. If
put to guess his calling and livelihood, I should have
taken him for a country schoolmaster as soon as
anything else."

Surely no portrait painter has given us any more
striking picture of Lincoln, than this painted by
Hawthorne's picturesque pen as he continues: —

"He was dressed in a rusty black frock-coat and
pantaloons, unbrushed, and worn so faithfully that
the suit had adapted itself to the curves and angu-
larities of his figure, and had grown to be an outer
skin of the man. He had shabby slippers on his feet.
His hair was black, still unmixed with gray, stiff,
somewhat bushy, and had apparently been acquainted with neither brush nor comb that morning, after the disarrangement of the pillow; and as
to a nightcap, Uncle Abe probably knows nothing

of such effeminacies. His complexion is dark and
sallow, betokening, I fear, an insalubrious atmosphere around the White House; he has thick black
eyebrows and an impending brow; his nose is large,
and the lines about his mouth are very strongly
defined.

"The whole physiognomy is as coarse a one as you
would meet anywhere in the length and breadth of
the States; but withal, it is redeemed, illumined,
softened, and brightened by a kindly though serious
look out of his eyes, and an expression of homely
sagacity, that seems weighted with rich results of
village experience. A great deal of native sense; no
bookish cultivation, no refinement; honest at heart,
and thoroughly so, and yet, in some sort, sly, —
at least, endowed with a sort of tact and wisdom
that are akin to craft, and would impel him, I think,
to take an antagonist in flank, rather than to make
a bull-run at him right in front. But, on the whole,
I liked this sallow, queer, sagacious visage, with the
homely human sympathies that warmed it; and, for
my small share in the matter, would as lief have
Uncle Abe for a ruler as any man whom it would
have been practicable to put in his place.

"Immediately on his entrance the President ac-
costed our Member of Congress, who had us in
charge, and, with a comical twist of his face, made
some jocular remark about the length of breakfast.
He then greeted us all round, not waiting for an
introduction, but shaking and squeezing everybody's hand with the utmost cordiality, whether the
individual's name was announced or not. His man-

ner towards us was wholly without pretence, but yet
had a kind of natural dignity, quite sufficient to
keep the forwardest of us from clapping him on the
shoulder and asking for a story. A mutual acquaintance being established, our leader took the whip out
of its case, and began to read the address of presentation. The whip was an exceedingly long one, its
handle wrought in ivory (by some artist in the Massachusetts State Prison, I believe), and ornamented
with a medallion of the President, and other equally
beautiful devices; and along its whole length there
was a succession of golden bands and ferrules. The
address was shorter than the whip, but equally well
made, consisting chiefly of an explanatory description of these artistic designs, and closing with a hint
that the gift was a suggestive and emblematic one,
and that the President would recognize the use to
which such an instrument should be put.

"This suggestion gave Uncle Abe rather a delicate
task in his reply, because, slight as the matter
seemed, it apparently called for some declaration, or
intimation, or faint foreshadowing of policy in reference to the conduct of the war, and the final
treatment of the Rebels. But the President's Yankee
aptness and not-to-be-caughtness stood him in good
stead, and he jerked or wriggled himself out of the
dilemma with an uncouth dexterity that was entirely in character; although, without his gesticula-
tion of eye and mouth, — and especially the flourish
of the whip, with which he imagined himself touching
up a pair of fat horses, — I doubt whether his words
would be worth recording, even if I could remember

them. The gist of the reply was, that he accepted the whip as an emblem of peace, not punishment; and, this great affair over, we retired out of the presence in high good-humour, only regretting that we could not have seen the President sit down and fold up his legs (which is said to be a most extraordinary spectacle), or have heard him tell one of those delectable stories for which he is so celebrated. A good many of them are afloat upon the common talk of Washington, and are certainly the aptest, pithiest, funniest little things imaginable; though, to be sure, they smack of the frontier freedom, and would not always bear repetition in a drawing-room, or the immaculate page of the 'Atlantic.'"

This picture, which for nine years slumbered in Mr. Fields's portfolio, is intensely characteristic both of Hawthorne, and the great statesman whom he describes, and in regard to whom he writes in the following paragraph: —

"Good Heavens! What liberties have I been taking with one of the potentates of the earth, and the man on whose conduct more important consequences depend than on any other historical personage of the century."

During their stay, the friends visited Alexandria, a little port on the Potomac, which they found thronged with Northern soldiery, who seemed to be regarded as unwelcome guests by the native population. Here they inspected the tavern in which Colonel Ellsworth was killed, saw the spot where he fell, and the stairs below, where Jackson fired the fatal shot, and where he was himself slain a moment after-wards. Already the memorial-hunters had completely cut away the original woodwork around the spot, with their pocket-knives; indeed, so much of the immediate environment had been carried off and renewed, that Hawthorne questioned whether the place of the murder still actually existed. Outside of Alexandria they stopped to inspect an old slave-pen, which was looked upon as one of the points of interest, and a little farther on they viewed an old brick church where Washington used at times to attend service.

They enjoyed a visit to Fort Ellsworth, where they looked out upon a beautiful view of the Potomac and the surrounding country, now so generally disfigured by those unsightly fortifications, of which Hawthorne asserted: "Their bare precipitous sides will remain as historic monuments, grass-grown and picturesque memorials of an epoch of terror and suffering: they will serve to make our country dearer and more interesting to us, and afford fit soil for poetry to root itself in: for this is a plant which thrives best in spots where blood has been spilt long ago, and grows in abundant clusters in old ditches, such as the moat around Fort Ellsworth will be a century hence. It may seem to be paying dear for what many will reckon but a worthless weed; but the more historical associations we can link with our localities, the richer will be the daily life that feeds upon the past, and the more valuable the things that have been long established: so that our children will be less prodigal than their fathers in sacrificing good institutions to passionate impulses and impracticable theories. This herb of grace, let us hope, may be found in the footprints of the war."

On March 20, Ticknor writes regarding two visits to the headquarters of General McClellan, which were established at Fairfax Seminary, on a gentle elevation amid very agreeable scenery. He says: "Each day I had a good opportunity of meeting General McClellan and taking him by the hand. I also met Mrs. McClellan yesterday, at a grand review of 12,000 troops at Fairfax Seminary. It was a grand affair. I have not time now to write about it. I went some out of my way to see John Whitney. He returned from Manassas on Saturday in the midst of a terrible storm, and was obliged to lie upon the wet ground without shelter, on Saturday night. He is well, and anxious, as are all the troops, to go forward. Great numbers are embarking for the South. It is supposed that General McClellan will take command of this expedition and that Banks will take charge of his post on the Potomac."

Hawthorne has registered his impression of General McClellan, as they saw him upon the field reviewing his troops on one of these occasions. He writes: "They received him with loud shouts, by the eager uproar of which — now near, now in the centre, now on the outskirts of the division, and now sweeping back towards us in a great volume of sound — we could trace his progress through the ranks. If he is a coward, or a traitor, or a humbug, or anything less than a brave, true, and able man, that mass of intelligent soldiers, whose lives and honor he had in charge, were utterly deceived, and so was the present writer;

for they believed in him, and so did I; and had I stood in the ranks, I should have shouted with the lustiest of them." Yet this expressed "belief" of Hawthorne's is not of long duration, for despite his having recorded this favorable impression of the enthusiasm evoked by McClellan when on parade, Hawthorne wrote home to his daughter shortly after, concerning him: "Tell mamma that the outcry opened against General McClellan, since the enemy's retreat from Manassas, is really terrible, and almost universal; because it is found that we might have taken their fortifications with perfect ease six months ago, they being defended chiefly by wooden guns. Unless he achieves something wonderful within a week, he will be removed from command, and perhaps shot, — at least I hope so; for I never did more than half believe in him."

Another excursion taken by Hawthorne and his publisher, was to Harper's Ferry; the directors of the Baltimore and Ohio Railroad having invited them to accompany a party on the first trip over the newly laid track, just completed after its breaking-up by the Confederate soldiers. The trip was made in a deluge of rain, and at the end of the route, the visitors were forced to flounder over portions of the track, which had not been restored, climb down an embankment, and cross the river on a pontoon-bridge, a thousand feet in length, over the narrow line of which, level with the river and rising and subsiding with it, General Banks had recently led his whole army. Below them lay the broken bridge and all

about were strewn quantities of wreckage. Having
reached their destination, the visitors were guided to
the little building which John Brown seized upon as
his fortress, and which, after it was stormed by the
United States Marines, became his temporary prison.
This, once an old engine-house, stood only a short distance from the river's bank, and on either side of the
door, in its front wall, were the loop-holes through
which John Brown had fired upon his besiegers, before
they succeeded in breaking down the door. This edifice had been turned into a prison for Confederate
captives, and upon these forlorn wretches the visitors gazed with compassion, subsequently conversing
with them for some little time.

A trip to Fortress Monroe proved exceedingly interesting to both travelers, although Ticknor suffered from a severe cold in consequence, which kept
him housed for a day or so after their return. As
mere pleasure parties were not allowed to cross the
river into Virginia, the friends were appointed upon
a special committee to visit the Fortress officially,
and their pass, autographed by Secretary Stanton,
was always preserved by Mr. Ticknor, who obtained
it as a souvenir of the occasion. They were received
with some ceremony by the commander of the Fortress, inspected the garrison, and then visited the
fleet, where the Monitor proved the object of special
interest, representing as it did an epoch-making advance in naval warfare which caused Hawthorne to
exclaim: "The wooden walls of Old England cease to
exist, and a whole history of naval renown reaches
its period, now that the Monitor comes smoking into

view; while billows dash over what seems her deck, and storms bury even her turret in green water, as she burrows and snorts along, oftener under the surface than above."

The various excursions ended with a trip to Manassas, and the rainy days which prevented their doing any sight-seeing were agreeably spent at Willard's hotel, which was, at that moment, the genuine center of Washington and the Union interests. Here assembled the representative men from all parts of the country, who were vitally interested in the great problem which was then being solved; here were generals, governors of states, orators, diplomats, journalists, wire-pullers and countless others, of equal interest to the author, who loved to study types, and to his friend, who, with a son at the front, was keenly interested in learning the character of the men striving to bring about a solution which should mean the firmer cementing of the Union. Ticknor did not share his friend's belief that all might be well, even if the Confederacy succeeded, nor could he acquiesce in such a suggestion as that put forth by Hawthorne, when he declared: "We woo the South 'as the Lion woos his bride'; it is a rough courtship, but perhaps love and a quiet household may come of it at last. Or, if we stop short of that blessed consummation, heaven was heaven still, as Milton sings, after Lucifer and a third part of the angels had seceded from its golden palaces, — perhaps all the more heavenly because so many gloomy brows, and soured, vindictive hearts, had gone to plot ineffectual schemes of mischief elsewhere."

At the end of the Washington visit, Hawthorne returned directly home, leaving his friend to continue his trip westward, as the latter had business to transact in Chicago, and elsewhere.

On Ticknor's return he received the following communication from his friend: —

"I am happy to hear from Julian that you have returned from your wanderings and are safely established at the Old Corner again. If the trip has done you as much good as it did me, it is worth the time and money.

"Bridge paid me (300) dollars on his note, and will pay the balance when you inform him what the amount is.

"I brought home some of your standing photographs (of which see a specimen), as it was taken at the photographer's request, and there was nothing to pay. I hold them at your disposal.

"I wish you would write Derby about my large photograph. You know he promised me (and you, too, for that matter), on behalf of Mr. Garden, that I should have a copy — that was my sole inducement for standing, because I knew that Mrs. Hawthorne would like to have it. But on speaking to Garden about it, the day before I left Washington, it appeared to me that he did not intend to give the copy.

"Do come and see me. I want to talk over our travels, and your subsequent adventures."

The "standing photographs" of both Ticknor and Hawthorne, taken by Brady at this time, were admirable likenesses. Hawthorne looks perchance a bit ethereal and delicate (and he complained that his

hair was "too white"), while his friend appears somewhat stouter than ordinarily represented, having declared about this time that he was adding too much
to his weight. Yet both pictures are very characteristic of the subjects.

During their stay in Washington, Hawthorne had
been persuaded to sit to Leutze for his portrait, and
in his own opinion the likeness obtained was very
satisfactory, the sitter asserting that the picture
was "the best ever painted of the same unworthy
subject."

The first glimpse of Leutze, then at work on the
Capitol, is described by Hawthorne: —

"In quest of him, we went through halls, galleries,
and corridors, and ascended a noble staircase, balus-
traded with a dark and beautifully variegated marble
from Tennessee, the richness of which is sufficient
cause for objecting to the secession of that State. At
last we came to a barrier of pine boards, built right
across the stairs. Knocking at a rough, temporary
door, we thrust a card beneath; and in a minute or
two it was opened by a person in his shirt-sleeves, a
middle-aged figure, neither tall nor short, of Teu-
tonic build and aspect, with an ample beard of a
ruddy tinge, and chestnut hair.

"He looked at us, in the first place, with keen and
somewhat guarded eyes, as if it were not his practice
to vouchsafe any great warmth of greeting, except
upon sure ground of observation. Soon, however, his
look grew kindly and genial (not that it had ever been
in the least degree repulsive, but only reserved), and
Leutze allowed us to gaze at the cartoon of his great

fresco, and talked about it unaffectedly, as only a man of true genius can speak of his own works. Meanwhile the noble design spoke for itself upon the wall."

Hawthorne came away from this visit to Leutze cheered by the consciousness that here was at least one artist, who could, despite the stress and turmoil about him, "Keep right on, firm of heart and hand, drawing his outlines with an unwavering pencil, beautifying and idealizing our rude, material life, and thus manifesting that we have an indefeasible claim to a more enduring national existence."

And so, at the conclusion of his trip to Washington, Hawthorne turned back again to his own work with renewed vigor of body and cheerfulness of spirit.

XVI

HAWTHORNE'S last days were closely identified with the pages of the "Atlantic Monthly." There appeared the final products of his pen, followed by the beautiful tributes to the writer's memory, contributed by his friends Longfellow and Holmes. And after the manuscript of his "Septimius Felton" had been deciphered by his daughter Una, who had been aided in her task by Robert Browning, once more the name of "Nathaniel Hawthorne" appeared within the table of contents of this magazine.

The story of the founding of the "Atlantic Monthly" has been frequently told, and the description of the famous little dinner, which took place at the Parker House in May, 1857, prior to the launching of the literary enterprise, is a familiar tale. This was, in truth, the actual beginning of the preliminary arrangements, but long before this time the forthcoming magazine had taken form and substance in the mind of its first projector.

This man was Francis H. Underwood, whose heart was set upon establishing a "Literary and Anti-Slavery Magazine," and who, as early as 1853, had tried to push his project. Just at this period, "Putnam's Magazine" was at the height of its prosperity, and kindred enterprises seemed likely to succeed, so that the founding of a good literary magazine in Boston was looked upon as a desirable undertaking. At this time the phenomenal success of "Uncle Tom's Cabin" (which Lowell wittily declared might then have fittingly assumed the title of "Mansion of Uncle Thomas") had emboldened its publisher, Mr. John P. Jewett, to attempt further literary ventures. Inspired by the enthusiasm of Mr. Underwood, who was then associated with him, he purposed to issue the first number of the "Literary and Anti-Slavery Magazine," in January, 1854.

In this new enterprise the aid of Mr. Lowell was eagerly solicited by Mr. Underwood, who had already planned a noteworthy list of contributors for this organ of literary Boston. Lowell took kindly to the scheme, and sent his poem, "The Nest," to be inserted in the first issue, which was, however, not destined to see the light. The failure of the luckless publishers of "Uncle Tom's Cabin" put an end to the project, and Mr. Underwood was for the time being obliged to relinquish his literary venture.

In view of Underwood's extreme disappointment at the disastrous outcome of his pet scheme, Lowell wrote cheerily of brighter prospects yet to come, asserting that he was "truly sorry to hear of the blowing-up of the magazine," which he declared was not "so irreparable as if it had been a powder-magazine." "Moreover," he remarked, "there are as good fish in that buccaneering sea of Bibliopoly as ever were caught, and if one of them has broken away from your harpoon, I hope the next may prove a downright kraaken, on whom, if needful, you can pitch your tent and live."

And thus it was, that, three years later, when the preliminary dinner was held at Parker's, two men, at least, in the small group assembled, had thought out and digested plans for furthering, and fathering, the proposed monthly. At this time Mr. Underwood had become literary adviser and reader for the firm of Phillips and Sampson, and had with some difficulty won over to his scheme Mr. Phillips, who had the practical man's distrust of new enterprises, especially when suggested by authors and other persons possessed of the artistic temperament.

At last, however, the interest of Mr. Phillips having been enlisted, a little dinner was planned by him at which the new project was to be launched. On the 5th of May, 1857, the memorable little company assembled at the Parker House to partake of a midday repast, which began at three o'clock and continued until eight. How much of that time was spent in the consumption of viands cannot be estimated at this late date, but the host afterwards declared it was "the richest time intellectually which he had ever been privileged to enjoy." The table was set for eight, with Mr. Phillips and Mr. Underwood at either end; the other six guests were Ralph Waldo Emerson, Henry W. Longfellow, James Russell Lowell, John Lothrop Motley, Oliver Wendell Holmes, and James Elliot Cabot.

It was not strange that such a brilliant coterie should have dined to some purpose upon that pleasant day in May. Granted that a new magazine was in the air, it could not have been materialized under more favorable auspices. The name "Atlantic" was suggested by Dr. Holmes, and Lowell was promptly selected as the desired editor-in-chief, to be assisted by Mr. Underwood. The cheering news that Mrs. Stowe would be among the first contributors brought added inspiration, and the success of the new enterprise seemed from the start assured. As the result of these preliminary plans, Lowell assumed the helm and Underwood was almost immediately dispatched to England to secure the coöperation of British authors.

Prior to Underwood's departure, Lowell had written to Professor Charles Eliot Norton, then in London, telling him of the new magazine, and asking him to secure for it some English contributors.

This kindly office was promptly performed by Professor Norton, who sailed for home a couple of months later, bearing with him numerous manuscripts which he had rather hastily collected from the lesser "lights" of London. At the end of the voyage, Professor Norton saw all his luggage delivered to the driver of an express wagon, who was to carry it to a certain hotel; but when the hotel was reached, the small trunk which contained the English manuscripts had disappeared.

A frantic search ensued, and the lost literature was hunted for in all directions; the offices of the express companies were ransacked in vain, and countless hotel officials were interviewed and questioned; handbills were printed and distributed, advertisements flew broadcast, and the police force of New York was vigorously employed in seeking for the "lost trunk." But the "lost" was not found, and Lowell, who had awaited its arrival with keen interest, pronounced its disappearance "mysterious and melancholy." Yet as weeks passed, and he inspected the admirable contributions tendered by his own countrymen, he began to perceive that this dark editorial cloud was not without its silver lining.

The "Atlantic Monthly" was destined to achieve fame through its gifted American contributors, and the small trunk which helped to compass this result by vanishing with its cargo of English articles, was truly the "mascot" of the magazine.

When the first number appeared, dated November, 1857, it had a proud list of contributors, whose articles, however, were unsigned, so that the public had the supreme pleasure of guessing which individual star in the bright galaxy, had furnished this, or that, delightful contribution.

It may be interesting to recall some of the special material contained in this first number. Whittier and Longfellow had each contributed a poem; Lowell his sonnet called "The Maple," as well as verses on the "Origin of Didactic Poetry," and various editorial pages; Emerson furnished four short poems, of which two were "Days," and "Brahma," besides his essay on "Illusions"; Mrs. Stowe and J. T. Trowbridge provided short stories, there was a paper by Motley, and there appeared the first installment of the "Autocrat of the Breakfast Table."

And then at once began the "guessing." In this age of innumerable periodicals, when almost every week brings the announcement of some new venture in this crowded field, it is difficult to conceive of the wide interest excited by the advent of the much-talked-of "Atlantic." One could find no more popular theme for discussion in literary circles than that which touched upon the veiled identity of its contributors. Especially was there great interest expressed in the discovery of the "Autocrat." This problem should have been one quite easy of solution for any "memory man," for over twenty years before this time a young medical student had furnished the "New England Magazine" with two papers by the selfsame title.

From the time of its inception, the "Atlantic" became one of the institutions of New England, and its aim, "the encouragement of and the production of literature," has ever been maintained to the best of its editorial ability. It is amusing to reflect that the "Atlantic," which in subsequent years came to be regarded as the stronghold of New England conservatism, was at the start looked at askance as almost too radical to be widely commended. Emerson's articles were viewed as most heretical, and Dr. Holmes was scouted as a reincarnation of the abhorred Voltaire. Emerson's poem, entitled "Brahma," called forth great controversy, and probably awakened more widespread discussion than any other poem which has ever appeared in the "Atlantic." "What does it mean?" was the inquiry put forth by puzzled readers throughout the land, and people passing others in a crowd would overhear voices exclaiming, "Tell me what all this is about? — 'If the red slayer thinks he slays,'" and so forth.

"The Atlantic" promptly asserted its opposition to slavery, and in its second number Edmund Quincy put forth a spirited denunciation entitled "Where will it End?"

In 1859, the breaking-up of the firm of Phillips and Sampson, through the death of Mr. Phillips, caused the magazine to be upon the market, and there ensued much lively discussion regarding its final destination. It was asserted that the Harpers had threatened to buy it and "suppress their rival," but in the end the purchase was completed by Messrs. Ticknor and Fields. In regard to this acquisition it is of interest to note that it was the project of the elder, and, one would have supposed, the more conservative, member of the firm, while it was opposed by the junior, whose literary tastes and delight in the association with authors would have seemed likely to render him predisposed in its favor.

The exact history of the transaction has been described by the late Governor Alexander H. Rice, who at the time of the failure of Messrs. Phillips and Sampson was their assignee, upon whom rested the responsibility of settling the business. Mr. Rice had sent letters to a number of publishers telling them that he would sell to the highest bidder whose offer should be received by noon on a certain day. The day arrived and not one bid had come. Mr. Rice walked over to the office of Ticknor and Fields, and said to Mr. Ticknor, "I have not yet received your bid for the 'Atlantic.'"—"No," replied the publisher, "and you will not, for we don't care to undertake the responsibility of the venture."

Mr. Rice still persisted and pointed to the clock on the Old South, which then registered half-past eleven. "I am about to go to my office to open the bids," he said, "and I am sure that Ticknor and Fields will be sorry if I find none there from them." Mr. Ticknor seemed at first immovable, but gradually displayed increasing interest in Mr. Rice's appeals. At five minutes of twelve, when that gentleman had concluded his remarks, Mr. Ticknor turned to his desk and wrote a line on a piece of paper, which he handed sealed to Mr. Rice. With the sealed paper in his hand the lawyer returned to his office, and at high noon solemnly opened the one and only bid received, which offered him the sum of $10,000 for the magazine. Mr. Rice hastened back to Mr. Ticknor exclaiming, "The 'Atlantic' is yours!"

When the war began, the spirit of the "Atlantic" was set forth on its cover, which from the opening of hostilities flew the flag of the Union, in token of its loyalty.

If, in those early days (when Unitarians were looked upon as heathen), the magazine was widely criticized for its rank heresy in printing such a study of "infidelity" as Holmes's "Guardian Angel" (which it is said cost the magazine many subscribers), what was not the effect of the exploiting of Anti-slavery propaganda? From the Southern subscribers came bitter denunciations of the magazine's standpoint, and threats were received by its proprietors such as would make it seem their lives were hardly safe in Boston, and would instantly have been forfeited had they dared show themselves on Southern soil.

"It's slow business," exclaimed Dr. Holmes, "this of getting the Ark launched. I love to hear the workmen knocking at the old blocks of tradition, and making the ways smooth with the oil of the Good Samaritan. I don't know, sir, but I do think she stirs a little, — I do believe she slides; and when I think of what work that is for the dear old three-breasted mother of American liberty, I would not take all the glory of all the greatest cities in the world for my birthright in the soil of little Boston!" And it was with the aid of such delightful workmen as Dr. Holmes that the "Atlantic" did its part towards knocking out some of the well-worn "blocks" of past tradition. Yet Dr. Holmes, even while recording with satisfaction the "Hub's" best attributes, trembled somewhat when contemplating her future; he looked askance at the unsavory foreign flood that was sweeping upon her like a tidal wave, likely to inundate her altogether, and voiced his "hope that the exchanges of emigrants and remigrants will be much more evenly balanced by and by than in the present."

Having helped to launch, as well as christen, the "Atlantic," Dr. Holmes stayed by the magazine, and to the end, favored it with his contributions, and one of his very last visits was made to its editorial precincts. When urged to contribute to other periodicals, he answered, "I do not wish to listen to outside temptations. My nature is a very loyal one, and (in Prior's words): —

'I hold it both a shame and sin
To quit the good old Angel inn.'"

In Mr. Howells's delightful picture of his first journey from the West, to what he regarded as the literary center, he writes of his conviction that all the
great New England group must be of easy access
when once the traveler reached the office of the
"Atlantic Monthly." And, after reflecting upon the
literary riches of New England at this time, he
declares: —

"New York had nothing distinctive to show
for American literature but the decrepit and dot-
ing 'Knickerbocker Magazine.' 'Harper's New
Monthly,' through Curtis, had already come from
the wreck of 'Putnam's,' and it had long ceased to
be eclectic in material, and had begun to stand for
native work in the allied arts, which it has since so
magnificently advanced, but it was not distinctively
literary, and the 'Weekly' had just begun to make
itself known. The 'Century,' 'Scribner's,' the 'Cos-
mopolitan,' 'McClure's,' and I know not what others,
were still unimagined by five, ten, and twenty years,
and the 'Galaxy' was to flash and fade before any of
these should kindle its more effectual fires. The
'Nation,' which was destined to chastise, rather than
nurture, our young literature, had still six years of
dreamless potentiality before it; and the 'Nation'
was always more Bostonian than New Yorkish by
nature, whatever it was by nativity.

"Philadelphia had long counted for nothing in the
literary field. 'Graham's Magazine' at one time
showed a certain critical force, but it seemed to
perish of this expression of vitality; and there
remained 'Godey's Lady's Book' and 'Peterson's

Magazine,' publications really incredible in their
insipidity. In the South there was nothing but a
mistaken ideal, with the moral principles all standing
on their heads in defense of slavery; and in the West
there was a feeble and foolish notion that Western
talent was repressed by Eastern jealousy. At Boston
chiefly, if not at Boston alone, was there a vigorous
intellectual life among such authors as I have named.
Every young writer was ambitious to join his name
with theirs in the 'Atlantic Monthly,' and in the lists
of Ticknor and Fields, who were literary publishers
in a sense such as the business world has known
nowhere else before or since. Their imprint was a
warrant of quality to the reader, and of immortality
to the author, so that if I could have had a book
issued by them at that day I should now be in the
full enjoyment of an undying fame."

Mr. Howells has entertainingly described his first
entrance through the portals which guarded the
approach to the "Atlantic," then under the editorial
management of Mr. Fields, who had succeeded
Lowell a few months after the transfer of the magazine, and whose editorial chair Howells was himself
destined to occupy a few years hence: —

"It was the Old Corner Book-Store on Washington Street that drew my heart as soon as I had
replenished my pocket in Cornhill. After verifying
the editor of the 'Atlantic Monthly,' I wished to
verify its publishers, and it very fitly happened that
when I was shown into Mr. Fields's little room at
the back of the store, with its window looking upon
School Street, and its scholarly keeping in books and

prints, he had just got the magazine sheets of a poem of mine from the Cambridge printers.

"He was then lately from abroad, and he had the zest for American things which a foreign sojourn is apt to renew in us, though I did not know this then, and could not account for it in the kindness he expressed for my poem; . . . He introduced me to Mr. Ticknor, who I fancied had not read my poem; but he seemed to know what it was from the junior partner, and he asked me whether I had been paid for it. I confessed that I had not, and then he got out a chamois-leather bag, and took from it five half-eagles in gold and laid them on the green cloth top of the desk, in much the shape and of much the size of the Great Bear. I have never since felt myself paid so lavishly for any literary work, though I have had more for a single piece than the twenty-five dollars that dazzled me in this constellation. The publisher seemed aware of the poetic character of the transaction; he let the pieces lie a moment before he gathered them up and put them in my hand, and said, 'I always think it is pleasant to have it in gold.'"

Following this memorable encounter with the head of the firm, came a dash of cold water upon the ardor of the young Western writer. Passing out through the office he was invited to glance over the sheet containing his poem just from the printer. It was "The Pilot's Story," and as he scanned the lines the author's heart sank rapidly into his boots. Something most grievous had happened to one of the lines now printed and about to be spread broadcast throughout the land! In this poem Mr. Howells had treated a most pathetic phase of the slavery question. The scene is on a Mississippi steamboat where a young planter has gambled away the slave-girl who is the mother of his child. When he informs her of her fate she breaks out upon him with the demand: —

"What will you say to our boy when he cries for me, there in St. Louis—"

This line, which to the writer seemed the most natural and pathetic outcry, had been changed in the printer's or proof-reader's hands to read: —

"What will you say to our boy when he cries for 'Ma,' there in St. Louis—"

The consternation visible upon the young man's countenance attracted Mr. Fields's attention, and he at once set about repairing the mischief. He found that the whole edition of that sheet had been printed, and a few lively minutes ensued during which the atmosphere was charged with inquiries and responses; it was found that the final proof-reader had endeavored to improve upon the line in question; the publisher at once decided that the sheet must be reprinted and the young author took his leave, his mind at rest, but feeling a sense of bodily weakness as if he had escaped some deadly peril.

The poetical calamity thus averted was of a kind that even the "Atlantic Monthly" could not hope to escape from, and there are now on record some notable examples of the masterly achievements of the proof-reader, who is never proof against the temptation to correct the seeming blunders of the author. The late Thomas Bailey Aldrich, who was for nine years a distinguished occupant of the editorial chair, has recorded some amusing occurrences; he was at one time appalled to see the line which he had penned, "The old wound breaks out anew," amended to read, "The old woman breaks out anew"; but even this was less startling than was the transformation of "Fair Auburn, loveliest village of the plain," into "Mount Auburn, loveliest village of the plain."

This brief glance backward towards the beginnings of the "Atlantic," when the magazine took its place among the institutions of New England, and established itself as a political, as well as a literary force, may fittingly be supplemented by the words put forth on its fiftieth birthday by the then President of Princeton University, Woodrow Wilson, who declared: —

"The 'Atlantic Monthly' has enjoyed the great distinction of supplying the writing of conviction throughout the deep troubles and perplexities of half a century of contest and reconstruction. . . . We are separated from the year 1857, as men of one age are separated from those of another. We live amidst scenes and circumstances to which the events of that day can hardly be made to seem even a prelude. A stupendous civil war and economic and political reconstruction of a nation have been crowded into the brief space of fifty years, — one era closed and another opened."

Hawthorne was of that earlier era, and yet it could by no means contain him, and he exclaimed as he looked out from under its shadow: —

"How narrow, scanty, and meagre is this record of observation, compared with the immensity that was to be observed, within the bounds that we prescribed ourselves! How shallow and small a stream of thought, too, compared with the broad tide of dim emotions, ideas, associations, which were flowing through the haunted regions of imagination, intellect, and sentiment. When we see how little we can express, it is a wonder that any one ever takes up a pen a second time."

As has been previously suggested, the closing chapter of Hawthorne's life was slipped between the covers of the "Atlantic Monthly"; following his essays from the "English Notes," came his delightful article upon "War Matters"; and just before his death, those first installments of "The Dolliver Romance." And one may search in vain for a tribute to Hawthorne more exquisite than that of Longfellow, which appeared in the August number of this magazine in 1864, and closes with the lines: —

"There in seclusion and remote from men
The wizard hand lies cold,
Which at its topmost speed let fall the pen,
And left the tale half told.

"Ah! who shall lift that wand of magic power,
And that lost clew regain?
The unfinished window in Aladdin's tower
Unfinished must remain."

XVII

HAWTHORNE'S LAST LITERARY WORK

FOLLOWING his return from Washington, Hawthorne did but a small amount of literary work besides finishing his article on "War Matters," previously referred to. He continued, however, to copy and rewrite his papers on England, which from time to time appeared in the "Atlantic Monthly." This work, which he had begun early in 1862, he continued through the early part of 1863, when he wrote to his publisher on February 22: "I mean to write two more of these articles, and then hold my hand. I intend to come to Boston before the end of the week if the weather is good. It must be nearly six months since I was there! I wonder how many people there are in the world who would keep their nerves in tolerably good order through such a length of nearly solitary imprisonment?"

Before settling down to this "solitary imprisonment," Hawthorne had, with his son, taken a little outing in Maine, where he stayed at West Gouldsboro', on the mainland opposite Mount Desert. His journey thither was marked by rain, fog, and various discomforts which made the trip hardly one of unmitigated pleasure for Hawthorne, but, in the end, it proved a beneficial change from the routine of the Concord existence.

Hawthorne penned the following, while en route:—

ELLSWORTH, August 8th, '62.

DEAR TICKNOR, — We have got thus far on our way, after many hardships.

I have determined not to go to Mount Desert for two or three weeks to come. My direction for the present will be, —

Care of Mr. Barney Hill,
Gouldsboro', Maine.

Fields said he should soon have proof-sheet for me. It may be sent as above.

In haste,
Your friend,
NATH^L HAWTHORNE.

P.S. The mail comes to Gouldsboro' only three times a week.

Hawthorne remained for a fortnight under the roof of Mr. Barney Hill, with whom he nightly carried on an animated political discussion. Mr. Hill was an ardent Abolitionist, and although his table manners might not have passed muster in the most refined circles, his companionship proved an enlivening element during this period of Hawthorne's enjoyment of the "simple life." The one drawback to complete satisfaction in discoursing with his host came in the guise of his host's daughter, Miss Charlotte Hill, who, despite the fact that she was decidedly deaf, yet displayed an intense desire to share with her father Hawthorne's enlightening remarks. As she invariably ensconced herself by her father's side, Hawthorne was forced to carry on his political disquisitions in a very loud tone of voice, which

made his evening's diversion not always a restful
process.

During the day Hawthorne went fishing and
boating with his son, attended the country picnics,
and took long walks along the picturesque coast, or
through the pleasant pasture lands. When, on the
1st of September, they took leave of their host, Hawthorne expressed his intention of returning the following year, not dreaming that this was the last
journey he was destined to take with his son.

The autumn found him indulging in some of the
social festivities of Concord, and even scribbling
occasional nonsense rhymes to amuse the young
people, while he continued with the preparation of
his "English Notes." He wrote Ticknor at the end
of October: —

"I want a hundred dollars before Saturday, having my taxes to pay then.

"How have you been this long while? I mean to
go to Boston for a day, when I get through with
some writing which I have now in hand."

A couple of months later, he again pens the
request: —

"I want (as usual) a hundred dollars; and I enclose
a tailor's bill of Devereux & Eager, which, at your
leisure, I should like to have you pay. It grieves me
to have to impose trouble of this sort upon you; but
it is the penalty of your own kindness, and kind
people will always be bothered by idle and incom-
petent ones.

I don't know whether I shall ever see you again;
for I have now stayed here so long that I find my-

self rusted into my hole, and could not get out even if I wished."

Hawthorne had usually been able to do his best work in the winter-time, and after completing his English sketches, he began the "Dolliver Romance," which he consented to have published serially in the "Atlantic," an agreement which he made against his better judgment, as he seemed from the first shadowed by the conviction that he should be unable to complete the work. "There is something preternatural," he writes, "in my reluctance to begin. I linger on the threshold, and have a perception of very disagreeable phantoms to be encountered if I enter."

In February, 1863, Hawthorne voices his dissatisfaction with a certain political appointment which has displaced his friend North: —

"I am very sorry for our friend North, but hope he will consider there is more honor and comfort in being turned out by such a miserable administration as this. We are going to have great changes in our administrations; and I trust that one result will be, to prevent upright and capable men from being sacrificed merely on account of honest political opinions.

"I have done nothing about my claim as Surveyor, and if Mr. North can push it through, I shall be glad both on his account and my own. He may make his own terms of remuneration. If he needs any information or assistance as to papers, or records, in the Salem Custom House, Burchmore would no doubt be able to give it to him, or get it for him. He is still, I suppose, a clerk in the Charlestown Navy Yard.

"As Mr. North has written you I return my answer through the same medium, and you may enclose my note to him if you think proper.

"When the weather gets a little more genial, I shall come and see you. What became of the visit from General Pierce and yourself which you promised me?"

That the response to this letter came in "spirit" rather than in person is attested by Hawthorne's next communication: —

DEAR TICKNOR: — I knew that nobody but yourself could have sent me the cider, and it tastes all the more deliciously for the knowledge. I never drank any that I liked so well, and my wife agrees with me in opinion. We sit down quietly together, when everybody is gone to bed, and make ourselves jolly with a bottle of it."

On April 30, Hawthorne expresses his thanks for another token of his publisher's regard.

He writes: — " I thank you for the excellent lot of cigars, and expect to have as much enjoyment as a man can reasonably hope for in this troublesome world, while smoking them after breakfast and dinner. Their fragrance would be much improved if you would come and smoke in company."

On this same day Hawthorne forwards the introductory article with which his volume of English sketches is to begin, declaring: "I can think of no better title than 'Our Old Home; a series of English sketches by,' etc. I send the article with which the volume is to commence and you can begin printing it whenever you like."

The following week the subject of the dedication for this book arises for discussion, and Hawthorne is torn between his desire to dedicate it to his dear friend Bennoch, in England, and his wish to pay tribute to his devoted friend Pierce; he realizes that the latter's political unpopularity must have a damaging effect upon the volume from a selling standpoint, yet he finally decides in favor of his old college chum, after writing to Mr. Fields: —

" I am of three minds about dedicating the volume. First, it seems due to Frank Pierce (as he put me into the position where I made all those profound observations of English scenery, life, and character) to inscribe it to him with a few pages of friendly explanatory talk, which would also be very gratifying to my own lifelong affection for him.

"Secondly, I want to say something to Bennoch to show him that I am thoroughly mindful of all his hospitality and kindness; and I suppose he might be pleased to see his name at the head of a book of mine.

"Thirdly, I am not convinced that it is worth while to inscribe it to anybody. We will see hereafter."

Hawthorne's decision to dedicate the book to Pierce was undoubtedly made from the start, in spite of his protest that he was " of three minds." It was useless for various friends to point out to him the inappropriateness of exploiting, just at this time, a man who was looked upon as a sympathizer with the cause of the South; such protests undoubtedly strengthened Hawthorne's determination, and on July 2, he finished the elaborate inscription which stands as a preface to the work. And thus handicapped, "Our Old Home" went forth to take its place among the classic productions of the time. It evoked a tempest in the English teapot because of its author's supposed uncomplimentary pictures of his British friends, and called forth regretful comments from the antagonists of Pierce, but time has obliterated these trivial objections, and to-day the reader of the volume, be he English or American, is totally untroubled by either the dedication to Pierce, or the sly reflections upon John Bull.

Just before finishing his dedication, Hawthorne wrote concerning an article for the "Monthly": —

DEAR TICKNOR, — I sent you a week ago to-day a sealed packet containing an article for the Magazine; and not hearing of its arrival, I deem it possible it may have miscarried — which would be a pity, as I have no other copy. For reasons connected with the publication of my volume, I wanted this article to appear in the Magazine as soon as possible.

But I suppose you do not concern yourself about the Magazine. I should have come to see you last week, if it had not been so rainy; and now it is so hot that I think I shall put it off till the autumn.

Your friend,
NATH^L HAWTHORNE.

P.S.   I hear nothing of Fields. Whereabouts is he?

The ever-present demand for the wherewithal to carry on his household, gave Hawthorne little respite from the tedious task of endeavoring to make both ends meet. No matter how earnestly he desired to withdraw into the recesses of his world of shadow and imagination, he was constantly recalled to the sphere of material mediocrity by the demand for commonplace dollars. He writes Ticknor at the end of July: —

"I have been looking over my quarterly bills, and find that it will take more than $250 to pay them, so, if you please, I should like $300 (three hundred), which will leave me very little in pocket. I expect to outlive my means and die in the almshouse. Julian's college expenses will count up tremendously. I must try to get my poor blunted pen at work again pretty soon; especially as Fields threatens me that nobody will buy the new book on account of my dedication."

In penning his dedicatory preface to the volume in question, Hawthorne had exercised all possible diplomacy in order to appease his publishers and to disarm the critics, who were prepared to pounce upon him and denounce him for thus paying tribute to a pro-slavery man. This tribute is entitled "To A Friend," and concludes with these words: —

"I dedicate my book to a Friend, and shall defer a colloquy with the Statesman till some calmer and sunnier hour. Only this let me say, that, with the record of your life in my memory, and with a sense of your character in my deeper consciousness as among the few things that time has left as it found them, I need no assurance that you continue faithful forever to that grand idea of an irrevocable Union, which, as you once told me, was the earliest that your brave father taught you. For other men there may be a choice of paths — for you, but one; and it rests among my certainties that no man's loyalty is more steadfast, no man's hopes or apprehensions on behalf of our national existence more deeply heart-felt, or more closely intertwined with his possibilities of personal happiness, than those of Franklin Pierce.''

From the time of his return to America, Hawthorne's physical strength had been gradually waning; he lost flesh rapidly, and found it difficult to shake off his languor and general weakness. He took few long walks and generally confined himself to his own grounds. He was, moreover, deeply oppressed by the progress of the war; every day brought him fresh news of disaster, and he could not escape into his cherished realm of imagination.

It was noticed that the expression of his face had changed, and he seemed to be brooding upon the approach of what he felt to be the end. He tried, however, to stem the tide setting against him and strove to exercise in various ways out of doors. A cord of wood had been cut upon the hill, and he deliberately dragged it, log by log, down to the lower level of the house. He would fasten two logs at a time to a cord, and then slowly descend, drawing his burden down the pine-flanked path; as he went, he would stop to muse upon some moral problem or pause to meditate upon some plot which was unfolding itself to his inner consciousness; meanwhile the cord of wood gradually changed its resting-place. But this and other practices did little to revive the vital forces, which were gradually failing. His splendid vigor paled, his hair grew snowy white, and he began to express certain wishes in regard to provisions to be made after his death and to burn up old letters, while his efforts to carry on his work proved almost futile.

Having begun the "Dolliver Romance" and then laid it aside for a while, he afterwards strove in vain to complete this task. One day would find him confident of soon finishing the romance, and the next would discover him helplessly asserting that he was powerless to go on with the work. He was undecided as to the best title for the book, and suggested that it might be called "Fragments of a Romance," which would leave him at liberty to make it as fragmentary as he might desire. He had written in the preface of "Our Old Home": "The Present, the Immediate, the Actual, has proved too potent for me. It takes away not only my scanty faculty, but even my desire for imaginative composition, and leaves me sadly content to scatter a thousand peaceful fantasies upon the hurricane that is sweeping us all along with it, possibly into a limbo where our nation and its policy may be as literally the fragments of a shattered dream as my unwritten romance."

Although he had not completed the romance in question, Hawthorne acquiesced in the arrangement that its first installment should appear in the "At-

lantic Monthly" for January, 1864, though he still
protested: "In this untried experiment of a serial
work, I desire not to pledge myself, or promise the
public more than I may confidently expect to
achieve. When the work is completed in the Magazine, I can fill up the gaps and make straight the
crookednesses, and christen it with a fresh title."

But the serial was doomed never to be completed.
During the summer and autumn of 1863, Hawthorne's condition showed no improvement; without
seeming to be afflicted with an organic disease he
nevertheless grew thinner and paler every day, and
seemed to be slowly relinquishing his hold on life
and its interests.

The New Year found him still more feeble, though
he maintained a cheerful demeanor and exercised a
gentle playfulness towards all around him, which
wrung their hearts even more than continual dejec-
tion would have done. Yet his professed hopeful-
ness did not conceal from those nearest to him that
Hawthorne himself believed that his life was ebbing
away. At the end of February he announced to Mr.
Fields his absolute inability to finish the "Dolliver
Romance," which had opened with such promise.

Hawthorne asserted that he should now never
finish the work, the launching of which he regretted;
then he proceeded to set forth in his own whimsical
manner the possible reasons which Mr. Fields was
presumedly to advance to the readers of the "Atlantic" as an excuse for the abrupt breaking-off of the
book. He wrote: —

"We are sorry to hear (but know not whether the

public will share our grief) that Mr Hawthorne is out
of health and is thereby prevented, for the present,
from producing another of his promised (or threatened) Romances, intended for this magazine"; or,
"Mr. Hawthorne's brain is addled at last, and, much
to our satisfaction, he tells us that he cannot possibly
go on with the Romance announced on the cover of
the January Magazine. We consider him finally
shelved, and shall take early occasion to bury him
under a heavy article, carefully summing up his
merits (such as they were) and his demerits, what
few of them can be touched upon in our limited
space."

In this humorous vein he penned several imagin-
ary excuses, any one of which he pretended might be
offered by his publishers, ending his communication
with the serious protest: —

"I cannot finish it unless a great change comes
over me; not that I should care much for that if I
could fight the battle through and win it, thus ending
a life of much smoulder and scanty fire in a blaze of
glory. . . . I mean to come to Boston soon, not for a
week, but for a single day, and then I can talk about
my sanitary prospects more freely than I choose to
write. I am not low-spirited, nor fanciful, nor freak-
ish, but look what seem to be realities in the face,
and am ready to take whatever may come. If I could
but go to England now, I think that the sea voyage
and the 'Old Home' might set me all right."

Hawthorne's prophecy that when once again
settled in his own land he would sigh for England
was pathetically realized, and towards the end he

frequently expressed the wish that he might be
again on British soil, where he had asserted that he
had "never felt so well in his life."

But at this juncture, while a foreign trip was out of
the question, it yet seemed eminently desirable that
a change of scene and climate should be tried. Looking back upon the trip to Washington, taken two
years previously, when Hawthorne had returned
greatly benefited by the journey, it seemed as if a
similar trip might be productive of renewed health
and vigor in the sick man.

Then, as on previous occasions, Hawthorne at
once turned to his publisher, as the never-failing
mountain of strength on which to lean. He would go
if Ticknor would accompany him as of old, and as
before, his tried friend did not fail him; he was
ready and willing to do all in his power in this time of
emergency for this dear friend, who relied with such
perfect trust upon his cheerful, watchful, and sagacious guardianship. Into his able hands, the family
of Hawthorne confidently surrendered their charge,
knowing that Ticknor would do for him everything
in his power, and not foreseeing that at the bidding
of a higher power the sturdy guardian would be
forced to relinquish his sacred trust.

XVIII

THEIR LAST JOURNEY TOGETHER

LIKE his own exquisite "Snow-Image," Hawthorne seemed to be slowly and imperceptibly melting from mortal sight into that sphere of the immortals, where there had been a place reserved for him from the beginning.

He had a dread of helpless old age, and when the moment came that failing physical faculties began to chain the freedom of his spirit, and he realized that he must be hemmed in by mere mortal complaints, there seemed for him but one alternative, that of escape. His spirit must prevail over his flesh, or it must fly away.

Yet he was truly docile and ready to please those that loved him, by acquiescing in their various suggestions as to what might prove beneficial to his health, and while it was not easy to awaken in him any keen interest in journeying to balmier climes with Mr. Ticknor, he cheerfully made ready for the experiment, knowing that as of old he could relinquish all responsibility when once in charge of his devoted friend from the "Old Corner."

It had been at this time suggested that Franklin Pierce should also make one of the party, but he responded that it would be impossible for him to join his two friends on their prospective journey southward, where it was hoped that they would meet the awakening spring hastening to greet them.

The last note penned by Hawthorne to his publisher and friend was written on receipt of Pierce's regretful message, stating his inability to join the party. He wrote: —

DEAR TICKNOR, — I have gained strength a little, and am otherwise as flourishing as can be expected of a man in my desperate condition, — still retaining rapturous remembrances of beefsteak and oysters. I am fully resolved to start on Wednesday, or any day thereafter that may suit your conscience. I have heard from Pierce, who does not go with us. Let me know your final decision as to the day,
Your friend
NATH^L HAWTHORNE.

Ticknor's response was one of hearty coöperation in the project which Hawthorne's family felt should be carried out as a last desperate measure.

On Monday, the 28th of March, Hawthorne arrived in Boston and spent one night at the home of his friend, James T. Fields, who was distressed by his apparent feebleness, and convinced of the seriousness of his condition. He afterwards declared: " I was greatly shocked by his invalid appearance. The light in his eye was as beautiful as ever, but his limbs seemed shrunken and his usual stalwart vigor gone."

It was no slight responsibility to undertake to pioneer the sick man back to better health and greater hope, but Ticknor gladly set himself the task, and so the two, the dreamy sick man, and his sturdy companion, set out on their last journey together.

Prior to their departure Mr. Ticknor had, at the urgent request of his wife, consulted his own physician in regard to a slight cold on his chest from which he had been suffering for some little time. After tapping him with professional skill, the doctor assured him, laughingly, that he "was good for twenty years."

The friends left Boston on the evening of March 28, and arrived in New York the next morning. There they stopped at the Astor House, where they remained for almost a week, being shut in by violently stormy weather, which had met them upon arrival and persistently dogged their footsteps upon this inauspicious journey.

Ticknor kept Mrs. Hawthorne posted regarding her husband's health, which, despite the inclement weather, seemed daily to improve. He wrote from the Astor House, twenty-four hours after their arrival: —

DEAR MRS. HAWTHORNE, — I regret that I am too late for the afternoon mail, but that can't be helped now. A worse than a northeaster has prevailed here to-day. I have hardly been out of the house; Mr. Hawthorne not at all. But we have been very comfortable within. He needed the rest, and the storm seemed to say that both he and I must be content, and we have not complained. I do not think that

Mr. Hawthorne suffered any inconvenience from the journey, but, on the contrary, I think he is better to-day than when we started. He is looking better, and says he feels very well. It will take a few days to see what effect this change will have upon him; but I can't but hope that it will prove the right medicine. I shall remain here two or three days, and perhaps more. The storm has prevented my doing what I intended to-day, and of course I cannot at once decide what shall be best to do. I can only say that I hope the trip may accomplish what we all desire; and I have great faith. I will keep you advised,

Sincerely yours,

W. D. TICKNOR.

Mr. Ticknor writes again the following day: —

DEAR MRS. HAWTHORNE, — The storm of yesterday continues, but not as violent. Mr. Hawthorne is improving, I trust. The weather makes everything very gloomy; notwithstanding we took a short walk this morning. I hope the sun will appear to-morrow, so that we may see something of New York. Mr. Hawthorne left me, saying that he proposed to sleep an hour before dinner. He seems afraid he shall eat too much, as he says his appetite is good. I assure him he is very prudent, and there is no fear of his eating too much. He slept well last night, and is evidently gaining strength. But it will take time to restore him.

Truly yours,

W. D. T.

P.S. Mr. Hawthorne said this morning that he thought he must write home to-day; but I hardly think he will do so.

April 3 finds the storm-bound travelers still imprisoned at the Astor House by the tempestuous elements, which seem bound to harass them to the uttermost. And Mr. Ticknor writes: —

MY DEAR MRS. HAWTHORNE, — Your letter has just arrived. The mail was very late. I handed it to our "King," and he read it with interest and delight and is now writing an answer. I assure you he is much improved, but he is yet very weak. The weather has been as bad as possible, and of course we have not been out much. I intended to have left New York yesterday, but I thought it best not to leave in a driving storm. We took quite a long walk this morning, and Mr. Hawthorne does not seem fatigued. I cannot say where we go next, as I shall be governed by what shall seem best for him. We shall float along for a while. Probably to Philadelphia to-morrow. I will keep you posted, though at this time I do not feel like laying out any definite plan. I shall be much disappointed if our friend does not return in much better health than when we left Boston. We have been very quiet here, and this, I am satisfied, was the right thing at first. He slept well last night. I write this short note now, as you will have from him his own account.

Sincerely and truly yours,
W. D. TICKNOR.

In the words, "I shall be governed by what shall seem best for him," Mr. Ticknor embodied the rule of his own line of conduct. Having surrendered his own interests in order to further those of Hawthorne, he did not for a moment allow his own preferences or personal comfort to stand in the way of anything which might seem to be beneficial to his friend.

Yet the cold which had worried Mrs. Ticknor prior to his departure continued to increase, and to his wife he wrote rather despondently, after a week of battling with the elements, and doing his best to enliven his enfeebled companion.

ASTOR HOUSE, April 4, '64.

MY DEAR WIFE, — You see I am still in New York. This morning it is very pleasant, almost the first time that the sun has showed himself since we left home. It has rained every day with cold east winds. I have been out very little and made but one call. . . . I have only written once before, as I really have n't felt like doing anything. Hawthorne, I think, is improving, but is very far from being well. I would have left on Saturday for Havana, but the storm was too severe. It has been terrific at sea.

I think I shall go to Philadelphia to-day. I have been here long enough and quite too long for comfort. I would much prefer to turn my face homeward, for I am truly homesick. I shall not soon start on a similar mission.

We went to the "Park" yesterday P.M. It was a cold and disagreeable ride. I have added somewhat to my cold, but hope soon to be rid of it.

The great Fair opens to-day and business generally, I understand, will be suspended.

If you do not hear often from me, just believe that
I am doing well. I cannot say where I shall go when
we reach Philadelphia — perhaps no farther.

With love to all the dear ones at home, I am as
ever,

Your loving husband,

W. D. Ticknor.

In reading over this, the next to his last home-
letter, those closing lines stand out as if penned by
some strange foreboding: "I cannot say where I
shall go when we reach Philadelphia — perhaps no
farther." And this, indeed, proved but too true a
prophecy.

Yet by this same mail Ticknor wrote cheerfully to
Mrs. Hawthorne: —

"I wrote you a short note yesterday upon receipt
of your letter. I have not much to add. The fact
that we have a bright sun to greet us this morning is
most cheering. Yesterday we went to Central Park,
in spite of the weather. Mr. Hawthorne seemed to
enjoy the drive, and was not much fatigued on our
return. We had a good cheerful evening in his room.
He retired as usual at nine, and I hope to find him
bright this morning. He is gaining strength, but very
slowly. I think we may go to Philadelphia to-day,
but am not certain. We could n't have had more unpleasant weather, but I tell him we will make up for
it by staying so much longer. Hearing from home did
him much good. He reads the papers, moderately,

to be sure, but at first he declined entirely. His appetite is very good, but he eats very moderately. Perhaps it is as well, at present."

Some days after the travelers' departure from Boston Mrs. Hawthorne wrote of their trip, to Hawthorne's close friend, Mr. Bridge: —

"Mr. Hawthorne has gone upon a journey, and I opened your letter this morning. . . . Alas! it was no 'author's excuse' which was published in the 'Atlantic,' but a most sad and serious truth. Mr. Hawthorne has really been very ill all winter, and not well, by any means, for a much longer time; not ill in bed, but miserable on the lounge, or sofa, and quite unable to read.

"I have felt the wildest anxiety about him, because he is a person who has been immaculately well all his life, and this illness has seemed to me an awful dream which could not be true. But he has wasted away very much, and the suns in his eyes are collapsed, and he has had no spirits, no appetite, and very little sleep. Richard is not himself, and his absolute repugnance to see a physician, or to have any scientific investigation of his indisposition, has weighed me down like a millstone. I have felt such terrible oppression, in thinking that all was not doing for his relief that might be done, that sometimes I have scarcely been able to endure it — at moments hardly able to fetch my breath in apprehension of the possible danger.

"But, thank Heaven, Mr. Ticknor has taken him out of this groove of existence, and intends to keep

him away until he is better. He has been in New
York at the Astor House since last Tuesday night,
a week from to-day. I have had six letters, five from
Mr. Ticknor, and one from my husband, written
with a very tremulous hand, but with a cheerful
spirit."

Ticknor's last communication, addressed to Mrs.
Hawthorne, was written from the Continental Hotel, Philadelphia, where the merciless elements had
continued to pursue them with storm after storm,
like some relentless destiny. It was dated April 7,
and in it the writer asserted: —

"You will be glad to hear that our patient continues to improve. He wrote to you yesterday. He
reads the papers, and sleeps well. The first real sunshine since we left Boston came upon us yesterday.
On Tuesday it rained and blew furiously. Mr. Hawthorne did not go out; I only for an hour, — by his
permission; but was glad to return and keep within
doors. It was too blue a day even to write. I hardly
know how we got through the day. The bright sun
of yesterday was a relief. We improved it. Made
calls on some of the publishers, then on Mr. John
Grigg, a retired *rich* bookseller. After dinner a gentleman called and invited us to drive to Fairmount,
Girard College, etc. Mr. Hawthorne seemed somewhat fatigued. Retired before nine. This morning
he is bright and said at breakfast he was feeling much
better. Now, I don't know exactly what next, but, if
he is inclined, I shall go to Baltimore. But it is not
best to lay out a business plan, or feel that so much

must be done in a given time. I tell him we will float along and see what 'turns up.' One thing is certain, it has been altogether too stormy to try the sea."

By this same mail went to Mrs. Ticknor her husband's last communication: —

MY DEAR WIFE, — Until yesterday we have had nothing but storm. I have wished myself at home many times. . . . We came here on Monday P.M.; Tuesday it stormed furiously. Yesterday we had the sun, but it was very cold. The sun is visible to-day, but I have not yet been out. I am yet undecided as to where to go next, but probably to Baltimore. Mr. Hawthorne is getting on very well. I have made but few calls and shall not make many. I gave up the idea of the sea on account of storms.

Excuse this short note, as I must look after my friend. I have a bad cold and feel disinclined to move at all. Love to all.

Hoping that you are all well, I am as ever,
Your loving husband,
W. D. TICKNOR.

This following day brought to the friends a strange reversal of relations; the strong man and the guardian was stricken down, and Hawthorne, the dependent and feeble, was forced to become the man of action. Upon him devolved the task of summoning doctors and nurses and of notifying the sick man's family, none of whom had time to reach his bedside before he passed away.

Although on Saturday evening Mr. Hawthorne

Cap

Phil^a Apl. 7. 64.

My dear Wife,

Until yesterday
we have had nothing but
Storm. I have wished myself
at home many times. $3.50
per day & shut up in a
Hotel is not very pleasant
We came here on Monday
P.m. Tuesday it Stormed
furiously. Yesterday we
had the Sun but it was
very Cold. — The Sun is risible
to day but I have not
yet been out. I am
yet undecided as to where
to go next, but probably
to Baltimore. Mr H. is
getting on very well
I have made but few
Calls & shall not make

morning. — I gave up
idea of the Sea on acc't
of the Storm. —

Excuse this
short note as I
must look after
my friend. — I have
a bad Cold & feel
disinclined to move at
all. Love to all
Hoping that you are
all well.
I Am, as Ever
Your loving Husband
M. D. Fickus

wrote to those at home announcing the serious illness
of his friend, he did not, even then, anticipate a fatal
result, and the news that reached the sick man's family of his illness was almost immediately supplemented by the announcement of Ticknor's death,
which occurred on Sunday morning.

Starting as he did from home with a cold upon his
chest, and adding constantly to this ailment by exposure to the inclement weather, the chilly drive to
Fairmount Park proved the last straw in precipitat-
ing what was pronounced congestion of the lungs by
the attending physicians.

Mr. Hawthorne was like one dazed, seemingly unable to realize that it could be possible that it was
Ticknor and not he, himself, who lay ill and helpless
in the Continental Hotel. He constantly reiterated
the words that there must be some mistake, and that
he must be the one to go and not his friend. He had
never seen any one die, and the experience, coming
at this time, proved a truly overwhelming one, as
must also have proved the knowledge that the life
ebbing away before his distracted vision was practically sacrificed for him.

And the sacrifice of the strong man, but fifty-three
years of age, at the height of his useful and active
career, was seemingly a useless one. Hawthorne at
the most had not long to remain; he would have
slipped away quietly from his study at the Wayside,
after a brief interval, and all this suffering need not
have been. Yet who dares say that any noble sacrifice has been in vain?

The thought of the grim irony, as well as the absolute futility, of the tragic occurrence took complete possession of Hawthorne, who could only reiterate over and over again that he should have died and not Ticknor. Yet even in those sad hours it is hardly likely that Hawthorne fully realized how directly the other's illness might be traced to his unselfish devotion. During the fatal drive to Fairmount Park, when the deceptive weather proved much colder than had been anticipated, Ticknor feared that his friend might take cold; he therefore took off his own coat and wrapped it about Hawthorne, regardless of the risk that he himself was running, afflicted as he was with a heavy cold. This little episode was not known by the members of Ticknor's family until many years afterwards, when the truth came back to them from a friend of the gentleman who had taken the visitors to drive.

And this instance of unselfish thought for Hawthorne was, in a lesser degree, paralleled by Franklin Pierce, at the time of his wife's funeral, which occurred in December, 1863. General Pierce was heartbroken at the great loss which he had sustained, but as Hawthorne stood near him, beside the open grave, grief-stricken as he was at the moment, he yet turned and drew up Hawthorne's coat-collar to shield him from the cold wind which was sweeping around them. In the moment of uttermost sorrow, Pierce could yet think of his friend's welfare; he did not forget him even in that absorbing moment, and this is, indeed, a true test of friendship. Pierce was ready to do all that he could for his friend, and Ticknor gave all that any man can give — his life.

In his last hours at the Continental Hotel, nursed by strangers, and realizing the seriousness of his own condition, Ticknor longed for the members of his family. He asked for them, and wished that he might look again upon their faces. It was a cruel fate which separated him at this moment from those he loved best, but his own guardian angel decreed that his last wish should seemingly be gratified. Suddenly the sick man's face lighted up with glad recognition. "They are all here," he exclaimed, "standing about my bed." Not one was missing from the group, in those last hours; he saw them all as clearly as if they had in reality been with him, and he was content.

A brief description of these last hours has been preserved in the communication sent to Mr. Fields by Dr. W. B. Atkinson, one of the attending physicians, to whom Mr. Ticknor's partner had forwarded a handsome book.

"The valuable work you were so kind as to send me is now at hand. Please accept my sincere thanks for this most beautiful token of your appreciation of my earnest though futile efforts in behalf of Mr. Ticknor.

"When at 11 o'clock on Saturday evening, in company with Dr. Turner, I saw Mr. Ticknor, I felt assured that he was dying, yet I earnestly resolved that if any effort on my part could aid in preserving his life, or promoting his comfort, it should be freely made.

"As the hours wore on, and despite the free use of stimulants, he continued to grow feebler, Mr. Ticknor, much against my wishes, declined to take any more, only allowing me occasionally to moisten his lips with cold water.

"At 11 o'clock, in conversation with Dr. Turner and myself, he assured us that he would not see the morning light, and his premonition was fulfilled, as he died about 5¼ A.M., on Sunday, April 10.

"His end was peaceful and happy. When asked if he desired the presence of a clergyman, he declined, saying that he was endeavoring himself to make his peace with God.

"While I could not but feel great regret at my utter helplessness and inability to preserve this valuable life, yet I was happy in the belief that I had been of some slight service in his last moments."

After the departure of Mr. Ticknor's remains, in charge of his eldest son, who had hastened on from Boston on receipt of the sad news, Mr. Hawthorne set out on his journey homeward. Of his arrival Mrs. Hawthorne has drawn the pitiful picture, in her communication to Mr. Fields, penned a few days after the invalid's return: —

"He came back unlooked-for that day; and when I heard a step on the piazza, I was lying on a couch and feeling quite indisposed. But as soon as I saw him, I was frightened out of all knowledge of myself, — so haggard, so white, so deeply scored with pain and fatigue was the face, so much more ill he looked than I ever saw him before. He had walked from the station because he saw no carriage there, and his brow was streaming with a perfect rain, so great had been the effort to walk so far. . . . He needed much to get home to me, where he could fling off all care of himself and give way to his feelings, pent up and kept back for so long, especially since his watch and ward of most excellent Mr. Ticknor.

"It relieved him to break down as he spoke of that scene. . . . He has more than lost all he gained by the journey, by the sad event. From being the nursed and cared-for, — early to bed and late to rise, — led as it were, by the ever-ready hand of kind Mr. Ticknor, to become the nurse and night-watcher, with all the responsibilities, with his mighty power of sympathy, and his vast apprehension of suffering in others, and to see death for the first time in a state so weak as his, — the death also of so valued a friend, — there are lines ploughed on his brow which never were there before.

"I do nothing but sit with him, ready to do or not to do, just as he wishes. The wheels of my small *ménage* are all stopped. He is my world and all the business of it."

Ticknor was buried at Mount Auburn, and on that occasion a truly distinguished company gathered to pay their last tribute to him who had won from all such genuine respect and warm personal affection, and whose sudden passing had caused widespread mourning in both the literary and business circles of his city. The departed had given freely to his friends the best that was in him, — love, loyalty, and unselfish devotion, — and their attitude towards him was expressed in the words which were forwarded from a high official at Washington, who said:

"I find, everywhere, they who best knew him, loved him best. And I know of no higher or worthier testimony."

Mr. Ticknor's cousin, George Ticknor, who was his senior by twenty years, was greatly shocked by the death of the younger man, whom he had looked upon as the embodiment of health and vitality. In the following words he expresses to the bereaved wife, his sincere sorrow at the sad news which has reached him at his summer home in Keene: —

KEENE, April 18, 1864.

MY DEAR COUSIN, — My heart is full of sympathy for you, for the heavy stroke which the Divine Hand has suddenly laid upon you. And yet I know of no one better prepared to receive it. I know your faith is bright, and your trust unshaken. And now in the sudden gloom of unexpected affliction, may the Heavenly Father appear more precious than ever. As He has transferred your beloved husband to the Spiritual world before you, may your burdens be lightened by the reflection that you will one day rejoin him and with him engage in those Celestial vocations which are the occupation of the good and true. It is by no means an unpleasant thought to me that earthly ties must be sundered, when I feel that those ties may be more strongly and happily united in the other world.

The last time I saw William, I little thought I should outlive him. Externally, he was the picture of health, and when I saw in the papers the so unexpected news of his sudden departure, away from

his home, his family, it almost overwhelmed me. I
felt thankful that one valued friend was beside him,
and if it were proper to weep for you, so far away, and
unconscious perhaps that he was passing through
his last trial, I had tears in store.

I have been expecting that my time is short, but
still I have a desire to live, if it please God, that I
may with His Gracious assistance make a far greater
progress in the Divine Life. No man could have a
better name than William and he was widely known.

Let me hope that the Grace of our Heavenly
Father may be sufficient for yourself and your children. They have enjoyed the incalculable benefit of
a father's counsel and aid until they have reached
the first limits of mature life, or most of them. That
is a blessing beyond measurement, and but a few
thoroughly appreciate it.

I hope you have comfortable health, and that
you may be spared many years to your children and
friends; and I am sure that as years pass away your
view of the spirit land, where your husband resides,
will be more extended, more satisfactory, become
more and more Heavenly.

Respectfully your cousin,
GEORGE TICKNOR.

After Ticknor's funeral it became evident that
Hawthorne must not remain in Concord, where he
was brooding mournfully upon the loss of his friend,
and living over and over again those last painful
hours. It was, therefore, arranged that he should
once more try a change of scene, though all felt that

it was doubtful if anything could at this stage prove really beneficial. A consultation with Franklin Pierce resulted in a plan to try what an excursion through northern New England would do for the sick man. Although almost too feeble to undertake the journey, Hawthorne consented to make this one last effort to please those that were so anxiously guarding his welfare, and about the middle of May the friends set out on this, Hawthorne's last, journey, which has been too often described to necessitate a further repetition of its final details.

Shortly before Hawthorne's departure, Dr. O. W. Holmes made him a visit, in compliance with an earnest request from Mrs. Hawthorne, who wished a final diagnosis made by this well-known authority, and an account of this visit, with the writer's impressions of the invalid, were later published in the pages of the "Atlantic." In the course of his remarks Dr. Holmes said: —

"It was my fortune to be among the last of the friends who looked upon Hawthorne's living face. Late in the afternoon of the day before he left Boston on his last journey, I called upon him at the hotel where he was staying. He had gone out but a moment before. Looking along the street, I saw a figure at some distance in advance which could only be his, but how changed from his former port and figure! There was no mistaking the long iron-gray locks, the carriage of the head, and the general look of the native outlines and movement; but he seemed to have shrunken in all his dimensions, and faltered along with an uncertain, feeble step, as if every movement were an effort. I joined him, and we walked together for half an hour, during which time I learned so much of his state of mind and body as could be got at without worrying him with suggestive questions; my object being to form an opinion of his condition, as I had been requested to do, and to give him some hints that might be useful to him on his journey. . . . His aspect medically was very unfavorable. . . . He was very gentle, very willing to answer questions, very docile to such counsel as I offered him, but evidently he had no hope of recovering his health. He spoke as if his work were done, and he should work no more.

"With all his obvious depression there was no failing noticeable in his conversational powers. There was the same backwardness and hesitancy which in his best days it was hard for him to overcome; so that talking with him was almost like love-making, and his shy, beautiful soul had to be wooed from its bashful prudery like an unschooled maiden. The calm despondency with which he spoke about himself confirmed the unfavorable opinion suggested by his look and history.

"A few weeks earlier he had left Boston on a similar errand in company with Mr. William D. Ticknor, who had kindly volunteered to be his companion in a trip which promised to be of some extent and duration, and from which this faithful friend, whose generous devotion deserves the most grateful remembrance, hoped to bring him back restored.

"Death joined the travelers, but it was not the invalid whom he selected as his victim. The strong man was taken and the suffering valetudinarian found himself charged with those last duties which he was so soon to need at the hands of others."

As has been frequently recorded, Hawthorne and Pierce set out upon their journey about the middle of May, traveling very leisurely until, upon the 18th of the month, they reached Plymouth, New Hampshire. Here they put up at the Pemigewasset House, and Hawthorne retired early and fell asleep; his friend, who occupied an adjoining room, looked in upon him from time to time and found him resting comfortably. Returning again, however, soon after midnight, he noticed that the sleeper had ceased to breathe. Pierce quickly laid his hand upon his friend's heart and found it had stopped beating.

In answer to his often expressed wish, Hawthorne had taken his departure in his sleep, without the final struggle which he had always dreaded, or any agonizing parting from his dear ones. Like that of his friend Ticknor, his spirit was destined to take its flight while away from home surroundings, in a hotel, far from his family circle; yet each one had beside him a loving guardian, who stood ready to render to the departing one all that devoted friendship could lovingly bestow at such a time. Upon the 23d of May, 1864, a little more than a month after the final tribute had been paid to Ticknor, Hawthorne was carried through the flowering orchards adjacent to his home in Concord.

Upon the lovely slope of "Sleepy Hollow," Hawthorne was laid, while almost the same circle gathered about his grave that had but a few weeks before followed the bier of his friend at Mount Auburn. By the gates of the cemetery stood with uncovered heads that most distinguished group, including Longfellow, Whittier, Lowell, Pierce, Emerson, Hoar, Agassiz, Channing, Alcott, Greene, and Hillard.

The sun shone brightly, and the birds sang cheerily; Hawthorne and his devoted friend and publisher had started out to "meet the spring," and lo! it had o'ertaken them in all its splendor.

> "How beautiful it was, that one bright day
> In the long week of rain!
> Though all its splendor could not chase away
> The omnipresent pain.
>
> "The lovely town was white with apple-blooms
> And the great elms o'erhead
> Dark shadows wove on their aërial looms
> Shot through with golden thread."

THE END

INDEX

Agassiz, Alexander, 27, 331.
Alcott, A. Bronson, 212, 331.
Aldershot, Camp, 166–69.
Aldrich, Thomas Bailey, 293.
Allen, John, 17, 20.
Allen and Ticknor, 20.
Allingham, William, 146, 147.
Andrew, John A., 267.
Appleton, William, 42.
Atkinson, Dr. W. B., 323, 324.
"Atlantic Monthly, The," Hawthorne's last work identified with, 283; founding of, 283–87; contributors to first number, 287; purchased by Ticknor, 290; Howells's description of, 292–96; contained "English Notes," "The Dolliver Romance," Longfellow's tribute to Hawthorne, 297.

Bacon, Delia, Hawthorne finances her book, 182; one thousand copies to be printed, 183; ignorant of Hawthorne's aid, 183; title-page of work, 184; book printed, 185; quarrels with Hawthorne, 188; accepts Hawthorne's preface, 191; "Shakespeare Problem" launched, 192; Hawthorne visits her, 197–99; displeased with Hawthorne, 200; unwilling to condense work, 201; work severely criticised, 202; afflicted with insanity, her death, 203.
Bailey, Dr. Gamaliel, 46.
Baldwin, Rev. Thomas, D.D., 20.
Banks, Nathaniel P., 276, 277.
Barrow, James, 25.
Barrow, Mrs. Frances Elizabeth, 25.
Beck, Mr., 151, 155.
Beecher, Henry Ward, 25.
Benjamin, Park, 127.
Bennett, William Cox, 154.
Bennoch, Francis, calls on Ticknor, 54; invites Ticknor to dine with The Lord Mayor, 58; greatly beloved by American friends, 60;

personal description of, 61; figures in "Doctor Grimshawe's Secret," 62; entertains the Hawthornes, 63; denounces Hawthorne's slanderers, 64; crosses to America, 65; association with Haydon, 65; "Passages from English Notes" dedicated to him, 65; invites Hawthorne, 67; entertains distinguished guests at garden party, 69; goes with Ticknor to visit Tupper and Miss Mitford, 70; aids Miss Mitford, 72–73; with Mrs. Bennock accompanies Ticknor, 74; conveys note to Ticknor from Miss De Quincey, 85; sends letter of introduction to Hawthorne, 119; entertains Hawthorne, 164; visits Aldershot with Hawthorne, 167, 168; offers Hawthorne "Blackheath," 170, 171; Hawthorne's gratitude for "Blackheath," 179; supervises Delia Bacon's book, 183; transmits title-page, 184; conciliates Delia Bacon, 189, 190; his misfortunes, 212, 213; Hawthorne's sympathy for, 222; Hawthorne writes of, 230; sends Hawthorne oysters, 233; again prosperous, 237; "Marble Faun" sent him, 238; Hawthorne wishes to dedicate book to, 303.
Bennoch, Mrs. Francis, 56, 63, 65, 72, 132.
Bentley (English publisher), 73.
Biscaccianti, 25.
Bishop (composer), 69.
Bixby (hotel-keeper), 41.
Blodgett, Mrs. (landlady), 66, 67, 151, 155.
Bohn, Henry G., 58, 67, 68, 105.
Bowman, Mr., 63.
Brady (photographer), 280.
Bremer, Frederika, 214.
Bridge, F. I., 32, 186, 191, 318.
Bridge, Mrs. Horatio, 34.
Bright, Henry A., description of,

offers Hawthorne Liverpool Consulship, 36; receives communication from Hawthorne, 38; "Tanglewood Tales" relinquished for work on "Life," 39; Ticknor calls on him at White House, 43; he offers to "change places" with Ticknor, 44; interviews with him, 45; aspersions cast on him by English critic, 64; "Old Home" dedicated to him, 65; Hawthorne writes of him, 124 ; recognition of Walker's Government, 170; praised by Hawthorne, 172; in Naples, 221; in Rome, 224; copy of "Marble Faun" sent him, 234, 241; to visit Hawthorne, 302; book dedicated to, 303–04; extract from dedication, 305–06; asked to take trip with Hawthorne, 311; cannot join party, 312; unselfish devotion to Hawthorne, 322; plans final trip with Hawthorne, 328; sets out on journey; Hawthorne dies at Pemigewasset House, 330; attends funeral, 331.

Pike, William B., 234.
Poore, Benjamin Perley, 266, 269.
Pope, Alexander, 68.
Procter, Adelaide A., 249.

Quincy, Edmund, 289.

Reade, Charles, 5, 21, 165.
Reed, John, Jr., 23.
Reid, Mayne, 248.
Reynolds, Mr., 75, 76.
Rice, Alexander H., 289, 290.
Ritchie, Anne Thackeray (Lady), 5, 161.
Roberts, David, 234.
Roberts Brothers, 23.
Russell, Mr., 75, 101, 102, 103.

Saxe, John G., 22, 25.
Scott, Sir Walter, 26, 61, 206, 253, 254, 255.
Shakespeare, William, 32, 199, 202, 203.
Shepard, Ada, 208, 222.
Shrimpton, Henry, 14.
Shurtleff, Dr. Nathaniel B., 14.
Silsbee, George, 49.
Skinner, Mr., 159.

Smith, Albert, 55.
Smith, William H., 196.
Sohier, Edward, 14.
Sohier, Susanna, 14.
Sparks, Mrs., 73.
Spiers, Mayor of Oxford, 175, 176, 177, 178, 195.
Stanton, E. M., 278.
Story, William W., 235.
Stowe, Mrs. Harriet Beecher, 25, 286, 287.
Sturgis, Russell, 79, 102.

Talfourd, Field, 49.
Taylor, Tom, 73.
Tennyson, Alfred, Lord, 3, 20, 21, 134, 146.
Thackeray, William Makepeace, 3, 24, 84.
Thompson, C. G., 224.
Thoreau, Henry D., 2, 32, 135, 165.
Ticknor, Benjamin, 19.
Ticknor, Caleb, 19.
Ticknor, Elisha, 18, 19.
Ticknor, Mrs. Emeline S., 20, 67, 262, 313, 316, 320, 326.
Ticknor, Frank, 19.
Ticknor, George, 18, 173, 174, 326, 327.
Ticknor, Howard Malcom, 9.
Ticknor and Fields, 23, 29, 94.
Ticknor, Reed and Fields, 23, 149.
Ticknor, William Davis, early ambition, 2; strove to establish international copyright, 4 ; birth and ancestry, 18–19 ; seeks fortune in Boston, 19; holds position in Columbian Bank, 19; partnership with John Allen; marriage and children, 20 ; first decade of publishing; purchase of "Atlantic Monthly," 21 ; partnership with Reed and Fields, firm becomes Ticknor and Fields, 23; journeys to Washington with Hawthorne, 40–46; sails for Europe with Hawthorne, 48; visits Bennoch, 54; attends party at Bennoch's, 69; visits Miss Mitford, 71; attends Napoleonic fête in Paris, 74–77; visits the Tomb of Napoleon, 78; inspects Bank of England, 79; visits Royal Stables, 80; goes to stay with De Quin-

𝕮𝖍𝖊 𝕽𝖎𝖛𝖊𝖗𝖘𝖎𝖉𝖊 𝕻𝖗𝖊𝖘𝖘

CAMBRIDGE . MASSACHUSETTS

U . S . A